Palgrave Studies in Globalization and Embodiment

Series Editors
Erynn Masi de Casanova
University of Cincinnati
Cincinnati, OH, USA

Afshan Jafar
Connecticut College
New London, CT, USA

This cutting-edge series will address how global forces impact human bodies and the individual and collective practices associated with them. Books in this series will explore the globalization of bodily practices as well as how the interaction of local and global ideas about bodies produces particular forms of embodiment. We are particularly interested in research covering the ways that globalization engenders in between spaces, hybrid identities and 'body projects.'

More information about this series at
http://www.palgrave.com/gp/series/15115

Claudia Liebelt · Sarah Böllinger
Ulf Vierke
Editors

Beauty and the Norm

Debating Standardization in Bodily Appearance

Editors
Claudia Liebelt
University of Bayreuth
Bayreuth, Germany

Ulf Vierke
University of Bayreuth
Bayreuth, Germany

Sarah Böllinger
University of Bayreuth
Bayreuth, Germany

Palgrave Studies in Globalization and Embodiment
ISBN 978-3-030-08191-1   ISBN 978-3-319-91174-8   (eBook)
https://doi.org/10.1007/978-3-319-91174-8

Cover photo: © Yassine Balbzioui

This Palgrave Macmillan imprint is published by the registered company Springer Nature
Switzerland AG
The registered company address is: Gewerbestrasse 11, 6330 Cham, Switzerland

We dedicate this book to Stella Young (1982–2014)

PREFACE AND ACKNOWLEDGEMENTS

Edited volumes are markers of the life-cycle of academic discourses. Like testimonies, they look back on lengthy debates: some might be interdisciplinary marriage certificates, while others are more like birth certificates. This volume certainly tends to be more like the latter, not only due to the fact that, during its production, at least five babies were born to its contributors. Bringing together hitherto rather separate debates in critical beauty studies, cultural anthropology, sociology, the history of science and disability studies, we feel that *Beauty and the Norm* has succeeded in mapping out an emerging discursive field.

Being positioned in different departments and disciplines at the University of Bayreuth, we were fascinated by how much we shared in our thinking about the body as praxis and its relation to both aesthetics and norms. The story of this book thus began with questions over cups of coffee such as, "What do you make of Stella Young's notion of 'Inspiration Porn'?" or "Have your read Garland-Thomson's book on staring?" The list could be continued, but the reader will find many of the works we found so inspiring for our debates in the lists of references in this volume. The discursive field we were targeting had just a few well-established authors, and it was a great pleasure to discover, while organizing a conference on the topic, the large number of young scholars from different disciplines and area studies who were enthusiastic about our project. Some of them went on to contribute to the present volume.

This collection thus builds on an international conference that took place at Iwalewahaus, University of Bayreuth, from 6 to 8 April 2016. Over the course of three days, scholars and artists from the Czech Republic, Germany, France, Israel, Kenya, the Netherlands, Portugal, South Africa, Turkey, the United Kingdom and the United States presented their current research on body aesthetics, representation, and gendered and racialized norms. Even though one might doubt whether "inspiration porn" qualifies as a solid analytical term, we feel that Stella Young, who passed away in 2014, would have loved to be part of our conference, not least because it was academia at its best, bringing together not just scholars in the strict sense of the term, but intellectuals in a broader sense, including artists and activists. We experienced the warm, friendly, yet intellectually sharp atmosphere as something unique. Presentations without the usual posturing, full of thorough and inspiring thoughts—we learned a lot, were moved, and continued to discuss and laugh together afterwards. Some of this spirit we feel has clearly made it into the present volume.

We would like to thank everyone who made this work possible. Claudia Liebelt is grateful to Erdmute Alber, who, on a train ride to Berlin, triggered the idea for this project by suggesting that greater attention should be paid to the generative operations of human standardization and normative looks. Liebelt would also like to thank the extraordinary support of the staff at the Chair for Social Anthropology at the University of Bayreuth for their remarkable editorial assistance, most importantly Severin Penger, Nadja Bscherer and Korbinian Baumer. With his rigorous and immensely quick language editing, Robert Parkin not only saved us from numerous mistakes, but also spotted errors as only a superb scholar can. Sarah Böllinger would like to thank Katharina Fink, who believed in the idea of artwork as disabled bodies and promoted this project with her all-embracing positive energy, as well as Sigrid-Horsch-Albert and Katharina Greven for their insights into the Ulli Beier heritage and for supporting the ideal of "Iwalewa" (Yoruba for "Character is Beauty").

Most of all, we are indebted to the contributors to this volume. We all profited from the insightful comments we provided to each other and the debates we had. This edited volume is a truly collaborative work. As mentioned above, it builds on a conference we co-organized in 2016 at Iwalewahaus in cooperation with the Chair for Social Anthropology at the University of Bayreuth. The conference was supported by the German Research Foundation (DFG), the Bayreuth Academy of Advanced African Studies and the Bayreuth International Graduate School of African Studies (BIGSAS). Our keynote speakers, Ann M. Fox and Maxine L. Craig, were the best speakers we could have hoped for: as our multiple references to their work throughout this volume testify, they were crucial for our thinking on *Beauty and the Norm*. While unfortunately she could not contribute to our volume or make it to the conference, we drew much intellectual inspiration from Rosemarie Garland-Thomson and would like to offer our thanks to her for her interest in and support of our book project. We also thank Anne-Christina Thiel for her outstanding organizational skills and Katharina Greven for her supportive design work for our cover. Indispensable was the support of the (former) staff of Bayreuth's Iwalewahaus and the Chair for Social Anthropology, especially Talea Schütte, Anisha H. Soff, Tamara Fick, Shirin Dünkel, Lena Naumann, Siegrun Salmanian, Gloria Igabe and Miroslav Martinka.

Bayreuth, Germany   Claudia Liebelt
                                                             Sarah Böllinger
                                                             Ulf Vierke

CONTENTS

NOTES ON CONTRIBUTORS

R. Arzu Ünal (Ph.D. Amsterdam, 2013) is a lecturer of Cultural Studies at Sabancı University and a postdoctoral researcher at the University of Amsterdam. She is currently conducting an ethnographic research project on 'Disengaging Marriage from Motherhood: Life stories of midlife single women and single mothers in Turkey'. She is the author of 'The Genealogy of Turkish Overcoat in the Netherlands' (in '*Islamic Fashion and Anti-Fashion*', 2013, E. Tarlo and A. Moors, eds.) and the co-author of 'Formats, Fabrics, and Fashions: Muslim Headscarves Revisited' (in *Material Religion: The Journal of Objects, Art and Belief,* 2012).

Sarah Böllinger (M.A.) is a Ph.D. candidate and Junior Fellow of the Bayreuth International Graduate School of African Studies. She is the director of *becks,* the administrative department for disabled and chronically ill students at Bayreuth University. Her research interests are Contemporary Arts, Disability Aesthetics, and Visual Culture, her main research focus is on Kenya.

Katharina Fink (Ph.D. Bayreuth, 2016) is a curator and postdoctoral Fellow at the Bayreuth Academy of Advanced African Studies, Bayreuth University. She is also affiliated to the Department of Historical Studies, University of Johannesburg, South Africa and part of a large-grant project on "Revolution 3.0—Iconographies of Utopias in Africa and its Diasporas." Her research interests are in aesthetics, popular culture, museum, memory, heritage, gender and feminism. She is the author of

Un/doing Sophiatown. Contemporary Reverberations of a Myth and in a Suburb (Himmelgrün, 2015).

Ann M. Fox is a professor of English at Davidson College (North Carolina), who specializes in twentieth- and twenty-first-century dramatic literature and disability studies. She teaches and publishes extensively on these topics and has co-curated three disability-related visual arts exhibitions. Her scholarship on disability and theatre has been published in *Legacy*, *Contemporary Theatre Review*, the *National Women's Studies Association Journal*, *Gendering Disability*, *The Journal of Literary and Cultural Disability Studies*, and *Disability Studies Quarterly*. Her current book project is entitled "Fabulous Invalids: Disability on the American Stage from Melodrama to Midcentury" and will be published by the University of Michigan Press.

Doreen Gordon (Ph.D. Manchester, 2009) is a lecturer in Anthropology in the Faculty of Social Sciences at the University of the West Indies, Mona, Jamaica. She was formerly a research fellow in the Human Economy Programme, University of Pretoria, South Africa. She received her Ph.D. in Social Anthropology from the University of Manchester for ethnographic work on race and class in Brazil. Doreen has carried out research in Tanzania, South Africa, Brazil, and Jamaica.

Filip Herza (Ph.D. Prague, 2017) is an assistant professor at the Charles University in Prague. He is particularly interested in representations of the ab/normal body in science and mass entertainment culture in nineteenth- and twentieth-century East Central Europe. In his dissertation research, Herza focuses on the nineteenth- and twentieth-century freak show culture in Prague. His latest publication, "Anthropologists and their Monsters: Body, Ethnicity and Ab/normality in the Early Czech Anthropology" appeared in *East Central Europe* (2016, volume 1–2).

Christopher Hohl (M.A.) is a Ph.D. candidate in Anthropology at the Johannes Gutenberg University Mainz. He is a member of the research project "Un/doing Albinism: Recodings of a bodily difference through historically shifting frames," within a larger research group funded by the German Research Foundation (DFG). For his dissertation, he studies the representation of persons with albinism within the fashion industry, photography, advertisement and popular culture.

Hieke Huistra (Ph.D. Leiden, 2013) is an assistant professor in the History of Science and Medicine at Utrecht University. She uses history of medicine to investigate how medical practices and objects shape the way we experience our bodies. In the past, she has researched the history of, among other things, obesity, medical museums, anatomical collections and scientific instruments. Her new project investigates how patients changed the role of medicine in birth and death in the twentieth century, with hospital birth and active euthanasia as the main case studies.

Matthias Krings is a professor of Anthropology and African Popular Culture at the Johannes Gutenberg University Mainz. His research interests include the study of African popular culture, representation, fashion, Albinism, as well as migration and diaspora; he conducted extensive fieldwork in Tanzania and Nigeria. He currently heads a large-grant project on the meaning of albinism in cross-cultural perspective. He published extensively and is the author of *African Appropriations: Cultural Difference, Mimesis, and Media* (2015, Indiana University Press), *Bongo Media Worlds: Producing and Consuming Popular Culture in Dar es Salaam* (co-edited with Uta Reuster-Jahn, Köppe 2014) and *Global Nollywood: The Transnational Dimensions of an African Video Film Industry* (co-edited with Onookome Okome, Indiana University Press 2013).

Nina Kullrich (M.A.) is a Ph.D. candidate and junior fellow at Bayreuth University and affiliated with the Department of Sociology at Delhi University, India. Her dissertation in Cultural Studies is on "Skin Color Politics and Social Stratification in India". Her research interests include Critical Race and Whiteness Studies, Feminist Theories and Indian histories, literatures and political movements. Prior to her dissertation, she worked as research assistant and lecturer at the Department for Modern German and Comparative Literature at Göttingen University.

Syowia Kyambi is an alumnus of the Art Institute of Chicago and has been the recipient of several awards and grants, including most recently the Smithsonian Artist Research Fellow, being shortlisted for the Financial Times Emerging Artist Award and the Art in Global Health Grant from the Wellcome Trust Fund in the United Kingdom. Her work examines how our contemporary human experience is influenced by constructed histories, creating installations that include a performative practice to narrate stories and activate objects, exploring cultural identities, and linking them to issues of loss, memory, race and gender. Her work has been shown in museums in Belgium, Finland, Kenya, Mali, the UK, Ireland, Sweden, Germany, Zimbabwe, France, South Africa and the US.

Claudia Liebelt (Ph.D. Halle, 2010) is an assistant professor in Social Anthropology at the University of Bayreuth. Her current primary research interest and teaching pertains to the gendered notions of beauty and aesthetic body modification in Turkey, extending to questions of normativity, intimate labor, class, embodiment and Islam in its lived and embodied aspects. She authored *Caring for the 'Holy Land': Filipina Domestic Workers in Israel* (Berghahn, 2011) and has published in the *Journal of Middle East Women's Studies, Ethnos, South East Asia Research, Diaspora, Critical Asian Studies, Feminist Review* and *Contemporary Levant*. Her current book project is entitled *Istanbul Appearances: Beauty and the Making of Middle Class Femininities in Urban Turkey*.

Anisha H. Soff (M.A.) is a coordinator of cultural projects with a focus on visual arts and music at the Goethe-Institut Kenya in Nairobi. She studied Curatorial Studies, Art and Cultural Anthropology at the University of Bayreuth, after having earned a degree in architecture from the Technical University of Darmstadt. Her research focuses on contemporary art in Nairobi, Kenya, in relation to postcolonial discourse, gender and queer theory, and the (performative) body. This research, together with her curatorial work, has led to several projects with the artist Syowia Kyambi.

Shirley A. Tate is Professor of Race and Education in the Carnegie School of Education, Leeds Beckett University, UK, Research Associate in the Institute for Reconciliation and Social Justice, University of the Free State, South Africa and Research Associate in the Centre for Critical Studies in Higher Education Transformation at Nelson Mandela University, South Africa. Her area of research is Black diaspora studies broadly and her research interests are institutional racism, the body, affect, beauty, 'race' performativity and Caribbean decolonial studies while paying attention to the intersections of 'race' and gender. She has written widely on these topics. Her monographs are: *Black Skins, Blacks Masks: Hybridity, Dialogism, Performativity* (2005), *Black beauty: Aesthetics, Stylization, Politics* (2009), *Black Women's Bodies* *and The Nation: Race, Gender and Culture* (2015), *Skin Bleaching in Black Atlantic Zones: Shade Shifters* (2015). Her co-written book is *Caribbean Racisms: Connections and Complexities in the Racialization of the Caribbean Region* (2015 with Ian Law), and her co-edited book *Creolizing Europe: Legacies and Transformations* (2015 with Encarnacíon Gutíerrez Rodríguez).

Ulf Vierke is the director of Iwalewahaus, Museum for Contemporary African Arts at Bayreuth University. He also acts as the Head of DEVA, the Digital Research Archive of African Studies. In his curatorial practice, he focuses on photography and contemporary media arts, mostly in the Eastern African and lusophone contexts.

LIST OF FIGURES

CHAPTER 1

Beauty and the Norm: An Introduction

Claudia Liebelt

Recent decades have seen the rise of a global beauty boom, with profound effects on people's bodies worldwide. The global beauty and fashion industries seem to disseminate mass-mediated images of men and women whose bodies have startling similarities, despite their differences in shade and attire. Against this background, some scholars have warned against an increasing regularization of the human body, indeed, of a 'pervasive smoothing out of human complexity and variation' (Garland-Thomson 2009, 30). On the other hand, an emerging literature on beauty practices and images worldwide has demonstrated that, in their quest for beauty, modernity or enhancement, bodies are shaped by particular, yet transnational body politics (Elias et al. 2017; Jarrín 2017; Nguyen 2011) and are embedded in culturally specific, collective fantasies that are neither exclusively local nor global, but may be both (cf. Jafar and Casanova 2013; Jha 2016). While certain hegemonic beauty norms and images are becoming increasingly prominent globally, the present volume argues that, for a nuanced reading of their diverse meanings and effects on and for bodies, we need to pay careful attention to the various ways in which normative beauty is manufactured in different contexts and across national boundaries. Techniques for measuring or weighing the body, lightening

C. Liebelt (✉)
University of Bayreuth, Bayreuth, Germany

© The Author(s) 2019
C. Liebelt et al. (eds.), *Beauty and the Norm*,
Palgrave Studies in Globalization and Embodiment,
https://doi.org/10.1007/978-3-319-91174-8_1

or tanning the skin, processing hair and altering eyelids, female breasts or noses may travel transnationally, but to understand their relationship to normative regimes of representation, it is crucial to analyse their multiple and changing meanings in specific locations.

Beauty and the Norm contains chapters based on empirical research across a wide range of geographical locations and cultural contexts, as well as shorter conversations between scholars that also include more personal reflections on scholarly debates, artistic representations and everyday experiences. Rather than engaging in the certainly futile attempt to provide a complete review of the literature on the relationship between the beautified/beautiful body and norms of appearance, in this introductory chapter, we seek to provide a framework that ties the various chapters together. In its attempt to expose the generative operations of human standardization and normative looks in everyday life to more systematic analysis this edited volume contributes to a debate that we feel is only just emerging. Not least, it brings together hitherto rather separate debates in critical beauty studies, cultural anthropology, sociology, the history of science and disability studies on the gendered, classed, (dis)abled and racialized body, normative regimes of representation and the global beauty economy. Before introducing the contributions to this volume, we begin with a brief history of the notion of the norm and of the closely related debates on standardization and normalization as well as a discussion of the global economy of gendered and racialized bodies.

Debating Norms, Standardization and Normalization

In their attempt to delineate a sociology of standards and standardization, Timmermans and Epstein (2010, 71) remark that standardization has a negative ring to it as it is perceived to create worldwide homogenization. While we may tolerate or even invite the standardization of consumer goods, bureaucratic policies, technical codes and even research methods as processes that make 'things work together over distance' (ibid.), the notion of a standard human is rather troubling and may trigger dystopian fears of enforced homogenization, designer babies and cloning. Far from being entirely dystopian, or utopian, for that matter, the notion of a standard human has in some domains long been an everyday reality. To Epstein, '[a]ttempts to construct a standard human are unavoidable, in part because other standards have spillover effects' (ibid., 36).

By citing the example of a new policy announcement by Southwest Airlines in 2002 that overweight passengers would be forced to purchase two adjoining seats and the controversy this triggered, Epstein explains that '[t]o standardize consumer goods is inevitably to standardize those who consume them; to standardize consumer goods is inevitably to standardize those administered by them' (ibid.).

From the perspective of disability studies, the insight that standardized material objects contribute to the construction of bodies as non-standard, extraordinary and indeed 'disabled' is hardly new (cf. Garland-Thomson 1997). Within disability studies, the notion of a 'disabling society' (Swain et al. 2003) has come to stand for both the analysis and the critique of the conceptual and material barriers that contribute to the impairment and exclusion of some members of society while they serve others. From such a perspective, the history of bodily standardization is intricately tied to that of the norm, the normal (and abnormal), normalcy, normality and the average—all notions, as Lennard Davis (1995, 24) suggests, that entered the English language rather late, in the mid-nineteenth century.

The history of human standardization is commonly traced back to the emergence of statistics in the mid-nineteenth century, and especially the works of Adolphe Quetelet (1796–1874), who developed the still powerful concepts of the average man and the body mass index. As ideological tools, these standards of somatic normalcy continue not only to describe, but also to prescribe human bodies today. With their help, Rosemarie Garland-Thomson remarks (2009, 28), generations of women, people of colour, the so-called handicapped and the poor have been measured, observed and evaluated, almost always being 'found wanting.' Up until the nineteenth century, when for Quetelet, as well as for artists like the Prussian sculptor Gottfried Schadow (cf. Döring 2011), the standardized or average human male came to signify beauty and vice versa, bodily beauty had been discussed in relation to the concept of the 'ideal' rather than the norm (Davis 1995, 24).

As Davis reminds us, in societies with bodily beauty ideals (rather than beauty *norms*), 'all members of the population are below the ideal. ... By definition, one can never have an ideal body. There is in such societies no demand that populations have bodies that conform to the ideal' (1995, 25). To illustrate his point, Davis (ibid.) recounts the story of the Greek artist Zeuxis lining up all the beautiful women in the town of Crotona to create the ideal figure of Aphrodite by combining their most beautiful body parts as individuals. While Zeuxis' creation of Aphrodite may sound not too far-fetched in an age when digital post-processing or 'image cosmetics' are routinely applied to the mass-mediated bodies and images of advertisement beauties and fashion models, there is nevertheless a great difference between his approach and ours: in contrast to Zeuxis' society, which idealized beauty as an unattainable ideal for any actual living body, in contemporary societies that measure and quantify beauty as a norm, each individual body is readily scrutinized in relation to others, whether in terms of its height, weight or complexion, or more generally its attractiveness.

The conceptualization of beauty as a norm has thus effected various forms of exclusion for those who fall short of, exceed or violate the normative parameters or else escape the pressure to 'correct' those aspects of their body that defy the norm. In his profound cultural history of aesthetic plastic surgery, Sander Gilman (1999, xvii) describes the basic motivation for aesthetic surgery as the desire to correct such 'deformations,' in the language of medical experts, and to 'pass' visibly. The idea of the averaged human being as physically attractive continues to be advocated by some evolutionary psychologists and neuroscientists, who, often on the basis of rather limited samples, claim to be able to measure physical attractiveness, linking it with averaged facial and bodily features (Pallet et al. 2010; Quinn et al. 2008; Rikowski and Grammer 1999), as well as reproductive strategies, fertility and, ultimately, evolutionary success (Buss 2003; Etcoff 1999).[1]

As outlined by Davis (1995), the rise of the concepts of the norm, the normal, the average man and normality is also bound up with the rise of eugenics and of larger processes of ordering bodies into clear-cut, typically binary categories such as able and disabled, male and female, black and white, rich and poor, and, often resulting from these, the beautiful and the ugly in the eighteenth and nineteenth centuries. Based on an 'ideology of containment and a politics of power and fear' (ibid., 4), eugenicists like the English Victorian Sir Francis Galton (1822–1911) conceptualized society as an organic body in need of perfection. In his work on cosmetic surgery in Brazil, Jarrín (2017, 28–53) speaks of the 'eugenesis' of beauty, showing how eugenic thought 'produced the backbone of the aesthetic hierarchy present to this day in Brazil' (ibid., 30). Social institutions such as hospitals, schools, prisons, barracks etc. became crucial in the process of creating ideal citizens and, indeed, of their normalization, which has been studied so prominently by Michel

Foucault (1990, 1995). Normalization, according to Foucault (1990), involves disciplinary power and social control rather than direct force. It is a process enforced by various authorities based on the concept of the normal 'as a principle of coercion' (1995, 184), eventually creating 'docile bodies' that self-monitor their compliance with the normative order. In an age of neoliberalism and humanitarian imperialism, Mimi Thi Nguyen (2011) argues, beauty is recruited as a part of imperial state-craft, a form of biopower that produces particular ways of managing the body, regulating not just appearances, for example of veiled women in Afghanistan, but moral character and feeling. As recent works that think beauty through affect theory have shown, it is not simply a disciplinary process, but an affective force that may also function to displace or disturb existing power hierarchies. For example, Rebecca Coleman and Mónica Moreno Figueroa (2010) conceptualize beauty as an affective aesthetic feeling that is intricately tied to the future 'as a more hopeful temporality' (ibid., 361). By looking at the resulting shifts and challenges, a field of paradoxes and contestations comes into view that speaks of the affective politics of beauty within a gendered and racialized global economy.

A GLOBAL ECONOMY OF BEAUTY

The global beauty market is often described as dominated by Western or Caucasian ideals of beauty promulgated by the mass media and multinational players. From such a perspective, beauty practices such as skin bleaching or toning, hair straightening or surgery such as the so-called 'correction of the negroid nose' (cf. Edmonds 2010, 145) or 'double eyelid surgery' in Asia and among Asian Americans are attempts to mimic Western or Caucasian beauty ideals (Jha 2016). While hegemonic beauty norms and images, for example, in respect of body weight and skin colour, clearly exist globally, the present volume argues for a nuanced reading of their diverse meanings and effects on and for bodies across the globe. In doing so, our volume contributes to an emerging debate in recent studies on the local ramifications and biopolitics of the global beauty boom as a transnational phenomenon.

For example, in her ethnography of Taiwanese bridal photography, Bonnie Adrian (2003) interprets the photographic staging of the bride as a 'Western baby doll' as creative response to a transnational visual imagery, which in this context is dominated by American representations of female beauty. Alex Edmonds (2007, 2010) studies the localized form of a beauty industry in Brazil that developed in the encounter 'between global media and medicine and a distinctive logic of aesthetics and race in Brazil' (2007, 374), speaking of it as a form of indigenization (ibid.). While Laura Miller (2006) describes Japan's beauty culture as 'unique,' drawing on Appadurai's (1990) notion of global flows and 'scapes', she also sees it as functioning in a global arena of transnational body aesthetics and practices in that Japanese women's beauty concerns 'are no different from the defects women all over the world are taught through global advertising and imagery to hide or correct' (Miller 2006, 5). Along these lines, in their multi-sited research on cosmetic surgery tourism, Holliday et al. (2015) speak of 'beautyscapes,' analyzing the assemblages that emerge in 'a particular form of coming-together' (ibid., n.p.) between surgeons, patients and their companions, different types of training and surgery sites, technologies, media and body images, as well as cash flows. To understand beauty practices and ideals in relation to normative regimes of representation, it is thus crucial to analyse their multiple and changing meanings in specific locations. Accordingly, all the contributors to our volume are part of an emerging debate among scholars on the representation of gendered and racialized bodies, as well as transnational beauty cultures and practices in an increasingly global market.

Not least, these chapters contribute to a debate on beautification as a tool for social positioning and upward mobility, especially for women, with standards for bodily appearance continually on the rise. Thus, physical beauty carries within it an affective force and a promise of social mobility that may be seen as challenging established power hierarchies. With the aid of aesthetic techniques, and speaking subjectively, aesthetic surgery *aficionados*, trans-people and those labelled as deviating from bodily norms—indeed, anyone who is ready to subject themselves to the demands of the market—may strive to become not ordinary, but outstanding, even spectacular. As Edmonds (2007, 2010) notes, for many Brazilian women cosmetic surgery and the beauty industry promise upward mobility and have become almost a prerequisite for finding a job in Rio de Janeiro's highly competitive service sector. Jarrín (2017, 16) emphasizes the affective quality of beauty as capital in Brazil, where 'both money and beauty are essential aspects of having worth in society, and they are understood as buttressing each other in fundamental ways.' In her study of cosmetic surgery in China, Wen Hua (2013) likewise analyses 'beauty capital' as being of great concern to young Chinese, who 'regard an attractive appearance obtained from cosmetic surgery as a form of capital that can give them an edge in the job market' (ibid., 80). In Venezuela, a nation that has repeatedly won the international Miss World beauty contest, beauty, glamour and what Ochoa (2014) calls 'spectacular femininities' are part of the political economy. For women entering the large beauty and entertainment employment sector, aesthetic body modifications are 'to a certain degree expected' (ibid., 194). In a recent volume on beauty politics in neoliberal times, Elias et al. (2017) argue that, by accumulating aesthetic capital, women are expected to become 'aesthetic entrepreneurs,' ever-vigilant about their outward appearance.

Are the fantasies and desires of beauty that accompany the normalization of 'corrective' measures thus part of a pervasive 'beauty myth,' as claimed by critical feminists, who argue that women's increased spending on their bodily appearance supports, rather than challenges, their subordinate position in patriarchal societies (cf. Wolf 1991; Jeffreys 2005)? Or rather, are they indeed effective, in that they function to disturb normative regimes of representation, if not by 'queering' (the look of) everyday life, then perhaps through the affective power of the sublime? While these questions cannot be completely resolved in the present volume, its various contributions all engage with this important debate by providing ethnographic and conceptual food for thought.

What is perhaps most important to argue in this regard is that hegemonic beauty and appearance norms affect people in different ways depending on their situated-ness within a gendered and racialized global economy. Norms of beauty and appearance affect both men and women, but not for nothing has there been a focus on femininity in the social science literature on beauty. While statistics suggest that men are also indulging in cosmetic surgery and spending on beauty products and services in growing numbers (Jones 2010, 294, 335), women continue to be its main consumers and make up the majority of cosmetic surgery patients. As the work of Judith Butler shows (1990, 1993), gender is produced in a process that is never completed or finished, but requires the constant performance and reiteration of gendered norms. For those who wish to be recognized as 'women,' norms of outer appearance and standards of feminine beauty play a crucial role in accomplishing this task. Much has been written on beauty as an external symbol of femininity that is intricately linked to female identity and the self, typically from a critical feminist perspective. In one of the foundational feminist works on beauty, Sandra Lee Bartky (1990) warns of the existentiality of the link between women's bodily appearance and femininity that the feminist critique of beauty norms calls into question:

> ... any political project that aims to dismantle the machinery that turns a female body into a feminine one may well be apprehended by a woman as something that threatens her with desexualisation, if not outright annihilation. (ibid., 105)

It is therefore hardly surprising that our call for the relationship between beauty and the norms of bodily appearance be debated almost exclusively attracted research on femininity, which also makes itself felt in the focus of the present volume.

The notion that beauty entails the promise of redemption, wealth and happiness for women is a kind of folk wisdom that provides the stuff fairy tales are made of, among them *Beauty and the Beast*, the French fairy tale first recorded in the eighteenth century that inspired our title. As Hamburger points out (2015), the story of *Beauty and the Beast* draws on a much older motif of 'beautiful girls and wild guys,' teaching its audience that beauty is essential for women, while for men lack of it may be transcended by wealth, charm and intelligence. In its history of oral, literary and visual transmission, the beast was often embodied by those who, due to their bodily otherness, were commonly presented as fairground 'freaks' throughout the eighteenth and nineteenth centuries. Examples include the 'ugly dwarf,' the syphilitic, with their typical facial deformations, or persons diagnosed with hypertrichosis, that is, an abnormal growth of hair on the face and body (Hamburger 2015).

To disentangle the multiple meanings of this fairy tale and its repercussions in contemporary media productions and urban legends all over the world, much more is needed than a simplistic notion of beauty as a form of power *or* a powerful myth. It requires, we argue, an understanding of beauty and the norm in their interrelatedness as a historical process of ordering and categorizing bodies into binary categories. However, as argued by Maxine Leeds Craig (2006) in an influential article, feminist work on the subject of beauty has often been limited by its use of 'individualist frameworks', as well as by a neglect of the (local) ramifications of race and class. Discussing the works of Sandra Lee Bartky (1988) and Iris Marion Young (1980) in particular, Craig shows that these started out from the position of a generalized woman 'that [is] racially unmarked, implicitly heterosexual [and] of unspecified class' (2006, 162). As Craig notes, '[t]he feelings of inadequacy produced by the presence of beauty standards in women's lives are, arguably, among the most personal manifestations of gender inequality in our lives' (ibid.). Following up on this, we argue that the study of (normative) beauty begins with the acknowledgement and analysis of inequality within the larger societal context. Such a perspective unavoidably leads us towards a notion of beauty as contested and paves the way for looking at the challenges and resistances of hegemonic norms, as well as at the 'multiple standards of beauty in circulation' (Craig 2006, 160).

As several contributions to this volume illustrate, while there are hegemonic beauty norms on an increasingly global scale, these are not at all going unchallenged, and their representation is far from monolithic. Instead, often as the result of political struggles, representations of beauty have come to include an increasing number of images of so-called 'alternative beauty' (cf. Tate 2009). Models may now include persons with albinism or of a darker complexion, or they may showcase specific subcultures or 'disability chic' (see Fox, Krings and Vierke in this volume). While the multiplicity of ways to be publicly recognized as beautiful may produce a more inclusive, affective belonging in the social and political spheres, we remain sceptical regarding the extent to which these representations are actually managing to reconfigure the dominant norms.

To sum up, standards of beauty, even when they become increasingly global, do not lead to a bodily standardization worldwide. As struggles against them change not only the standard itself, but the social, political and economic premises on which they are based, new standards emerge in what is an ongoing and contested process within an increasingly global economy.

Scope and Outline

As Timmermans and Epstein have noted (2010, 74), few scholars have analyzed specific (bodily) standards directly. Thus, this volume starts off with two contributions on the historical emergence and, indeed, the manufacturing of bodily standards in two particular contexts, namely masculine hairiness in late nineteenth- and early twentieth-century Prague (Herza), and body weight around the same time in the

Netherlands (Huistra). In his contribution to this volume, Filip Herza examines turn-of-the-century freak shows to consider the broader field of performing the masculine body. He shows that such shows were important sites for the negotiation and reproduction of gendered norms, as well as of bodily ab/normality. Against the background of an emerging professional dermatology and a growing cosmetic market, spectators of the so-called hairy wonders of early twentieth-century Prague freak shows 'learned' to think about the beautiful, clean and respectable masculine body in terms of criteria of normality and abnormality. Moreover, by staring, they could both distance themselves from the figure of the freak and self-identify as 'normal,' and feel threatened by the uncertainty of gender performances and the imminent sanctions tied to any transgression of the associated norms.

In her contribution to this volume, Hieke Huistra analyses the creation of what is arguably the most powerful standard of beauty today, namely body weight. As Huistra shows, body weight was not always relevant even where and when ideals of slimness were (already) in place. She also shows that, while body size, as in fatness or slimness, and body weight are commonly conflated, they are not the same. There is a paradox implied in the contemporary focus on body weight that is not easily apparent because weight as a beauty standard, according to Huistra, has become 'naturalized'. Thus, Huistra points out that body weight is not directly visible (and indeed, is commonly hidden), which prompts her to ask 'why do so many of us expect to be admired for something other people cannot see?' Analyzing late nineteenth- and early twentieth-century Dutch newspaper reports on fairs, beauty manuals and advertisements for slimming products, she describes the shift in the approach to body weight from a bodily curiosity on Dutch fairgrounds to a 'securely established ... beauty standard' in the Netherlands around 1930.

By doing so, she also describes a moral economy of beauty standards. As Jacqueline Urla and Jennifer Terry noted (1995, 1), the idea 'that moral character is rooted in the body' is ingrained 'in Western scientific and popular thought.' This becomes especially clear in light of the recent global campaign by the World Health Organization (WHO) to tackle the so-called global obesity epidemic. Huistra's contribution underlines the fact that the bodily standards that continue to inform, guide and indeed haunt biopolitics globally today are far from 'natural' or self-evident, but emerged as a historical process and under very specific circumstances.

Following this first set of chapters on the manufacturing of beauty norms is a closely connected second group on the representation of extraordinary bodies as 'alternative' forms of beauty. Christopher Hohl and Matthias Krings (this volume) look at the representation of the albinotic body from a social constructivist and comparative perspective. More particularly, they analyse three different forms of 'framing' the albinotic body to illustrate how these go hand in hand with either its spectacularization or normalization. In the first framing, that of nineteenth-century freak shows, albinotic bodies, like the hairy wonders described by Herza, function to transform the viewer into an 'undifferentiated mass of onlookers, bestowed with normality by the figure of the freak on stage.' Reacting to a process of medicalization and the pathologizing of the albinotic body in the early twentieth century, in the second frame, in the 1990s fashion photographers, with Rick Guidotti leading the way, attempted to redefine persons diagnosed with albinism as beautiful. And finally, in contemporary fashion modelling, the albinotic body is recoded as a valuable aesthetic quality to be celebrated for its glamorous and extraordinary beauty. Models diagnosed with albinism like Shaun Ross are now framed within a success story of overcoming stigmatization in a way that also constitutes an opportunity for the fashion-beauty industry, 'whose body politics are frequently subjected to heavy criticism.' While art photography and fashion modelling have indeed reduced the stigma of albinism by representing it as 'alternative beauty,' the authors point out that, as glamorous fashion models, albinotic bodies are once again represented as detached from ordinary everyday life, and like other bodies on the walkways of the global fashion scene, they leave their viewers feeling incomplete and insufficient.

Sarah Böllinger, in this volume, likewise focuses on the representation of bodies defined as disabled, namely in contemporary African art. Drawing on the concept of disability aesthetics (Siebers 2010), her chapter looks closely at the depiction of disabled human bodies by two African artists, namely the Kenyan painter Hezbon Owiti and the Moroccan sculptor, painter and performance artist Yassine Balbzioui, whose broken porcelain cups—one of which can be seen on the cover of this volume—speak of metaphorical disability. Böllinger discusses the 'disability gain' (Garland-Thomson 2015) that one may experience by analyzing artworks related to disability, and she shows how, by contesting established conceptions of the disabled body, anthropology, art and visual cultural studies can contribute to our understanding of the complex relationship between beauty and bodily norms.

Coined in an attempt to reframe disability as a source of gain rather than loss, the notion of 'disability gain' also constitutes the starting point of the conversation following Böllinger's chapter between Ann Fox, Matthias Krings and Ulf Vierke. As becomes clear, the notion of 'disability gain' raises a number of questions, including that of what happens when disabled bodies are commodified in an attempt to represent 'alternative beauty.' While some of these representations certainly do contain inclusionary moments, among them an appreciation of bodily difference as a source of beauty (Fox), others may be based on what Krings calls a beauty 'in spite of' disability, or which may even constitute 'inspiration porn' (Vierke). The conversation shows that, while the stakes for the fashion-beauty industry in extending aesthetic norms, pluralizing beauty and mainstreaming diversity are high, it manoeuvres within the economic logics of a capitalist market that, in its celebration of 'difference,' often reproduces forms of Othering. Finally, the figure of the cyborg, which has experienced a comeback in the recent debates over human enhancement, is discussed as a dystopian model for our bodies, which, from this perspective, are all in need of (aesthetic) enhancement through technology.

Indeed, cosmetic surgery, as Liebelt shows in her contribution on reshaping 'Turkish' female breasts and noses in Turkey, is now commonly conceptualized as a form of aesthetic enhancement, especially when it comes to the 'needs' of racialized and gendered bodies for what surgeons commonly term 'ethnic plastic surgery.' In Turkey, aesthetic body modification and surgery have become ever more normalized forms of consumption, and women may engage in surgery in an attempt to enhance and indeed 'normalize' their bodies. Given the common construal of large female breasts and noses as national defects linked to rural backwardness, this rings especially true for breast reduction and nose surgery. Finally, female breasts and noses are scrutinized by a patriarchal society that seeks control over the sexual female body; by altering them, women hope to reduce dominating stares at their bodies. This contribution illustrates that, when ideals of beauty travel transnationally, they are imbued with changing and varied meanings in different locations.

In the following contribution, which is also on the self-fashioning and beauty practices of young Muslim women in part three of this volume, Arzu Ünal shows how, in wearing the pious *Tesettür* style, the young daughters of Turkish immigrants to the Netherlands carefully manage their outer appearance to conform to both Turkish-Muslim gender norms and the normative expectations of themselves as 'presentable' employees and fashionable young women in the wider society. Due to older female relatives' reluctance to use make-up and the mainstream beauty and fashion industry's failure to countenance an Islamically proper outer appearance, their role models are limited. Thus, in a process of ever-changing compliance with gendered and moral ideals, as well as through a process of 'trial and error,' the young women that Ünal describes develop their own *Tesettür*-conforming styles and make-up practices, thus adapting the beauty and fashion mainstream to their needs.

Perhaps similar to what the young women Ünal describes might feel, the Nairobi-based performative artist Syowia Kyambi, in conversation with Anisha Soff in this volume, reflects on a situation where she often feels that 'the product is not for me,' given the fact that most of the products of the beauty and cosmetics industry continue to be produced for a white, Western market. Conversing about a public performance Kyambi developed for the conference that preceded this volume,[2] Kyambi and Soff analyse a 'flux in the relationship between beauty, as a personal assessment, and the hegemonic norms that people struggle with' (Kyambi). Recounting her own experiences of racism and of struggling with gendered and racialized beauty norms in an ageing body, Kyambi reflects on the frustrations and the feelings of 'insufficiency' imposed on one within a competitive labour market or when confronted with the beauty and cosmetic industry's marketing campaigns. Because they are established so early in life and are so substantive for the ways we see ourselves, Kyambi asserts, beauty norms are especially 'hard to break free from ... even if it is not necessarily a positive representation of your identity for you.' Because beauty is such a personal and yet public and embodied aspect of the self, Kyambi and Soff agree, it is a particularly 'tricky' topic for scientific investigation.

The conversation between Kyambi and Soff is the first of a final part of contributions that focus on skin colour politics across a variety of geographical settings. In her contribution to this volume, Doreen Gordon writes on the comparative meanings of beauty among emerging non-white elites in South Africa, Brazil and Jamaica. Against the background of an immense growth in the hair and skin bleaching or toning industry among black people across the diaspora, for Gordon's respondents the consumption of beauty products and services is vital in their efforts to 'become visible' and respected. While in all three settings self-identified black respondents 'crossed or blurred racial boundaries through their beauty discourses and practices,' her material shows that this is easier in Brazil and Jamaica than in post-apartheid South Africa, where those categorized as black experienced enforced segregation. Brazilians and Jamaicans, she writes, now 'privilege a brown, mixed raced appearance,' shifts in racial thinking having made it less problematic to identify with blackness, whereas in South Africa, 'indigenous cultural practices have mixed with western hegemonic discourses about beauty as well as discourses and practices from the African diaspora.'

The complex meanings of skin colour within a racialized global economy likewise become clear in Nina Kullrich's contribution to this volume. In India, where Kullrich studied skin colour politics and beauty practices, normative beauty, especially for women, is ever more closely linked to fairness of skin, despite awareness campaigns such as 'Dark Is Beautiful' rejecting and fighting the ideal of fairness and warning of the health risks of bleaching. Understanding the Indian ideal of 'fairness'—rather than 'whiteness'—solely as an imitation of western beauty standards or as a kind of colonial legacy, Kullrich argues, would be wrong because this perspective ignores 'both pre-colonial and non-western perspectives on beauty' and risks reproducing Eurocentric ideas. Instead, Kullrich traces the changing and situational meanings of fairness, adopting a performative perspective on skin-bleaching practices and the desire for a fair skin. She shows that fairness as an Indian ideal of beauty is closely linked with the imaginations of an (upper) middle-class, urban and cosmopolitan lifestyle that, for her respondents, materializes most clearly in the marriage and job markets.

Shirley Tate (2016), arguably one of the most prolific writers on contemporary skin colour politics and Black skin tone practices, likewise proposes to think about the variety of motivations underlying the practices of skin bleaching, lightening or toning. In a conversation with Katharina Fink that forms the final contribution to this volume, she reflects on the current resurgence of white supremacist ideas in the US American public sphere and its underlying racist-colonial imaginary that denies 'Black beauty, dignity and grace.' Beauty, she asserts, 'is not just a matter for the individual,' but socially constructed and as such 'has always been a political issue' for Black thinkers, 'engaged in thinking through what Black anti-racist aesthetics could and should be about politically, in terms of beautification practices and theoretically, in terms of critiquing white supremacist beauty norms.' In spite of decades of collective struggles against such norms, Tate comes to the conclusion that 'we still drag colonial conceptions of skin colour and beauty into the twenty-first century,' and she attributes a central role in this to the work of multi-nationals, which, by claiming to 'open up' new markets, are helping to create new beauty norms on a global scale, even though these might now include 'mixed looks' rather than just whiteness. Tate's thoughtful questions towards the end of the conversation are in many ways similar to those we had in mind when embarking on this book project, and they will certainly stay with us in future investigations, as well as in the politics of beauty more generally. What happens to people whose bodies defy dominant beauty norms or are found lacking in respect of what counts as an ordinary appearance? What does the increasing consumption of aesthetic body modifications mean for the particularities of our bodies, our everyday lives and the ways in which we determine what is good, beautiful, healthy and 'normal'? Under such circumstances, can we ever be truly content with how we look, or are we doomed to keep trying for perfection until our bodies simply cannot take it anymore?

The present collection thus seeks to open up rather than conclude the debate on bodily standardization and the normative implications of the global beauty boom. It is based on a notion of the body that questions the dichotomy between the social and the biological as long maintained and reproduced within Cartesian thinking. Instead, drawing on the work of Judith Butler, it foregrounds the materiality of the body as something that is 'less an entity than a relation, [one that] cannot be fully dissociated from the infrastructural and environmental conditions of its living' (Butler 2016, 19). From such a perspective, the body can only be understood as malleable and in a state of becoming, rather than being; interdependent on social relationships and embedded in particular bio-political economies. Moreover, such a perspective recognizes no 'natural' or 'given' body, in contrast to one that has artificially been modified, altered or enhanced to conform with dominant ideals. This is not to say that beauty norms, or any other gendered and racialized norms for that matter, can be changed easily or at will. Indeed, all the contributions to this volume speak of the deeply affective and embodied aspects of normative beauty that inform our everyday lives and desires, are tied to subjectivities in a deep and abiding manner and are 'tricky' to change or challenge, even collectively. Norms, including beauty norms, significantly shape and indeed support our bodies long before they come into material existence.

Against the background of a global boom in beauty services and products, all our contributions speak of the meanings of beauty for people across the globe and the immense costs and efforts of achieving it. This fact calls for scholarly consideration, yet so far it has received surprisingly little attention in the academic literature outside feminist and gender studies. Our edited volume brings together ethnographic and conceptual approaches from a variety of disciplines and across a large number of geographical locations to debate issues of standardization in bodily appearance. It calls for a politics of beauty that is wary of the way lookism, racism, ableism, ageism or classism, to name but a few normative regimes, affect the ways we look and how we represent ourselves. It sets out to analyse the meanings of beautification and aesthetic body modification for the particularities of bodies and people's everyday lives worldwide. Finally, it proposes to initiate an interdisciplinary and ethical debate on how we determine what is good, beautiful, healthy and 'normal' and what the implications are of doing so.

NOTES

1. To our knowledge, such claims have not been subject to any profound critique from the perspective of critical beauty studies.
2. 'Beauty and the Norm: Debating Standardization in Bodily Appearances,' Bayreuth University, 6–8 April 2016.

REFERENCES

Adrian, Bonnie. 2003. *Framing the Bride: Globalizing Beauty and Romance in Taiwan's Bridal Industry.* Berkeley and Los Angeles: University of California Press.

Appadurai, Arjun. 1990. "Disjuncture and Difference in the Global Cultural Economy." *Theory Culture Society* 7: 295–310.

Bartky, S. L. 1990. *Femininity and Domination: Studies in the Phenomenology of Oppression.* New York: Routledge.

Bartky, S. L. 1988. "Foucault, Femininity, and the Modernization of Patriarchal Power." In *Feminism and Foucault,* edited by I. Diamond and L. Quinby, 61–86. Boston: Northeastern University Press.

Brunsson, N., and B. Jacobsson (eds.). 2000. *A World of Standards.* Oxford: Oxford University Press.

Buss, David. 2003 [1994]. *The Evolution of Desire*. 2nd ed. New York: Basic Books.

Butler, Judith. 1990. *Gender Trouble: Feminism and the Subversion of Identity*. New York and London: Routledge.

Butler, Judith. 1993. *Bodies That Matter: On the Discursive Limits of 'Sex'*. New York and London: Routledge.

Butler, Judith. 2016. "Rethinking Vulnerability and Resistance." In *Vulnerability in Resistance*, edited by J. Butler, Z. Gambetti, and L. Sabsay, 12–27. Durham and London: Duke University Press.

Craig, Maxine L. 2006. "Race, Beauty, and the Tangled Knot of Guilty Pleasure." *Feminist Theory* 7 (2): 159–77.

Coleman, R., and M. M. Figueroa. 2010. "Past and Future Perfect? Beauty, Affect and Hope." *Journal for Cultural Research* 4 (4): 357–73.

Davis, Lennard J. 1995. *Enforcing Normalcy: Disability, Deafness and the Body*. London and New York: Verso.

Döring, Daniela. 2011. *Zeugende Zahlen. Mittelmaß und Durchschnittstypen in Proportion, Statistik und Konfektion*. Berlin: Kulturverlag Kadmos [German].

Edmonds, A. 2007. "'The Poor Have the Right to Be Beautiful': Cosmetic Surgery in Neoliberal Brazil." *Journal of the Royal Anthropological Institute* 13 (2): 363–81.

Edmonds, A. 2010. *Pretty Modern: Beauty, Sex, and Plastic Surgery in Brazil*. Durham and London: Duke University Press.

Elias, Ana Sofia, Rosalind Gill, and Christina Scharff, (eds.). 2017. *Aesthetic Labour: Rethinking Beauty Politics in Neoliberalism*. London: Palgrave Macmillan.

Epstein, Steven. 2009. "Beyond the Human Standard?" In *Standards and Their Stories: How Quantifying, Classifying, and Formalizing Practices Shape Everyday Life*, edited by Martha Lampland and Susan Leigh Star, 35–53. Ithaca: Cornell University Press.

Etcoff, Nancy. 1999. *Survival of the Prettiest: The Science of Beauty*. New York: Doubleday.

Foucault, Michel. 1990. *The History of Sexuality, Volume 1: An Introduction*. Translated by Robert Hurley. New York: Vintage Books.

Foucault, Michel. 1995. *Discipline and Punish: The Birth of the Prison*. 2nd ed. Translated by Alan Sheridan. New York: Vintage Books.

Garland-Thomson, R. 1997. *Extraordinary Bodies: Figuring Physical Disability in American Culture and Literature*. Columbia: Columbia University Press.

Garland-Thomson, R. 2009. *Staring: How We Look*. Oxford: Oxford University Press.

Garland-Thomson, R. 2015. "A Habitable World: Harriet McBryde Johnson's 'Case for My Life.'" *Hypatia* 30 (1): 300–6.

Gilman, S. L. 1999. *Making the Body Beautiful: A Cultural History of Aesthetic Surgery*. Princeton and Oxford: Princeton University Press.

Hamburger, Andreas. 2015. "Beautiful Beasts—Motif Tradition and Film Psychoanalysis in Jean Cocteau's LA BELLE ET LA BETE (F 1946)." In *Women and Images of Men in Cinema: Gender Construction in La Belle et la Bete by Jean Cocteau*, edited by A. Hamburger, 43–95. London: Karnac.

Holliday, R., D. Bell, O. Cheung, M. Jones, and E. Probyn. 2015. "Brief Encounters: Assembling Cosmetic Surgery Tourism." *Social Science and Medicine* 124: 298–304.

Hua, Wen. 2013. *Buying Beauty: Cosmetic Surgery in China*. Hong Kong: Hong Kong University Press.

Jafar, A., and E. M. de Casanova. 2013. *Global Beauty, Local Bodies*. New York: Palgrave Macmillan.

Jarrín, A. 2017. *The Biopolitics of Beauty: Cosmetic Citizenship and Affective Capital in Brazil*. Oakland: University of California Press.

Jeffreys, S. H. 2005. *Beauty and Misogyny: Harmful Cultural Practices in the West*. London and New York: Routledge.

Jha, M. R. 2016. *The Global Beauty Industry: Colorism, Racism and the National Body*. New York and Abingdon: Routledge.

Jones, Geoffrey. 2010. *Beauty Imagined. A History of the Global Beauty Industry*. Oxford and New York: Oxford University Press.

Miller, L. 2006. *Beauty Up: Exploring Contemporary Japanese Body Aesthetics*. Berkeley, Los Angeles, and London: University of California Press.

Nguyen, M. T. H. 2011. "The Biopower of Beauty: Humanitarian Imperialism and Global Feminisms in an Age of Terror." *Signs* 36 (2): 359–83.

Ochoa, M. 2014. *Queen for a Day: Transformistas, Beauty Queens, and the Performance of Femininity in Venezuela*. Durham and London: Duke University Press.

Pallet, P., S. Link, and K. Lee. 2010. "New 'Golden' Ratios for Facial Beauty." *Vision Research* 50: 149–54.

Porter, Theodore M. 1986. *The Rise of Statistical Thinking 1820–1900*. Princeton and Chichester: Princeton University Press.

Quetelet, L. A. J. 2013 [1842]. *A Treatise on Man and the Development of His Faculties*. Cambridge: Cambridge University Press.

Quinn, P. C., D. J. Kelly, K. Lee, O. Pascalis, and A. M. Slater. 2008. "Preference for Attractive Faces in Human Infants Extends Beyond Conspecifics." *Developmental Science* 11: 76–83.

Rikowski, A., and K. Grammer. 1999. "Human Body Odour, Symmetry and Attractiveness." *Proceedings of the Royal Society B* 266 (1422): 869–74.

Siebers, Tobin. 2010. *Disability Aesthetics*. Ann Arbor: University of Michigan Press.

Swain, John, Sally French, and Colin Cameron. 2003. *Controversial Issues in a Disabling Society*. Maidenhead and New York: Open University Press.

Tate, S. H. A. 2009. *Black Beauty: Aesthetics, Stylization, Politics.* Farnham, Surrey and Burlington, VT: Ashgate.

Tate, S. H. A. 2016. *Skin Bleaching in Black Atlantic Zones: Shade Shifters.* London: Palgrave Macmillan.

Timmermans, Stefan, and Steven Epstein. 2010. "A World of Standards but Not a Standard World: Toward a Sociology of Standards and Standardization." *Annual Review of Sociology* 36: 69–89.

Urla, J., and J. Terry. 1995. "Introduction: Mapping Embodied Deviance." In *Deviant Bodies: Critical Perspectives on Difference in Science and Popular Culture,* edited by J. Terry and J. Urla, 1–18. Bloomington: Indiana University Press.

Wolf, Naomi. 1991. *The Beauty Myth: How Images of Beauty Are Used Against Women.* New York: William Morrow and Company.

Young, I. M. 1980. "Throwing Like a Girl: A Phenomenology of Feminine Body Comportment, Motility and Spatiality." *Human Studies* 3: 137–56.

PART I

Doing and Undoing Norms

Faces of Masculinity: Shaving Practices and Popular Exhibitions of 'Hairy Wonders' in Early Twentieth-Century Prague

Filip Herza

As with so many other ideas, the impetus for this chapter came from reading the daily press, in this particular case, the major liberal German- and Czech-language newspapers,[1] published in the 1900–1910s in Prague, back then a provincial capital of the Austro-Hungarian Empire.[2] My reading was initially motivated by a search for news items about freak shows[3] in Prague, involving one person in particular, a man called Stephan Bibrowski (1890–1932). In his time, Bibrowski was better known as the 'Lion Man', a professional 'hairy wonder' who performed on freak show stages throughout early twentieth-century Europe.[4] What struck me at first sight, while browsing through the pages of these

The research on which this chapter is based was supported by an SVV grant, no. 260 468, 'Imagining "the Other": collective representations and politics of exclusion in Czech lands after 1750' at the Faculty of Humanities, Charles University in 2017.

F. Herza (✉)
Faculty of Humanities, Charles University, Prague, Czech Republic

© The Author(s) 2019   23
C. Liebelt et al. (eds.), *Beauty and the Norm*,
Palgrave Studies in Globalization and Embodiment,
https://doi.org/10.1007/978-3-319-91174-8_2

newspapers searching for news features on Bibrowski, was a prominent conglomeration of three different types of advertisement that all somehow related to hairiness. First, there were ads for beauty products offered to both women and men, among them different sorts of facial balms, miraculous pills to induce the growth of facial hair and various items of shaving equipment, such as shaving foam and razor blades. The second group consisted of advertisements published by medical professionals, often dermatologists, offering their products and services to women and 'gentlemen' suffering problems with their skin and with facial hair. What I felt was significant is that, in many cases, right next to these ads, there was a third type of picture and advertisement, namely of freak performers such as 'Lion Man Lionel' (*Der Löwenmensch/Lví muž Lionel*) mentioned above. Bibrowski was an eighteen-year-old man whose body was covered completely in thick hair and as a result was presented and advertised as a freak, 'half man, half lion'.[5] In a rare but significant case, these three sets of texts and images merged to form a coherent whole: in an advertisement for 'Mos Balm' (*Mosův balzám*) from 1911, bald and beardless readers are encouraged to cheer up and try out 'the one and only product of modern medicine, which—within just eight to 14 days—stimulates the hair bulbs and thus leads to an amazing growth of facial hair.'[6] To visualize the efficacy of the medicine, the ad showed images of a man and a woman with lush hair and, in the man's case, a long, vigorous beard (see Fig. 2.1). Between the two is a smaller inset depicting another face, reminiscent of a furry dog, but possibly also recognizable as an unusually hairy human similar to the 'hairy wonders' that were often on display in contemporary freak shows, such as Bibrowski.

This conjunction of images and texts related to body hair, and particularly to male facial hair, was certainly no coincidence. I wondered what it was that gave facial hair such significance at the turn of the century and how we should interpret the obvious popularity of 'hairy' performers such as Bibrowski? Thus, my initial research into the culture of the nineteenth- and twentieth-century freak shows eventually led me to consider the much broader field of performances of the masculine body, as delineated by early twentieth-century concepts of beauty and cleanliness. As I argue, such considerations are worth studying not only with regard to the understanding of the popularity and significance of European freak shows as important sites of the negotiation and reproduction of gendered norms. More generally, embodied masculinity is a subject that, to date, has received little attention compared to

Fig. 2.1 Advertisement for *Mosův balzám* (Mos balm), *Rozvoj*, 15 December 1911, 10

the burgeoning research on female embodiment. By linking masculine beauty ideals, shaving practices and the popularity of hairy wonders in early twentieth-century Prague, I hope to contribute to the ongoing project of masculinity studies, initiated some twenty years ago by publications such as Raewyn Connell's *Maculinities* (1995) and Michael Kimmel's *Politics of Manhood* (1995). At the same time, by linking the debate about the normative masculine body to that of the freak, I seek to address the role of ab/normality in defining the clean and beautiful masculine subject, thus deepening our understanding of gender performance in the field of masculinity and beauty studies.

Recent literature on beards and shaving practices offers a good starting point for these considerations. Probably due to the glorious comeback of beards in the current hipster fashion, which would itself be worth critical examination, scholarly research on the history of the beard has recently proliferated just as much as the facial hair on the faces of today's men. So far, scholars have focused on how grooming and shaving practices have served as a gendered language or performance in particular historical periods (Walton 2008; Tapley 2014).

Special attention has been given to the significance of the beard in relation to what Connell and others termed hegemonic, counter-hegemonic and subordinated masculinities (Connell 1995; Connell and Messerschmidt 2005). Others have explored historical continuities and analysed the changing meanings of sporting a full beard, trimming a moustache or shaving the whole face. For example, Oldstone-Moore (2005, 2016) suggested that the beard has a cyclical history in Western culture and that these cycles coincide with repeating crises of masculinity, for example, the crisis commonly associated with the industrialization of the mid-nineteenth century or the late nineteenth-century struggles over women's suffrage. More recently, Alexander Maxwell (2015) has linked the politics of shaving not only to re-negotiations of gender and social hierarchies, but also to national identities. Referring to the specific case of Hungary, Maxwell demonstrates how the moustache demarcated the borders of an imagined Hungarian nation throughout the nineteenth century (see also Lafferton 2007). Building upon these debates, this chapter asks: What does the synchronicity of the popular hairy freak Lionel, the emergence of professional dermatology and the growth of the cosmetic product market tell us about the development of ideals of male beauty, and particularly about the changing relationship between beauty ideals and the medical notion of the ab/normal body in turn-of-the-century Bohemia?

By posing the question in this way, I subscribe to a concept of masculinity that emphasizes the idea of historical change. My approach thus differs from that employed by George L. Mosse in his influential *The Image of Man* (1998). In this work, Mosse describes the modern masculine ideal as a set of definite characteristics that emerged during the Napoleonic wars of 1803–1815 and that continued to affect European society up until the mid-twentieth century. Rather, my conceptualization of masculinity adheres to the ideas of Connell and Messerschmidt (2005), noted above, which give greater space to dynamic change, negotiations of power hierarchies and the multiplicity of masculinities.

The gender performance according to which one is distinguished as a male thus, I argue, intersects with performances of other social differences, such as race, ethnicity, class and dis/ability, making it an aspect of the negotiation of power hierarchies in society. Therefore, there are a range of masculinities that include some positions that can assume a privileged position of power, usually temporarily: that is, hegemonic masculinity (Connell and Messerschmidt 2005, 851). How would one then conceptualize the relationship between this hegemonic masculinity and shaving practices? An important clue to answering this question comes from feminist research on beauty.

In recent decades, feminist scholars have put a great deal of effort into theorizing beauty and studying the effects of beauty ideals on the lives of women (Coleman and Figueroa 2010). Based on this rich body of work, we can theorize beauty as a contested symbolical resource that is closely connected to the production of gender, class and racial differences (Craig 2006). Considered as such, beauty, or at least proper appearance, can be considered an important resource for hegemonic masculinity, although it is not the only one. Indeed, in the context of nineteenth-century Europe, and particularly in relation to the male body, we scarcely read about male 'beauty,' but rather of the 'cleanliness' or 'respectability' of the male body. In personal letters from nineteenth-century Bohemia, mothers usually advise their sons to maintain a 'respectable' and 'clean' appearance, which was considered more appropriate for men than beauty, which had a female ring to it (Lenderová et al. 2014, 105). In the following, I will thus concentrate on cleanliness as the central ideal of male beauty of the time.

Finally, I would like to complete my conceptual outline of the relationship between hegemonic masculinity, beauty and cleanliness by briefly discussing the concepts of normativity and ab/normality. Following Butler (1993), the concept of gender performance already includes a notion of normative scripts that must be followed to produce a successful gender performance. I argue that the normative scripts of hegemonic masculinity in late nineteenth- and early twentieth-century Prague were informed by contemporary notions of the ab/normal body. There is a consensus among historians of disability that bodily normality is a concept that emerges around the middle of the nineteenth century, chiefly defined by statistics and modern medicine, which gradually influenced European society (Davis 1995). Regarding the beard and shaving practices, I ask how the emergence of this biomedical notion of a bodily norm, and of ab/normality more generally, had an impact on male hairiness in Bohemia and, if it did, what were its consequences for men's daily practices of bodily grooming and the making of a proper male body?

To sum up, in this chapter, the exhibition of Lionel, the 'hairy freak', in the Prague of the 1910s, serves as a point of departure for debating the transformation of masculinity in the context of early twentieth-century Bohemia. My main objective is to understand the popularity and meanings generated by the figure of Bibrowski in this regard. At the same time, I am trying to understand the significance of beards and shaving practices for the performance of hegemonic masculinity, as well as in demonstrating class and national belonging. In the following, I focus on three interconnected areas: the freak show culture, the emergence of a male cosmetic market, and the rise of expert dermatological knowledge in late nineteenth-century Bohemia.

FREAK SHOWS AND 'HAIRY WONDERS' IN THE NINETEENTH AND TWENTIETH CENTURIES

Before we can move on to discuss the changing significance of beards and shaving practices in the performance of masculinity, and specifically the notion of the norm, we need to familiarize ourselves with the culture of exhibiting so-called 'hairy wonders' in the nineteenth-century freak show tradition. Performers with excessive facial and/or body hair, sometimes called 'hairy wonders', formed only a part of a much larger group of 'human marvels' that constituted the cast of freak shows, popular exhibitions of 'otherness' organized in Europe and the USA throughout the nineteenth and early twentieth centuries. As Rosemary Garland-Thomson suggested (1997), freaks were the products of their staging, that is, performative constructs referring to the boundaries of what was considered normal by their contemporaries. For example, popular 'Lilliputian' performers put into question the boundary between children and adults, 'Siamese twins' that between the individual and society, and 'bearded ladies' that between male and female. The interaction between the audience and the ambiguous figures of freaks, which oscillated between differentiation and identification, enabled the audience to rest in the subject position of the normal, while at the same time projecting its suppressed fears and desires on to the figure of the freak (Garland-Thomson 1997, 61).

'Hairy wonders' constituted a specific category of professional freaks, which could be related to the troubling boundaries between masculinity and femininity, civilization and barbarism, humanity and animality. Besides the 'bearded ladies' already mentioned, people with extremely long hair and beards were also exhibited on the freak show stages. As in many cases they had been brought from the colonies, their ethnic difference played an important role and actually interacted with the perceived bodily difference to form a complex image of 'the Other' that underpinned the idea of civilization, ultimately legitimizing Western colonial rule. Since the middle of the nineteenth century, Darwinism started to play an important role in imagining 'the colonial Other', as is also witnessed by the freak show culture at this time. Particularly after the publication of Darwin's *Descent of Man* in 1871, 'hairy' exhibits started to be presented as 'living proofs' of the theory of evolution (Hamlin 2011). The most famous of these alleged evolutionary 'throwbacks' was Krao Farini (1876–1926), a female performer from Siam (today's Thailand), who, throughout her career, was exhibited as the 'missing link' in the evolutionary lineage between man and ape (Durbach 2010). The figure of Krao, with her extraordinary body and her 'exotic' origins and race, not only contributed to the dissemination of evolutionism among popular audiences in Europe, it also fitted into the orientalist imagery of the Far East as an exotic backwater of the world, to be colonized by the 'civilized' white European.[7]

This specifically orientalist and exoticizing imagery was also seen with Stephan Bibrowski (1890–1932), the so-called 'Lion Man', who appeared in Prague in 1912, as well as with his predecessor Fedor Jeftichew (1868–1904), the famous 'Jo-Jo the Dog-Faced Boy' from the Barnum and Bailey circus, who performed in the USA and Europe in the second half of the nineteenth century. Both men were presented in a very similar way, as 'half man, half animal', brought about by the styling of their facial hair, their costumes and a particular form of staging or choreography. Both performers appeared styled up in a way that made them resemble furry animals, a lion and a dog respectively, and they also wore colourful embroidered costumes reminiscent of those worn by contemporary circus animal tamers. The main narratives introducing these two 'abnormalities' were rather similar; in both cases it was claimed that they had come from 'the East': Jeftichew was born in St. Petersburg, Russia; Bibrowksi in Bielsk, part of Poland occupied by the Russian Empire. Eastern exoticism was therefore part of their performance.

However, there were also important differences in how these two freaks were presented, differences that point to some important shifts in freak show presentations and their context in the 1870–1890s and the first two decades of the twentieth century respectively. While the presentation of Jeftichew was based on the evolution narrative and stressed his savage-like personality, which allegedly could not be civilized even after he had spent many years in the US and Europe, in the case of Bibrowski evolutionary theory no longer played an important role. Rather, the official story devised for Stephan Bibrowski played with the ancient narrative of the so-called 'maternal impression'. As described in practically every article about him, his unusual appearance bore testimony to the fact that, while she was pregnant, his mother saw her husband, himself the owner of an animal menagerie, torn to shreds by one of his own lions. Affected by the horror of the scene, the mother gave birth to a lion-like boy, covered from head to toe with thick hair.

When Bibrowski came to Prague to perform in the Lhotka Cabaret (*Kabaret U Lhotků*) at Wenceslas Square in April 1912, his performance was based on a radical contrast between his animal-like appearance— as mentioned above, supported by a particular stylization—and the 'civilized demeanour' that Lionel supposedly demonstrated in his conversations and interactions with his audience.

This framing of Lionel's presentation in Prague becomes obvious in an advertisement that appeared in several issues of a major newspaper in the city in March and April 1912 (see Fig. 2.2). In this ad, Bibrowski is depicted lying on a sofa, leaning on a pillow and holding a book in his hand. The animal-like pose, the styling of his hair and the minimal dress—again we see parts of an animal trainer's costume—evoke his animality, while the book in his hand signifies his civilized character. Most importantly, the slogan used to lure the audience to visit the exhibition describes him as 'Halb Mensch halb Löwe—Der Liebling der Frauen und Kinder,' i.e. 'half-man, half-animal—the darling of women and children'.

This representation of Bibrowski, I suggest, should be read with respect not only to the obvious binaries of civilization and nature, and of man and animal respectively, but also regarding the changing significance of beards and shaving practices at the beginning of the twentieth century. If the presentation of Bibrowski is to be understood as a collective ritual of looking that served to release the anxieties of its audience (Garland-Thomson 1997, 61), what were the anxieties related to beards and hairiness in the society of Bohemia at this time? In the following two sections, I will explore the changing meaning of the beard in relation to gendered norms in the late nineteenth century along three interrelated lines that at the same time help explain the popularity of 'hairy wonders' in this historical period. In the first section, I will concentrate on the changing meanings of the beard in relation to its bearer's political and class position. In the second section, the focus turns to the rise

Fig. 2.2 Advertisement for 'Lionel the Lion Man', *Prager Tagblatt*, 30 March 1912, 10

of professional knowledge about ab/normal bodies and body hair, particularly in the discipline of professional dermatology, and on the emergence of a consumer culture, namely a market for cosmetic products that catered to both women and men.

The Politics of Beards in Bohemia and Austria in the Nineteenth Century

In the first half of the nineteenth century, shaving or sporting a beard signified one's occupation and affiliation to a particular sociocultural group in the late estate-based society of Habsburg Austria. Thus, members of particular craftsman's guilds, such as tailors and shoemakers, sported a beard on their necks, while wealthy proprietors and intellectuals of the emerging urban middle classes preferred a shaved chin and bushy sideburns. Among the employees of the Habsburg administration and in the army a shaved face was the rule, except in Hungary, where the moustache had specific national and class connotations (Maxwell 2015). The 1848 revolution and the subsequent sociopolitical changes brought about a pan-European fashion for growing a full beard. This beard now signified a revolutionary attitude and opposition, whether socialist or liberal in inclination, to the *ancien régime* (Oldstone-Moore 2005; Walton 2008). Specifically, in the context of Austria and Bohemia, full beards were a symbol of a liberal political orientation, as opposed to the supposedly reactionary, monarchical *Kaiserbart*, a combination of bushy sideburns and a moustache that was worn by Franz Joseph I and his loyal servants (Machar 2013, 80).

As pointed out by Josef Machar, a turn-of-the-century poet and publicist and himself a faithful wearer of a thick moustache, from the late 1850s to the 1880s, a long beard signalled affiliation with the liberal bourgeoisie. Moreover, it also had nationalist connotations. During the second half of the nineteenth century, parts of the bourgeoisie in Bohemia developed a distinct national identity based on the idea of a coherent national culture, language and history, which, in their eyes, justified their claims to power in relation to the existing Habsburg rule. For these Czech nationalists, long beards became a symbol of their national identity, like the style of beard worn by their alleged forefathers, the ancient Slavs.[8] Wearing a full beard in the second half of the nineteenth century thus signified male gender identity, a liberal political inclination and a bourgeois class position, as well as, in some cases, a Czech national identity. František Ladislav Rieger (1818–1903), one of the founders and most influential personalities of the Czech National Liberal Party (*Staročeši*), can be seen as a typical representative of this particular type of bearded liberal masculinity. His contemporaries described Rieger as 'having a friendly and genuinely Slavic face, a pale complexion ... dark, poignant eyes, a vigorous beard and dark-brown curly hair' (Jahn 1861, 134). In Rieger's case, the association between virile masculinity, liberalism and devotion to the national cause through facial hair was also made into a caricature in 1860, the year he re-entered the political arena as a deputy for the *Reichsrat* in Vienna. In it, Rieger was jokingly depicted as a lion—a heraldic animal of the historical kingdom of Bohemia—protecting the Bohemian royal crown. Obviously, this image was a commentary on the fact that the politics of the National Liberal Party in this period was concentrated on achieving the recognition of the historical rights and privileges of the kingdom of Bohemia within the Habsburg Monarchy. At the same time, the caricature also seemed to depict masculinity, animal virility, liberalism and nationalism, all embodied by Rieger's long beard.

Reading the abovementioned literature, it is tempting to link the success and decline of the fashion of wearing a full beard in Austria and the Bohemian lands to the political careers of the liberal bourgeoisie, who suffered a political crisis at the end of the nineteenth century (Judson 1996). Elsewhere in Europe and the USA, the end of the century was marked by a general shift towards the shaved face and/or a cultivated moustache (Walton 2008, 229). According to scholars of masculinity, however, this trend towards shaving the face should be seen not only in its relationship to the changing of political ideologies of a younger generation, but rather with respect to a more general late nineteenth-century crisis of masculinity. Michael Kimmel (1987, 1996), for example, suggests that the end of the century brought about a crisis in the gender order caused by rapid modernization and the demands of the first wave of feminism. This crisis, according to Kimmel and others, also reflected on the fashion of male beard styles. Kimmel specifically talks about the rise of the 'outdoor man' as a new type of masculinity, one that emerged in the USA as a response to the perceived gender crisis. In their search for an 'authentic' masculinity unspoiled by the 'diseases of modern life', these men embraced the romantic cult of nature, as well as military discipline and martial values. The cleanly shaven face or trimmed moustache, which had for a long time been restricted to army officials, became the hallmark of this movement and an important sign of revolt against the generation of their liberal fathers (Kimmel 1996).

While I agree with Kimmel about the significance of rapid social change and transformations in the imaginations of gender in the late nineteenth century, I doubt that the idea of a gender crisis can sufficiently explain the increased significance of shaving in early twentieth century Prague. Kimmel's approach can be criticized for two reasons. First, as pointed out by John Tosh (1994, 2005), the notion that there was a gender crisis rests on the idea of a stable core of individual identity that can be potentially shaken by an external crisis. Secondly, since Butler (1993) advanced the notion of gender performance, it makes little sense to speak about one particular gender crisis. Instead, from such a perspective, gender is always in crisis, always in danger of failing to reproduce the normative script that pervades a given historical period. For our understanding of beards and shaving practices, this means that it may be more productive to think of changing beard styles in terms of changing scripts of masculinity, rather than historical crises.

In any case, research into the history of gender in the Bohemian lands in the nineteenth and twentieth centuries, which is still rather scarce, does not hint at a gender crisis in the public discourse, nor in the personal testimonies of individual men (Filipowicz and Zachová 2009; Mareš 2012). Instead, local newspapers and personal correspondence between men addressed a more general fear of degeneration of manhood comprised of several aspects, such as the perceived decline of morality and good behaviour, the spread of 'civilization diseases' such as alcoholism and prostitution, and other negative trends that allegedly threatened the physical and mental health of the Czech 'national body' (Mareš 2012).

Moreover, contrary to the emergence of shaved faces in the US and Britain observed by Walton (2008) and Oldstone-Moore (2005), in Bohemia there was no noticeable trend towards shaved faces in the early twentieth century. Instead, the work of Josef Machar (2013) and the professional journals of barbers' associations published in Bohemia at that time[9] provide a much more complex picture of various trends and practices of shaving emerging before the First World War. Instead of one changing fashion—that is, a transformation from the liberal full beard to a post-liberal shaved face—what we witness is a pluralization of beard styles: the 'traditional' patriarchal full beard of different shape and size, alongside many other possible types of moustaches, as well as the cleanly shaven face. The pluralization of beard styles coincides with a pluralization of the political scene in Austria and the Bohemian lands in the late nineteenth century, with the rise of social movements and popular nationalist parties, such as Lueger's Christian Socialists, on one side of the political spectrum, and social democrats on the other. Nevertheless, these emerging beard styles never clearly corresponded to the emerging political parties, although there were groups, such as the communists, that used long beards as a distinguishing characteristic (Strobach 2015). Most importantly, facial hair was always to be kept 'clean' and properly shaped. It was the nicely trimmed and clean beard that distinguished the respectable gentleman from the disreputable vagrant.

Thus, to sum up, beard fashions cannot be reduced to a single hegemonic form of masculinity, nor a single masculinity crisis. Instead, beards and shaving practices were part of the ongoing social, political and national struggles in turn-of-the-century Bohemia. Besides, the practice of caring for one's appearance, and especially one's beard, referred to the concept of a clean, respectable male body, as well as to the anxiety generated by failing to comply with these normative scripts. In the next section I will examine this anxiety about facial hair more thoroughly, focusing particularly on the role of the concept of ab/normal hair that originated in contemporary medicine.

Shaving Practices, Expert Knowledge and the Rise of the Beauty Market in Early Twentieth-Century Bohemia

The pluralization of the political scene and the political fragmentation of the Czech national movement were not the only developments that challenged the social order in turn-of-the-century Bohemia. With rapid urbanization, industrialization and the rise of the capitalist market, the existing social structures seemed to have been thrown into flux (Urban 1978). As outlined above, many contemporaries, particularly the liberals, whose political hegemony was under threat, interpreted this in a discourse of moral panic, that is, as moral 'degeneration'. In the atmosphere of uncertainty, personal appearance became an important orienting point and, at the same time, an important source of social capital. The attention given to beards in Prague at the beginning of the twentieth century must therefore be read with respect to these social and political developments. In the following, I want to focus more closely on two interrelated arenas that had important effects on shaving practices in Bohemia before First World War (WWI): first, the emergence of expert medical knowledge about body hair; and secondly, the rise of a beauty market with special hair care products and services offered to both women and men.

From the beginning of the nineteenth century, medical science developed as an important power-knowledge affecting the everyday lives of people, political discourses about society and the very image of the human as a living being (Porter 1997). The trend towards specialization in medicine brought about a fragmentation of the body into different parts that were now entrusted to their respective specialists. Dermatology developed within eighteenth- and nineteenth-century clinical medicine as a specialization that dealt with the skin, predominantly skin ailments caused by venereal diseases such as syphilis. During the nineteenth century, dermatologists, including the leading figure of the discipline in Austria, Ferdinand von Hebra (1816–1880), also became interested in the question of body hair. Like other parts of the human body, hair became subject to medical inquiry. As such, from the middle of the nineteenth century onwards, it was described and examined through the concept of the norm. Although there is insufficient research about the discipline of dermatology and its history in the context of the Habsburg Empire, we know that hypertrochosis, defined as abnormal hairiness, figured in expert discussions as early as the publication of Hebra's *Atlas der Hautkrankheiten* (Atlas of Skin Diseases) in 1856. Unlike earlier interpretations of hairiness, which saw superfluous hair as an atavism pointing to an earlier phase of human development, or, later, linked it to evolution, dermatological knowledge diagnosed hypertrichosis as an individual 'abnormality', either congenital or acquired.[10]

From a rather cursory search of the medical journals of the time, we can see that late nineteenth-century dermatology introduced and developed a certain taxonomy of pathological hairiness. For example, in an article published in Prague in 1898[11] on 'Deviations in the Growth of Hair', we learn about the classification of abnormal hairiness used at that time. *Heterochrony* described a medical condition consisting of a mismatch between the growth of body hair and the 'normal' development of an individual, that is, when it appears in a wrong moment of the individual life cycle. *Heteromorphia* described body hair of an unusual shape or colour. The category of *Heterotopia* was used for a displacement of body hair, that is, its appearance on 'unusual' parts of the human body. *Atrichia* indicated a lack of hair and finally, *Hypertrichosis* stood for an abnormal abundance of body hair, a deviation that 'hairy performers,' such as Stephan Bibrowski, were usually diagnosed with.

Medical expert knowledge thus projected a complex notion of ab/normal facial hair, one that influenced masculinity performance at the end of the nineteenth century in at least three ways. First of all, it increased the attention placed on facial hair, itself perhaps being a result of this heightened attention. Secondly, it affected the notion of the cleanliness of the masculine face by delineating what was considered a normal growth of facial hair and vice versa—what could not be considered clean and beautiful. Finally, by pathologizing certain bodily conditions, such as the lack of or abundance of facial hair, it reinforced unequal power relations between those in the possession of beauty and those situated outside this category.

In order to understand the significance of shaving practices for the performance of proper masculinity, we need to address yet another aspect of late nineteenth-century culture, one closely connected to professional medicine, namely the beauty market. For the greater part of the nineteenth century, beauty services and products remained the domain of traditional artisans' guilds such as barbers, perfumers and other ancient professions, which mainly served the demands of the aristocracy, and later also of the bourgeoisie (Herzig 2015). With the establishment of industrial capitalism and consumer culture by the end of the nineteenth century in Austria, we see the emergence of a mass market for beauty products catering to a much broader circle of consumers, both male and female. Advertisements in the newly emerging popular mass media of the time promoted a large variety of different beauty products. Some of them advertised items to improve the aesthetics and style of facial hair, such as moustache holders and waxes. Others claimed to improve the healthy growth of facial hair by means of different balms and oils, among them the 'Mos Balm' mentioned above. Apparently, these products increased the pervasiveness of medical knowledge in society and reinforced the authority of medical professionals. In many cases, advertisements for or brand names of beauty and health products featured the names of individual medical professionals, feeding on their professional credit, while at the same time advertising the product's medically proven efficiency. Traditional artisans and barbers tried to keep up with the development of the beauty market, even when the spread of home shaving items in the first decades of the twentieth century seriously threatened their professions.[12]

In any case, the growth of the male cosmetic market, which was also connected to the medicalization of beards and shaving practices, seems to have contributed to the growing pressure placed on individual men to care for their appearance, particularly with regard to their beards. These anxieties about one's beard and more generally one's proper appearance can also be read from the literary genre of manuals concerned with etiquette, the so-called *Knigge*,[13] as they were called in German-speaking areas. These manuals, prescribing proper conduct in 'respectable' society, had already started to be published at the end of the eighteenth century,[14] and they peaked, at least in Bohemia, at the turn of the nineteenth century. Between the late 1870s and 1910s, 23 such manuals were published in Prague in the Czech language, and probably many more in German, some being original works, others being translations from other languages (Lenderová 2012).

Most of these manuals emphasized cleanliness as the most essential quality of a proper appearance for men. Men, it was generally felt, should not be too concerned about beauty, which was considered feminine, but they should nonetheless keep themselves clean and tidy, with particular attention to their hair and beards. 'Nobody should enter respectable society with unkempt and untidy hair. Get your hair and beard be nicely done, according to the current fashion', was the advice of Antonín Konstantin Viták (1885, 190–91), author of one of these manuals. These manuals were rather critical of the new cosmetic market and often advised men to be careful and cautious when applying new products, mainly because their efficacy had not yet been proved.[15] One of the most successful Czech-language manuals, Jiří Guth Jarkovský's *Společenský katechismus* ('Catechism of Social Conduct'), first published in 1914, referred to yet another technical novelty that was to have a major impact on the faces of respectable men, particularly after the WWI: the safety razor.

The safety razor, which used blades of stainless steel, was first introduced by King Camp Gillette in 1895 in the USA, from where it spread throughout the world. The success of this new technology is usually explained with reference to the widespread use of safety razors on the battlefields of the First World War (McKibben 1998, 429). As we learn from the fact that Jarkovský had already mentioned safety razors in 1915, they must have been known and used in the Bohemian lands even before then. In the 1915 edition of his authoritative work, Jarkovský also commented on the rarity of full beards in the early twentieth century and at the same time appealed to men to keep their facial hair clean and nicely trimmed, even if they wore their beards long. He considered the safety razor an instrument that made shaving more convenient. As he pointed out, the 'modern inventions of the safety razor de-legitimized the previously common excuse, that one could not, for whatever reason, visit a professional barber' (Jarkovský 1915, 38). As in the case of other health and beauty products launched on to the early twentieth-century beauty market, safety razors ultimately contributed to the increased appeal for men to care for their proper appearance, most importantly in respect of cleanliness, in order to be considered 'respectable' individuals in this hierarchically ordered society.

Conclusion: Bibrowski, the Beard and the Beautiful/Clean Masculine Face

However cursory and in many ways incomplete, the previous discussion gives us a few hints to understand both the meanings generated by the figure of Stephan Bibrowski and the changing norms of masculinity in relation to bodily appearance and beauty, particularly with regard to beards and shaving practices in the Prague of 1912.

In an atmosphere of dynamic change and uncertainty at the beginning of the new century, commonly expressed by the notion of 'degeneration', personal appearance became an increasingly important social resource and a matter of great anxiety. As the medical notion of the ab/normal pervaded many aspects of everyday life, including existing beauty practices, people learned to think about the beautiful, clean masculine body in medical terms of what is normal and what is pathological. The performances of Bibrowski and other 'hairy wonders' capitalized on these anxieties and at the same time contributed to firmly establishing a normative masculine appearance. What the audience learned from these shows, however, remains debatable. The performances of 'hairy wonders', their images and the narratives surrounding their bodies always remained ambiguous.

Still, given the context sketched out above, we can at least guess at possible ways of reading Bibrowski's body. Clearly, his presentation informed his audience about what was normal and what was abnormal regarding the male body, particularly with respect to male facial hair. Staring at Bibrowski, however, entailed not only the dynamics of differentiation, by which the men in the audience could distance themselves from the figure of the freak and self-identify as normal. Bibrowski's performance, I argue, also commented on the uncertainty of the masculine gender performance and on the possible sanctions against transgressing the normative boundaries of hegemonic masculinity. Bibrowski's face pointed to the fact that beards can grow beyond one's control. Moreover, it exemplified what happened when one failed to manage one's facial hair, which placed one not just beyond the category of cleanliness, but also beyond the very category of the civilized human. When uncontrolled, the growth of facial hair could turn one into a grotesque beast, neither human nor animal, and not even masculine. Remember that Bibrowski was presented as a kind of domestic pet, 'a sweetheart of women and children', and thus as a feminized man. Nevertheless, we cannot exclude yet another possible interpretation, such as an evolutionary one, of Bibrowksi as a 'missing link'—or even other readings. Could Bibrowski's superfluous hair, as some viewers interpreted it, possibly point to a kind of super masculinity, or to some inner animality, supposedly the essence of 'authentic masculinity,' which some contemporaries regarded as endangered by the political activity of women in trying to 'tame' and thus dominate men? Or, alternatively, did Bibrowski play the role of a queer figure, subversively eroding the image of the normative male, pointing to spaces of freedom beyond the heteronormative matrix (cf. Tromp 2008; Chen 2012)?

In any case, we can conclude that the popularity of 'hairy wonders' such as Bibrowski coincided with the increased significance of beards and shaving practices as means of masculinity performance in early twentieth-century Bohemia. As we have seen, the cleanliness of the male body—a basic requirement of hegemonic masculinity—came to be gradually affected by the notion of ab/normality, proposed by medical science. The quest for respectable masculinity thus became a struggle of individual men with their own bodies by means of shaving, the consumption of different beauty products and the necessity to conform to gendered norms defined by medical experts, such as dermatologists. Importantly, in this struggle for a respectable appearance, individual men did not all have the same starting positions and equal chances. The concept of cleanliness, which was also informed by the imagination of class and racial differences, apart from the notion of ab/normality, automatically excluded many individual men. Among them were those with disabilities or a non-white complexion and those who did not belong to the urban middle-class. Beautification practices such as shaving were important means of improving their allegedly 'ugly' appearance, though in many cases with uncertain results.

The figure of the hairy freak Lionel embodied the abovementioned concerns with beauty and ab/normality as tied to the racial and class differences between men in early twentieth-century Bohemia. A mixture of disgust and attraction induced by the ambiguous figure of Bibrowski both reinforced the sway of gender norms while perhaps at the same time opening up ways for subversive alternatives.

Notes

1. *Národní listy* (est. 1861) and *Národní politika* (est. 1883) were considered tribunes of the Czech liberal bourgeoisie. The German liberal press in Prague was represented by *Bohemia* (est. 1830) and *Prager Tagblatt* (est. 1877).
2. Prague was the capital of Bohemia, one of the three historical lands (the others being Moravia and Silesia) that made up the historical lands of the Bohemian Crown, ruled by the Bohemian king. From 1867, the Bohemian lands became part of the western half of the Austro-Hungarian Empire (Cisleithania). Throughout the article I use Bohemia to refer to all three Bohemian lands.
3. The word 'freak', which is nowadays considered derogatory and thus unacceptable, was part of the normal vocabulary of past centuries. Throughout this chapter, I use the word solely when referring to the language of my sources, as an English translation of Czech terms such as *zrůda*, *abnormita* or *lidská kuriozita*, commonly employed at the time. Here the word 'freak' is treated as a performative construct, not as a condition of an individual's body.
4. This chapter forms part of my dissertation project, entitled *Imaginations of Bodily 'Otherness' and Prague's Freak Show Culture 1850–1930*, at the Faculty of Humanities, Charles University in Prague.
5. See the advertisement for 'Lionel the Lion Man' in *Prager Tagblatt*, 30 March 1912, 10.
6. Advertisement for 'Mos Balm' (*Mosův balzám*) in, for example, *Rozvoj*, 15 December 1911, 10. All translations from primary sources are mine.
7. Already during the late 1880s, the figure of Krao became part of the freak show culture in Austria. Her wax figurines were displayed in museums of natural curiosities travelling around the Bohemian lands (cf. advertisement in the local South Bohemian daily newspaper *Karla Gabriela Panoptikum*, Budivoj, 19 January 1888, 4). Already in 1888, she was described, with a nod to evolutionary theory, as a 'missing link'. The dominance of this evolutionary framing persisted also during her visit to Prague in 1902. Her display at Nový Bazar was followed the next day with a public lecture on evolutionary theory, prepared as part of a

popularizing lecture series offered by the Czech Charles Ferdinand University in Prague (see 'Castanovo Panoptikum', *Národní listy*, 14 December 1902, 26).

8. Cf. also 'O zvyku nošení vlasů a vousů', *Nový Kadeřník*, 1902 (14), 5–6.

9. I am here referring to a journal article, 'On hair and beard customs', published by the Czech-language professional barbers' association in Prague ('O zvyku nošení vlasů a vousů', *Nový Kadeřník* 1902 [14], 5–6).

10. See the entry 'Hypertrichiasis' in the digitalized version of Herbra's Atlas on DermIS, the Dermatological Information System (http://www. hebra.dermis.net/content/e404/e454/index_ger.html, last accessed 24 October 2017).

11. I am citing here from the classification offered in the pages of the Czech scientific journal *Živa* ('Odchylky u vzrůstu vlasů a vousu', *Živa*, 1898 [9], 283).

12. The anxieties of professional barbers and their strategies in reaction to the emergence of a mass market of beauty products might be further analyzed by studying their professional journals, such as *Kadeřník* ('The Barber') and *Nový kadeřník* ('The New Barber').

13. The name refers to Freiherr Adolph Franz Friedrich Ludwig Knigge (1752–1796), author of an authoritative work, *Über den Umgang mit Menschen* (*On Human Relations*, 1788), that laid the grounds for the genre.

14. The first of such manuals published in Prague was Karl Seibt's *Klugheitslehre oder die Kunst aus dem Umgang mit Menschen die möglichst grössten Vorteile zu ziehen* (*The art of wisdom: using the advantages of proper conduct towards other people*) of 1799; cf. Lenderová (2012).

15. Kodym, František, 1896. *Kniha o slušném chování: Průvodce společností i životem*, Prague, 12.

REFERENCES

Butler, Judith. 1993. *Bodies That Matter: On the Discursive Limits of Sex*. New York and London: Routledge.

Chen, Mel Y. 2012. *Animacies: Biopolitics, Racial Mattering, and Queer Affect*. Durham, NC: Duke University Press.

Coleman, Rebecca, and Mónica Moreno Figueroa. 2010. "Past and Future Perfect? Beauty, Affect and Hope." *Journal for Cultural Research* 14 (4): 357–73.

Connell, Raewyn. 1995. *Masculinities*. Berkeley: University of California Press.

Connell, R. W., and James W. Messerschmidt. 2005. "Hegemonic Masculinity: Rethinking the Concept." *Gender* 19 (6): 829–59.

Craig, M. L. 2006. "Race, Beauty, and the Tangled Knot of a Guilty Pleasure." *Feminist Theory* 7 (2): 159–77.

Davis, Lennard J. 1995. *Enforcing Normalcy: Disability, Deafness, and the Body.* London and New York: Verso.

Durbach, Nadja. 2010. *Spectacle of Deformity: Freak Shows and Modern British Culture.* Berkeley: University of California Press.

Filipowicz, Marcin Łukasz, and Alena Zachová. 2009. *Rod v memoárech: Případ Hradec Králové.* Červený Kostelec: Pavel Mervart.

Garland-Thomson, Rosemarie. 1997. *Extraordinary Bodies: Figuring Physical Disability in American Culture and Literature.* New York: Columbia University Press.

Hamlin, Kimberly A. 2011. "The 'Case of a Bearded Woman': Hypertrichosis and the Construction of Gender in the Age of Darwin." *American Quarterly* 63 (4): 955–81.

Herzig, Rebecca M. 2015. *Plucked: A History of Hair Removal.* New York: New York University Press.

Jahn, Jiljí Vratislav. 1861. *František Ladislav Rieger: obraz životopisný.* Prague: Tiskem a nakl. Antonina Augusty.

Jarkovský, Jiří Guth. 1915. *Společenský katechismus.* Prague: Hejda a Tuček.

Judson, Pieter M. 1996. *Exclusive Revolutionaries: Liberal Politics, Social Experience, and National Identity in the Austrian Empire, 1848–1914.* Ann Arbor: University of Michigan Press.

Kimmel, Michael S. 1987. *Changing Men: New Directions in Research on Men and Masculinity.* Newbury Park, CA: Sage.

Kimmel, Michael S., ed. 1995. *The Politics of Manhood: Profeminist Men Respond To the Mythopoetic Men's Movement (And the Mythopoetic Leaders Answer).* Philadelphia: Temple University Press; Newbury Park, CA.: Sage.

Kimmel, Michael S. 1996. *Manhood in America: A Cultural History.* New York: Free Press.

Kodym, František. 1896. *Kniha o slušném chování: Průvodce společností i životem.* Prague: František Vlastimil Kodym.

Lafferton, Emese. 2007. "The Magyar Moustache: The Faces of Hungarian State Formation, 1867–1918." *Studies in History and Philosophy of Science Part C: Studies in History and Philosophy of Biological and Biomedical Sciences* 38 (4): 706–32.

Lenderová, Milena. 2012. "Genderové Stereotypy a konstrukt maskulinity ve společenských katechismech." In *Konstrukce maskulinní identity v minulosti a současnosti: Koncepty, metody, perspektivy,* edited by Slabáková Radmila et al., 224–40. Prague: Nakladatelství Lidové noviny.

Lenderová, Milena, Daniela Tinková, and Vladan Hanulík. 2014. *Tělo mezi medicínou a disciplínou.* Prague: Nakladatelství Lidové noviny.

Machar, Josef Svatopluk. 2013. *Z Dějin Vousu.* 2. vyd., 1. samost. Prague: Akropolis.

Mareš, Jan. 2012. "Český skauting jako důsledek krize maskulinity?" In *Konstrukce maskulinní identity v minulosti a současnosti: Koncepty, metody, perspektivy*, edited by Radmila Slabáková et al., 194–207. Prague: Nakladatelství Lidové noviny.

Maxwell, Alexander. 2015. "The Handsome Man with Hungarian Moustache and Beard: National Moustaches in Habsburg Hungary." *Cultural and Social History* 12 (1): 51–76.

McKibben, Gordon. 1998. *Cutting Edge: Gillette's Journey to Global Leadership*. Boston, MA: Harvard Business School Press.

Mosse, George L. 1998. *The Image of Man/The Creation of Modern Masculinity*. Oxford: Oxford University Press.

Oldstone-Moore, Christopher. 2005. "The Beard Movement in Victorian Britain." *Victorian Studies* 48 (1): 7–34.

Oldstone-Moore, Christopher. 2016. *Of Beards and Men: The Revealing History of Facial Hair*. Chicago: The University of Chicago Press.

Porter, Roy. 1997. *The Greatest Benefit to Mankind: A Medical History of Humanity*. New York: W. W. Norton.

Strobach, Vít. 2015. *Židé: Národ, rasa, třída: Sociální hnutí a 'židovská Otázka' v českých zemích 1861–1921*. Knižnice Dějin a Současnosti. Prague: Nakladatelství Lidové noviny, s.r.o.

Tapley, Heather. 2014. "The Making of Hobo Masculinities." *Canadian Review of American Studies* 44 (1): 25–43.

Tosh, Peter. 1994. "What Should Historians Do with Masculinity? Reflections on Nineteenth-Century Britain." *History Workshop Journal* 38 (1): 179–202.

Tosh, John. 2005. *Manliness and Masculinities in Nineteenth-Century Britain: Essays on Gender, Family, and Empire*. New York: Pearson Longman.

Tromp, Marlene. 2008. *Victorian Freaks: The Social Context of Freakery in Britain*. Columbus: Ohio State University Press.

Urban, Otto. 1978. *Kapitalismus a česká společnost: K otázkám formování české společnosti v 19. Století*. Prague: Svoboda.

Viták, Antonín Konstantin. 1885. *O obcování s lidmi. Nový průvodce dobrou společností. Díl I. Kniha pravidel pro cvik dobrých a jemných mravů, společenských vtipův a domácích povinností. Na základě díla šlechtičny F. Hohenhausenové vzdělal a pořekadly, příslovími a výroky čelnějších básníkův a spisovatelů českých valně rozšířil Ant. Konstantin Viták, gram. učitel a redaktor*. Prague: Fr. A. Urbánek.

Walton, Susan. 2008. "From Squalid Impropriety to Manly Respectability: The Revival of Beards, Moustaches and Martial Values in the 1850s in England." *Nineteenth-Century Contexts* 30 (3): 229–45.

CHAPTER 3

Standardizing Slimness: How Body Weight Quantified Beauty in the Netherlands, 1870–1940

Hieke Huistra

When anthropologist Rebecca Popenoe volunteered in a Nigerien clinic in the 1980s, she noticed that local nurses put on additional clothing before stepping onto the scales in order to increase their body weight. Popenoe (2005) uses the anecdote in a piece on living in a culture with an ideal of beauty opposite to her own. Whereas Nigerien women wanted to be fat, Popenoe, an American woman, wanted to be slim.[1] Yet, although their desired weights differed, both Popenoe and the Nigerien women used scales to determine their level of beauty. Body weight is a powerful beauty standard for women in communities around the world—and increasingly for men as well.

But as beauty standards go, body weight is not a particularly visible one. We can see the shape of someone's nose, the colour of someone's skin, the style of someone's hair, but our eyes cannot establish someone's exact weight; for that, we require a set of scales. Yet, when we as scholars analyse weight as a beauty standard, we often focus on the visual: we

H. Huistra (✉)
Descartes Centre, Utrecht University, Utrecht, The Netherlands

© The Author(s) 2019
C. Liebelt et al. (eds.), *Beauty and the Norm*,
Palgrave Studies in Globalization and Embodiment,
https://doi.org/10.1007/978-3-319-91174-8_3

understand the desire to lose or gain weight as a desire to change our appearance and as something propagated by visual representations of the body in magazines, movies or music videos. Susan Bordo, for example, in her new 2003 preface to the classic *Unbearable Weight*, situates Western ideals of both weight loss and slenderness in the late modern 'empire of images' (Bordo 2003, xiii–xxxvi)—but what visual imagery presents as 'unbearable' is fatness, not weight. And although fatness, slimness and weight have come to be closely connected in many contemporary cultures, they are not the same. Stepping onto the scales may tell us something about our body size, but by no means does it reveal everything: it does not tell us whether the weight consists of muscles or of fat, nor whether it is located on our hips or on our belly. Nonetheless, weight has become a powerful standard for body size and the link between body size and weight, between slimness and the scales, seems natural to many of us.

Like other strongly established standards—for example, blood pressure as a standard for health—weight as a standard for body size may seem inevitable. But historians and sociologists of science, technology and medicine have shown time and again that standards are neither natural nor neutral (Lampland and Star 2009; Timmermans and Epstein 2010). Establishing them takes time and effort, and once established, they change the things they claim to measure. Researchers in the emerging field of fat studies—or, as some scholars prefer, critical weight studies—build on such historical and sociological work to challenge the use of body weight as a measurement for health, as do fat activists and the Health at Every Size movement (Bacon 2010; Cooper 2010; Lupton 2013, 18–31; Rothblum and Solovay 2009). Fat studies scholars have shown that the current dominance of the body mass index, which is based on body weight, as a health indicator is not the inevitable result of biomedical research but instead the contingent outcome of social and historical processes (Dawes 2014; Fletcher 2012, 2014; Gard and Wright 2005; Jutel 2005, 2006; Lupton 2013; Saguy 2013)—or even, some argue, a profitable lie nurtured by big pharmaceutical companies (Campos 2004; Oliver 2006).

In this chapter, I show that in addition to not being a self-evident standard for health, weight is also not a self-evident standard for body size. As fat studies scholars have noted before, fatness and slimness are not necessarily measured in kilos or pounds; instead, they can be expressed in inches, dress size or the number of compliments or insults received, to name but a few. I believe that a distinction between fatness, slimness and weight is important because it enables us to address some urgent questions about body weight as a beauty standard, including: How could a bodily quality that is visible indirectly at best be such a powerful beauty standard? Why do so many of us expect to be admired for something other people cannot see? We cannot address these questions as long as we conflate body size (which is visible) and body weight (which is not visible). Unfortunately, scholars working on beauty and the body do not always carefully distinguish between the two—Bordo's link between desired weight loss and visual imagery is just one example; another can be found in a chapter of the *Routledge Handbook of Body Studies*, which lists 'increased body weight' as one of the 'visible effects of aging' (Dumas 2012, 380). However, what our eyes see when looking at 'old' people is not increased body weight, but fatness.

To increase our sensitivity to the differences between weight and body size, slimness and fatness, it helps, I think, to study the history of weight as a beauty standard. Hence, this chapter addresses two historical questions: first, when did we learn to link body weight and body size? And second, how did this change the character of beauty in so far as it came to be determined by body size? Obviously, my answers are not full and universal, but partial and local. In the following I focus on the Netherlands, where Dutch men and women learned to weigh themselves in the early twentieth century (whereas the Nigerien women described by Popenoe [2005, 11] quoted above did so much later, around the 1970s). And whereas the Nigerien women wanted to be fat, the actors in my case study, like many westerners, were striving to remain or become slim.

My case study consists of two parts. The first part shows that body weight is not a natural standard of slimness. I analyse the non-medical use of scales in the late nineteenth and early twentieth centuries in the Netherlands to show that things used to be different: weight had not yet become a beauty standard but functioned instead as a bodily curiosity. This was the case even when slimness had already become a beauty ideal. The link between weight, being slim and beauty emerged later, in the Netherlands in the 1920s. The second part of my case study focuses on advertisements for slimming remedies in the 1930s. It demonstrates that by then weight was securely established as a beauty standard. It also investigates how advertisers—who, as we will see, relied on beauty as a visible characteristic—dealt with this invisible beauty standard.

METHODOLOGY

My research is based on sources that include newspaper reports on fairs, beauty manuals and newspaper advertising campaigns for slimming products. A significant number of these sources were selected with the help of digital search techniques. I worked with the newspaper database of the Dutch National Library and extracted my sources from this database using keyword searches before its most recent updates (April 2016 and December 2017). When I carried out my searches, this database contained over eight million newspaper pages published between the early seventeenth and late twentieth centuries.[2] Although that places it among the largest in Europe, it contains only ten percent of all the newspapers ever published in the Netherlands. The percentage differs between periods, and my focus here, the early twentieth century, seems to have above-average representation, although it is hard to give an exact figure. What can be said is that for this period the database's spread of newspapers is substantial, ranging from the regional, socialist *Zaans Volksblad* to the national, liberal *Algemeen Handelsblad*, and from the Catholic *De Tijd* to the national-socialist *Volk en Vaderland*. I have offered a detailed discussion of my approach in searching these newspapers elsewhere, including an overview of the limitations of these techniques: in particular, digital repositories help us find more and different sources than before, but they offer neither completeness nor objectivity (Huistra 2017; see also Bingham 2010; Brake 2012; Hitchcock 2013; Putnam 2016). After selecting the sources, I analysed them manually.

This analysis is informed by theoretical work on standards, standardization and quantification. Building on the work of sociologists Stefan Timmermans and Steven Epstein (2010), I define a standard as a property, or a set of properties, that a certain object, procedure, person or process should meet according to the person, institution or social group that has set the standard. Standards can be set and enforced either formally, for example, by professional organizations or the state, or informally (Timmermans and Epstein 2010, 71). Beauty standards are informal: there is no Agency of Beauty issuing official guidelines on our appearance that have been established through carefully arranged committee meetings involving all stakeholders. Their informality makes it harder to track their history, and this may tempt us to take them for granted, but informal standards are neither more natural nor less powerful than formal standards.

All standards change the world around them, including the qualities they standardize, but each standard does so in its own way (Espeland and Stevens 2008; Lampland and Star 2009; Timmermans and Epstein 2010). A standard's effects depend on its type (e.g., quantitative standards differ from qualitative ones), on what is being standardized and on the social domain in which the standard functions. Therefore, Timmermans and Epstein call for specific, empirical analyses that enable us to compare standards and standardization across distinct social domains (Timmermans and Epstein 2010, 84–85).

In the last two centuries, ever more products, procedures and processes have been standardized, from scientific measuring units to fruit and vegetables, from ethical behaviour to child seats. Some types of standardization have received more attention than others. Body weight is a quantitative standard regulating the body. Quantitative standardization of the body has been studied extensively by historians and sociologists of medicine (Czerniawski 2007; Dawes 2014; Fletcher 2014; Jorland et al. 2005; Jutel 2001, 2006; Porter 1995), but mainly in the domain of medicine and health. Quantitative standardization of the body in the domain of beauty, the topic of this chapter, has received less attention. Yet the introduction of quantitative standards poses specific challenges for actors in this domain. Quantitative standardization results in what Lorraine Daston and Peter Galison (1992, 2007, 115–90; see also Porter 1995) have called 'mechanical objectivity,' that is an objectivity produced by mechanical means (in the case of quantitative standardization, this means measuring instruments) that in theory exclude all human involvement, although in practice, this is an unattainable ideal. The mechanical objectivity produced by scales contrasts with a crucial aspect of beauty: beauty is about being seen through the *subjective* eyes of other individuals— exactly the human observers that mechanical objectivity aims to exclude. This tension is less prominent in the domain of modern health and medicine, which is why quantification of the body in the domain of beauty deserves to be studied in its own right. To do so, we will now return to the late nineteenth-century Netherlands, just before weight became what it is now: the most prominent quantitative beauty standard.[3]

SLIMNESS AROUND 1900: A QUALITATIVE BEAUTY IDEAL

Historians of the body have dated the rise of being slim as the dominant beauty ideal in Western Europe and the United States in the mid- to late nineteenth century (Stearns 2002). The Netherlands seems to fit this pattern. An 1898 Dutch beauty manual describes corpulence as 'disturbing … the harmony of forms,' although it stresses that being too thin is no good either: 'With the notion of perfect beauty, a certain "too much or too little" with regard to the curves of the forms of the body cannot be reconciled' (Goupy 1898, 96). Advertising campaigns for slimming remedies from the early twentieth century show that slimness had by then been firmly established as a beauty ideal.

Take the campaign for the Boranium berry, which ran in the 1910s. The Boranium berry was a slimming product that was introduced in 1914, presented as the newest discovery from England. This little brown berry was, the ads claimed, 'the most pleasant and easiest method' to lose fat: just one berry after every meal (or three to four per day), and the rest would take care of itself (*Rotterdamsch Nieuwsblad*, 20 July 1914, 10).[4] This paints a rather rosy picture of how things worked. First, the berry was not actually a natural berry, but an artificial pill that looked like a berry. The main active ingredient was phenolphthalein, a laxative; in addition, it contained peppermint oil and sugar, to help the medicine go down. The laxative no doubt helped people to become thinner, but as far as slimming methods go, it was not 'the most pleasant … method one can think of' (ibid.): the laxative effect was strong, and it had serious side effects. None of this was mentioned in the ads—and wisely so. Instead, the ads focused on explaining to the reader why he or she would want to become thin. Beauty was one of these reasons; health was another major reason. This chapter focuses on advertisements discussing beauty, but beauty ideals and health ideals cannot always be separated, and they often influenced each other.

The most prominent example of the use of the beauty frame in the Boranium campaign is the ad '*Dit is het geheim van mijn mooi figuur*' ('This is the secret of my beautiful figure'), which is formatted as a testimonial (*Nieuwe Rotterdamsche Courant*, 19 July 1914, 7). The nameless user states: 'A few months ago I was just as fat and plump as hundreds of others and, having tried all advertised remedies available, I had almost, filled with despair, given up all hope to ever regaining my past slenderness and beautiful figure.' Then, of course, the person encountered

Boranium berries, which delivered excellent results within a month. Here, the explicit aim is a 'beautiful figure.' In other ads, it was not so much being beautiful as looking young that counted—being slender was strongly linked to appearing young, an important value at the time. The ad '*Eet en wordt mager*' ('Eat and become thin'), for example, explains that 'women in particular will value this advice [to take Boranium berries], because continued use will quickly enable her [sic] to follow fashion better and to appear years younger with regard to features and posture' (*Het Nieuws van den Dag*, 18 February 1914, 5).

Most of the Boranium ads that link slenderness to beauty also link it to health. In another early twentieth-century campaign, the Tonnola campaign, the focus on beauty was more exclusive. The campaign ran between 1912 and 1915, and was relaunched in the early 1920s. It had three different advertisements (most campaigns had more; the Boranium campaign had ten, and the campaigns in the 1920s and 1930s sometimes had around one hundred different advertisements), though only one of them was used between 1912 and 1915. This campaign focuses on appearance and frames being slim as being beautiful. In particular, the ad promises the Tonnola user a 'slender, elegant figure' and a 'graceful waist,' instead of a 'broad body' with 'broad hips' (*Rotterdamsch Nieuwsblad*, 15 October 1913, 8). The ad is illustrated with two male figures (one fat, the other thin). Fatness was not just a female issue in early twentieth-century Europe (Zweiniger-Bargielowska 2005). Most of the advertising campaigns discussed in this chapter addressed both men and women, although not to the same extent: the majority of the advertisements, especially in the 1920s and 1930s, focused on women.

It is striking that in both the Boranium and the Tonnola campaigns, body weight is absent. The Tonnola advertisement does not mention it at all. Two of the Boranium advertisements do so, but they only talk about 'weight loss' as a general goal and do not quantify the amount of body weight lost (*Rotterdamsch Nieuwsblad*, 16 April 1914, 14; *Het Nieuws van den Dag*, 15 April 1914, 10). They focus instead on a loss of *fat*, and some of the Boranium ads do quantify this: they state that one berry will remove thirty grams of fat from the body. But although the loss of fat is quantified, the loss of weight is not, nor are slimness and fatness as such. Apparently, fatness was not expressed in kilos in early twentieth-century advertising; weight had not yet entered the domain of beauty. Instead, it could be found elsewhere, in a place we may find surprising: the fairground.

WEIGHT AROUND 1900: A FAIRGROUND CURIOSITY

In the Netherlands around 1900, one could hear the fair coming days before it arrived from the fairground songs sung in the streets (Bruin 2002, 29). The cheerful songs anticipated the experiences the fair would bring to town. While some of these experiences have not changed much in the past century—such as having a ride on the merry-go-round, eating traditional pastries, and making advances at potential partners—others might now seem out of place at a fairground. Take this suggestion in a fairground song from Groningen, a city in the north of the Netherlands: '*Of anders, stap de weegschaal op, die twee cent maakt u ook niet dop*' ('Or else, step on the scale, the two cents won't kill you;' Huizinga [1900?]).

The song represents having oneself weighed as a standard fairground attraction, as do newspaper reports and other fairground descriptions from this period, the late nineteenth and early twentieth centuries. The fair in Groningen, to which the song above refers, was at the time one of the largest in the Netherlands, but other, often smaller fairs across the country had scales as well, including those in Tilburg, Wormerveer, Zaandam, Leeuwarden and Hoorn (Oers et al. 1986, 106; Tjeertes Sr. 1978, 204; Maas 1950, 12; Schat 2005, 88; Zoonen 1996, 51). The author of a local newspaper report on the fair in the northern city of Zwolle in the 1870s explains why he left out the personal scales from his overview of attractions: 'I have kept silent about the scales with the stereotypical "get on and have yourself weighed!" or "this is where you weigh the heaviest." ... Such enterprises can be found everywhere, and they are the same everywhere' (*Provinciaalse Overijsselsche & Zwolsche Courant*, 31 July 1873, 3). The quotation suggests not only that scales for weighing the individual were common at fairs, but also that their presentation and framing did not differ much between the different fairs. Indeed, the phrase 'Get on and have yourself weighed!', which occurs both in the Zwolle newspaper report and in the Groningen song, was used regularly to describe this attraction. The exclamation mark suggests an enthusiasm for weighing oneself that many of us nowadays do not share. Most of us do not weigh ourselves for pleasure and thus would never expect to find scales at a fairground, which we consider a site for entertainment instead.

Until the early twentieth century, however, fairs were about more than just entertainment (Jacobs 2002; Jansen 1987; Keikes 1978; Keyser 1978). Take the Leeuwarden fair around 1850 (Schat 2005), which took place in July and lasted for two weeks—not uncommon for fairs at the time. During the fair, visitors could ride on the merry-go-round, eat waffles, drink wine and enjoy music, but they could also have themselves weighed, study anatomical wax models to learn about the human body, gaze at panoramas informing them about historical and current events, have their teeth pulled and buy shoes, hats, books, scissors and umbrellas. Fairground experiences varied from the pleasant to the painful, but what they shared was their uniqueness. The stalls and stands offered objects and experiences that could not easily be found elsewhere.

Having oneself weighed was one such unique experience. At the time, scales were not yet household instruments. Bathroom scales did not yet exist, and weighing people was usually done with platform scales or weighing chairs. Both types of scales are large and expensive instruments and thus not suitable for individual purchase. To weigh themselves, most adults depended on scales in public spaces; and in the late nineteenth and early twentieth centuries fairgrounds were a major space for weighing. Travellers had yet another option: they might encounter scales when visiting spas. Furthermore, scales also started appearing in doctor's offices, but around 1900 many doctors still did without them (Horstman 2001, 85; Stearns 2002, 27).

When the fair came to town, the atmosphere changed: fair time was accompanied by a specific set of norms and customs, often involving reversals. In many towns, for example, women asked men out to the fair instead of the other way around. The reversal of norms and the uniqueness of the experiences on offer supports a conceptualization of fairgrounds as Foucauldian heterotopias, counter sites that represent other sites but at the same time contest and invert them (Foucault 1986; Stallybrass and White 1986, 27–43).

But the boundary between the fairground and other, non-heterotopian sites was permeable. The fair did not just mirror society as it was; it also anticipated society as it might become. Philosopher Petran Kockelkoren (2003, 26) has argued that fairs should not be seen as places letting people escape 'cultural conditioning' but as 'cultural normalization machines,' places that offered people the opportunity to get used to unfamiliar technologies and practices. The fair introduced visitors to new objects and experiences, thus preparing them for the incorporation of these objects and experiences into their daily lives. Many new technologies were first introduced at the fairground. In the early days of cinema, for example, the fairground was a major site for movie screenings. Once permanent cinemas emerged and the moving image lost its uniqueness, it disappeared from the fairgrounds (Hemels 2002).

Between roughly 1850 and 1920, many of the non-entertainment elements at fairs became available elsewhere and throughout the year: newly established department stores sold products until then only available at the fair, emerging mass media made world news accessible to a large audience, and public museums replaced travelling exhibitions. Together, these changes modified the character of the fair, resulting in a predominance of entertainment (Schat 2005). Thus, the period discussed here was a transitional period, when the multi-layered character of the fair was still present, although slowly dissolving. This provides the context in which we should understand the fairground scales and the bodily quality they measured: a context of entertainment and education, of uniqueness and normalization.

In this context, fairground scales enabled people to become acquainted with weighing and quantifying their bodies, but they did not (yet) standardize their bodies. Stepping onto a set of scales was something out of the ordinary, a unique experience, to be done once a year at most. The limited accessibility of scales made it difficult to monitor one's weight. Moreover, not only did incidental weighing prevent people from checking regularly whether they adhered to the standard, they also lacked any standard to adhere to. A common slogan for the weighing attractions was '*hier weegt men 't zwaarst*' ('this is where you weigh the heaviest'). This slogan focuses on an extreme bodily state—'the heaviest'—instead of a normal one, or a standard. The focus on extraordinary bodies could also be found in the fairground shows exhibiting 'freaks' (Sliggers 2002), that is, (living) persons with unique bodily properties, such as the very short or very tall, Siamese twins and bearded women (see Herza, this volume). A common feature in the freak shows were people billed as 'fat' (or even 'the fattest'), whose weights were listed in the shows' announcements. When fair visitors stepped on the scales, these weights were what they had in mind—perhaps they even strove to compete with 'the heaviest' or 'the fattest' man or woman in town.

Thus, while interpreting weighing oneself at a fairground as a form of plain entertainment might be too simplistic, the experience was certainly something (still) out of the ordinary. Furthermore, the resulting measurement was not compared with a standard weight since the only weights available for comparison were the extraordinary weights of the fat men, women and children in the curiosity cabinets. Hence, the weights measured on fairground scales were curiosities, not standards of beauty. This does not mean that people did not care about their body sizes though. As we have seen, being slim had already become a qualitative ideal of beauty: it was simply not yet measured in quantitative terms. This changed in subsequent decades. In the next section, I will show how, contrary to slimming remedy ads from the 1910s, those from the 1920s and the 1930s express a new consciousness of body size in kilos.

How exactly slimness and body weight came to be linked to each other is a complex question, and to disentangle the multiple causes involved we require more research on this topic. Possible causes include the growing importance of weight as a measurement of health, driven in part by the life insurance industry, and the wider availability of scales. We might think that the latter is simply a consequence of the emergence of weight as a norm, but, as science and technology studies have shown, we should be careful not to underestimate the power of instruments to shape the world instead of the other way around (Latour 1988, 1992; Pickering 1995; Verbeek 2005). In what follows, I focus not on the causes of the emergence of weight as a standard of beauty but on one of the consequences, namely that it complicated the character of beauty by objectifying beauty mechanically and thus separating it from the gaze of others. Nevertheless, as we shall see below, slimming remedy advertisers still relied on this gaze as an incentive for their potential customers to reduce weight, while at the same time propagating weight as a standard of beauty in their advertisements.

WEIGHT IN THE INTERWAR PERIOD: A QUANTITATIVE BEAUTY STANDARD

Advertising campaigns in the 1920s and 1930s regularly express body size, or a change in body size, in kilos or pounds. The extent to which someone meets the ideal of slimness is increasingly expressed in quantitative terms, namely in body weight. In this section, I analyse the most influential slimming remedy campaign from this period, the Bonkora campaign, occasionally supplementing my analysis with examples from other prominent campaigns of the era. Bonkora was a slimming cure sold internationally. Its ingredients were kept a secret, as was common with these kinds of remedies, but analysis by the Association Against Quackery revealed that its active ingredients were simple laxatives ('Bonkora' 1936; 'Het wondervermageringsmiddel "Bonkora"' 1937; 'Bonkora' 1938). It was introduced in the Netherlands in the 1930s and became well known, judging from newspaper articles mentioning the brand without further explanation. One example is the preview of an upcoming hockey game in the regional newspaper *Nieuwe Tilburgsche Courant* (21 October 1939, 12). The newspaper writes mockingly: 'But the goal of the Pelicans [team name] is narrow, given their large goalkeeper. Or could it be that "Bonkora" has meanwhile offered a helping hand?'

The Bonkora campaign has the most advertisements of all the campaigns I have analysed. When searching for advertisements on slimming remedies between 1918 and 1940 in the National Library's newspaper database, I found approximately 1150 advertisements for Bonkora. For other prominent campaigns in this period, such as for Richter's tea, Remmler's de-fattening beans and Facil tablets, I have found a few hundred advertisements each at most.

Virtually all the Bonkora advertisements use weight to indicate a change in body size.[5] Regularly, the headings mention specific cases of amounts of weight supposedly lost through taking Bonkora. For example, one ad prominently describes a user with the words: 'Has lost 18 pounds in barely 2 weeks' (*De Gooi- en Eemlander*, 11 May 1936, 4). This ad contains a letter signed by a Mrs. F. Cole, whose portrait is also included. It says: 'I am so grateful for what Bonkora has done for me that I would like to shout it from the rooftops. By using just 2 phials I have already lost 16 pounds [8 kilos] in 2 weeks. My weight has decreased from 167 pounds [83.5 kilos] to 151 [75.5 kilos].'[6] Such user testimonials were printed regularly, not just in the Bonkora campaigns but in other campaigns as well. Producers of slimming remedies liked to employ lay users as external authorities in their advertisements to convince potential customers to buy their products (Huistra 2017). Most Bonkora advertisements contain one or more user testimonials, but references to weight occurred outside user testimonials as well. Several Bonkora advertisements make general claims about the amount of weight that can be lost in taking Bonkora: for example, 'Thousands of people … have lost dozens of pounds without a diet' (*De Graafschap-bode*, 17 May 1937, 7) or 'How to reduce a pound a day without a diet' (*De Telegraaf*, 31 July 1936, 20).

In the Bonkora advertisements, body size is expressed first and foremost in terms of weight. This distinguishes them from earlier advertising campaigns, such as Boranium and Tonnola discussed above, which did not quantify body size at all. Moreover, in the Bonkora campaign weight is more than a matter of quantification, it is also a standard. Bonkora users do not just express their body size quantitatively, they also strive to meet a specific value for this quantitative measurement. In some

Bonkora advertisements this is very explicit, as they encourage people to take Bonkora until they have reached their 'normal, healthy weight' (see, for example, *Nieuwsblad van het Noorden*, 27 July 1936, 12; *De Gooi- en Eemlander*, 26 May 1938, 7; *Limburger Koerier*, 7 May 1937, 4).

As Ian Hacking (1990, 160–69) has explained, the modern concept of 'normal' is a not a neutral description referring to a statistical average, but a morally loaded term prescribing how things ought to be. Defining the 'normal', healthy body then becomes a way to exert what Foucault (1990) has called biopower, i.e. control over people's bodies (either individual bodies or populations).[7] When advertisements mentioned a 'normal weight,' they referred to a standard that their readers had to make their bodies adhere to. The fact that the term was used regularly in advertisements shows that people were now familiar with this standard, that they knew their own 'normal' weight and that they were aware they should strive for it. The advertisements could refer to a 'normal weight' because their audience was familiar with this concept; through these references, the advertisements reinforced the importance the public attached to having a normal weight—advertisements not only reflect, but also shape the society that produces them (Huistra 2017; Lears 1994; Marchand 1985).

With weight becoming a standard measurement for slimness and fatness, scales changed from fairground attractions into essential instruments to determine whether one has met the new beauty standard: weight. The Bonkora campaign indeed presents scales as such, not just because most advertisements express body size and the success of slimming in pounds, but also because some advertisements explicitly depict scales as judges of beauty. A striking example is displayed in Fig. 3.1, where we see a woman standing on a scale. Compared to the type of women explicitly labelled 'slender' in other Bonkora ads, she has a rather large body size. She also has a troubled look on her face, looking down at the scale dial. The dial, depicted as a face, also looks troublesome, staring back at the woman, and uttering a warning: 'You are really becoming too fat.' The advertisement is entitled 'My scale has warned me' (*Nieuwe Tilburgsche Courant*, 25 September 1936, 15).

The illustration in another advertisement, 'Lose 13 pounds in 11 days,' shows two women, one fat, the other thin (*Leeuwarder Courant*, 23 October 1936, 8). The first is standing on a scale, looking worriedly at the dial. The second, smilingly, tells her: 'Take a cure too; in a week's time you will be amazed.' The implicit message is that the scale is a judge of the too-fat woman urging her to do something about it.

Fig. 3.1 Advertisement for the Bonkora slimming cure, captioned 'My scale has warned me.' The scale says: 'You are really becoming too fat.' *Limburger Koerier*, 26 February 1937. The Hague, National Library of the Netherlands

The scales-as-judge motif required weighing practices different from those of scales as fairground attractions. Instead of weighing themselves occasionally at the fairground out of curiosity, people now were supposed to monitor their weight regularly, either to ensure they were not deviating from the beauty standard or to check whether they were indeed getting closer to that standard. The claims made in the Bonkora testimonials about losing a pound a day, or '21 pounds in 6 weeks'

(*Het Vaderland*, 11 May 1936, 8), '9 pounds in 10 days' (*Limburgsch Dagblad*, 12 November 1937, 10), '18 pounds in barely 2 weeks' (*De Tijd*, 12 February 1937, 8) etc., cannot be made based on an annual weighing at the fairground, nor even on irregular weighing in the doctor's office whenever the doctor considers it necessary. Regular weighing was facilitated by personal scales moving from the fairgrounds first into the streets and later into private households (Bivins and Marland 2016). The scale, like other technologies such as the cinema before it, changed from a unique fairground experience into an ordinary practice or household staple. This required different types of scales.

The first type of scale that enabled regular weighing was the penny scale, a platform scale that required the user to put in a small amount of money and then disclosed his or her weight (Schwartz 1990, 165–68). Penny scales could be found on the streets and in public buildings such as department stores, post offices, railway stations, drugstores and apothecaries. That these scales were supposed to be used regularly is illustrated by the 'weight booklet' published by a druggist from Eindhoven in the southern Netherlands ('Gewichtsboekje' 1918). The booklet offered customers the possibility to record their weight on subsequent dates so as to monitor changes closely. Because of their size, platform scales (such as the penny scales) were not suitable for household use. Weighing at home would become possible only after the introduction of bathroom scales. The scales depicted in the Bonkora advertisements are the size of bathroom scales. Moreover, those shown weighing themselves on these scales are often wearing minimal amounts of clothing, which suggests that by then, in the late 1930s, at least some people were also weighing themselves at home.

As weighing became more common outside the fairground context, weight ceased to be a curiosity. People no longer compared their weight with the extreme weights of human 'freaks,' but with those considered 'normal' for their age, height and gender. In 1932, the journal of the Dutch medical association described a 'standard [public] personal scale' as having 'some lights and mirrors, a dial, and tables of normal weights in relation to age, sex and length' (Pinkhof 1932). Such scales told you not only what your weight was, but also what it ought to be. The tables with normal weights that were used for this were first introduced in the Netherlands (as in many other European countries and the US) through the life insurance industry and then travelled into the public domain (Czerniawski 2007; Stearns 2002, 111). Many scales not only displayed weight tables on the instrument itself, but also printed out cards with one's actual weight—a recording that in itself was an incentive to keep track of one's weight—alongside one's 'normal' weight. Unlike the weighing chairs at the fairs, these scales strongly communicated the message that there existed such a thing as a 'normal' or standard weight and that this was something one should actively strive for. Weight tables could be found elsewhere as well, for example, in personal diaries (Byrdal 1939, 93). The references to 'normal weight' in the Bonkora advertisements mentioned above suggest that people were indeed supposed to know what their 'normal' weight was.

This shows that, by the time the Bonkora campaign was running in the 1930s, beauty had been standardized in quantitative terms. The quantitative standard was body weight; the accompanying measuring instruments were scales. What should be emphasized here is that neither the standards nor the instruments that measure them simply reflect an existing reality. Instead, as historians and sociologists of science, technology and medicine in particular have shown repeatedly, standards and instruments actively co-shape that reality, changing the qualities they quantify, standardize and measure. How, then, did weight and the scale change ideals of slimness and beauty?

QUANTIFYING BEAUTY

To investigate the effects of weight as a beauty standard and the scale as a measuring instrument, it is instructive to consider the medical historian Volker Hess's (2005) study of the thermometer and the quantitative standardization of body temperature. Hess has shown how, in the second half of the nineteenth century, standardization of the thermometer and the accompanying measuring practices shifted the balance of power in the doctor–patient relationship. Because the thermometer 'objectified' fever, patients could use their temperature readings to convince their doctors that they required treatment. They no longer needed to phrase their complaints in a language the doctor could understand, a requirement that constituted a strong impediment to lower-class patients, who were not skilled in the art of conversation as practised by the upper classes to which the doctors belonged. Thus, with the spread of the thermometer, whether a patient received medical treatment and the treatment he or she received became less dependent on the doctor's subjective judgment.

Just as thermometers objectified fever and separated it from the doctor's subjective judgment, scales objectified slimness, enabling it to be established without relying on the subjective judgment of others.

Until then, slimness had been judged quantitatively only in the medical sphere, where doctors used other tools for quantification, such as measuring tapes. Outside the medical sphere, it had been established qualitatively, in the eye of the beholder. Thus, one needed to see oneself through the eyes of others to determine whether one was fulfilling the prevailing standard of beauty. This could be done either by actually encouraging others to judge, or through imitating their judgment by looking in a mirror. Either way, there was a strongly subjective, interpersonal element in assessing beauty as determined by body size. When slimness came to be quantified and the scale partially replaced the eye as the judge of beauty, one no longer needed to *be seen* to establish to what extent one met the beauty standard. This partially separated beauty from looking and thus to some extent individualized the assessment of beauty. In so far as body shape was concerned, all one required was an instrument; involving other people became superfluous.

This individualized assessment of beauty contrasts with what, in the advertising campaigns for slimming products, was presented as a major incentive for becoming beautiful, namely avoiding social exclusion. Take, for example, an ad promoting Facil tablets entitled '*Gaat u dansen, dan moet u slank zijn*' ('If you go dancing, you have to be slender'; *De Telegraaf*, 15 November 1934, 13). The ad shows a dancing couple, both smiling; the woman in particular has a slim figure. The accompanying text explains that women especially have to be slender to fully enjoy dancing. Slender women, it states, are 'admired' (and even 'envied'); corpulent women 'are usually asked to dance solely out of courtesy.' In a Bonkora advertisement, the situation is presented as even more dire: corpulent women are not asked to dance at all (*De Telegraaf*, 8 August 1938, 8). The advertisement opens with a drawing of several couples dancing and one woman sitting on a bench on her own. The accompanying text states: 'People scrupulously avoid her; she is too fat and dances too heavily.' Other Bonkora advertisements likewise regularly depicted fat persons as being excluded from social events. The advertisements show fat women standing apart or even being ridiculed, while other, slimmer women are dancing or enjoying themselves at the beach or the swimming pool. In many advertisements, product users explain how unhappy they were until they finally managed to become slim. Being fat, according to these advertisements, leads to unhappiness resulting from being laughed at, not being able to participate in social occasions and having difficulties, especially as a female, in finding a partner.

Fat people, however, were said to risk even more than social exclusion. An ad from the campaign for Dr. Richter's slimming tea from 1933 (Fig. 3.2) is a case in point. It shows a slim man in a suit and tie, presumably drinking a cup of Dr. Richter's tea. Appearing in the middle of the economic crisis following the 1929 stock market crash, the ad warns: 'Your appearance is your capital' (*Algemeen Handelsblad*, 21 September 1933, 4). A 1935 beauty manual confirms the importance of appearance in finding employment in these difficult times: 'The large number of persons in search of employment has no doubt created the wish to look young. Exhausted, weak, fatigued people do not inspire confidence in employers' (Alsen 1935, 38–39). Thus, fulfilling beauty standards is presented as crucial not only in participating in social life, but also in getting a job.

The advertisements' stress on the importance of beauty for social inclusion is somewhat at odds with their propagation of weight as a beauty standard. Since weight as a standard objectifies and individualizes beauty, it separates it from the judgments of others. Yet, beauty can only play a part in social inclusion if it is readily accessible to others. The advertisers' examples of being asked to dance, not being ridiculed and using your appearance as your capital only make sense if a person's body size and shape can be judged by outside observers. But someone else's body weight can only be known if that person decides to share it. Thus, if weight were the main beauty standard related to slimness, all one had to do to hide one's lack of beauty in this respect was hide one's body weight. The advertisements make it clear that things are not that simple: although they stress the importance of body weight, they also make clear that a lack of beauty due to fatness will ultimately be noticed by others.

The advertisements commonly confront readers with situations in which fatness cannot be hidden, even if they keep their weight a secret from others. Particularly popular for this purpose were advertisements situated at the beach, a new travel destination in the early twentieth century (Pater and Sintobin 2013). As an advertisement for Facil tablets puts it: 'The bathing costume betrays one's figure' (*Algemeen Handelsblad*, 21 July 1930, 3). Figure 3.3 reproduces an illustration used in several Bonkora advertisements, sometimes as a photograph, sometimes as a drawing (e.g., *De Gooi- en Eemlander*, 11 May 1936, 4;

Fig. 3.2 Advertisement for Dr. E. Richter's herbal slimming tea, captioned 'Your appearance is your capital!' *Nieuwsblad van het Noorden*, 30 November 1933. The Hague, National Library of the Netherlands

Fig. 3.3 Advertisement for the Bonkora slimming cure showing how fat persons risk social exclusion. *Limburger Koerier*, 12 June 1937. The Hague, National Library of the Netherlands

Nieuwe Tilburgsche Courant, 28 August 1936, 8; *Limburger Koerier*, 7 May 1937, 4). In it, we see three people: a slim man and woman, and a fat woman. The slim man is holding the arm of the slim woman as they run through the water smiling. Separated from them, in the front, stands the fat woman on her own, looking sad. The illustration depicts the social exclusion of fat people once more, and it also suggests that, when they cannot hide beneath layers of clothing, fat people can be identified even without scales. Finally, another Bonkora beach advertisement depicts two slim women in bathing suits and a more corpulent woman in a summer dress (*Zaans Volksblad*, 14 June 1939, 11). The accompanying text states '[She] would have liked to wear a bathing costume as well, but ... her figure does not allow her. The excess fatness gets onlookers laughing.' The message here is again that fatness leads to social exclusion—in this case, not just by being ignored, but by actively being mocked. Once you are dressed in a bathing suit, your fatness will be impossible to hide.

Yet another Bonkora advertisement (Fig. 3.4) suggests that even minimal clothing does not reveal everything (*Leeuwarder Courant*, 23 April 1937, 8). The illustration shows two women, one fat, one thin, both wearing short, tight underwear—clothing comparable to bathing suits when it comes to its ability to hide fatness. The fat woman is standing on a scale, worriedly looking down, reading the dial. The other woman asks her 'How are you planning on hiding all this ugliness this summer?' On the one hand, the advertisement stresses that there are situations when ugliness cannot be hidden, namely in summer, because it then becomes easily accessible even without scales. On the other hand, it stresses the importance of the scales. The fat woman is not asking the other woman, presumably a friend, to assess her appearance, although her clothing, comparable to beachwear, would enable this. Instead, she looks down at the scale, letting the dial make the assessment. This advertisement nicely illustrates the combined standards that existed for judging to what extent someone fulfils the beauty ideal of slimness. The woman steps onto the scales because, by the 1930s, weight had become a prominent beauty standard. Yet, she must fear the coming of summer because weight was not seen as the only way to establish fatness: visual judgment continued to be a valid way to do so as well. A combined standard existed: the quantitative standardization of the body in the domain of beauty, with its reliance on the visual, did not replace the qualitative judgment by outside observers to the extent it did in the domain of health.

Fig. 3.4 Advertisement for the Bonkora slimming cure. The woman on the right asks: 'How are you planning on hiding all this ugliness this summer?' *De Gooi- en Eemlander*, 23 April 1937. The Hague, National Library of the Netherlands

Conclusion

Today, many of us use weight as a quantitative beauty standard. In the Netherlands, weighing is no longer done at fairgrounds but as in other Western countries has become a private act, to be carried out alone, naked, in the bathroom or bedroom. Women in particular can be reluctant to share the results. This can take extreme forms: in a US survey of female medical personnel, over ten percent of the respondents reported that they had cancelled or delayed medical appointments because they expected to be weighed—the higher a woman's weight-height ratio, the more likely she was to cancel or delay her appointment (Olson et al. 1994). These women were unwilling to share their weights with their doctors and perhaps even wanted to hide these weights from themselves. As long as no one knows your weight, it is impossible to judge whether you meet this beauty standard, and thus your beauty, or lack of it, becomes invisible. Yet, like their historical counterparts in the Bonkora advertisements, many present-day Western women fear the summer, the beach, the swimming pool: the fewer clothes they wear, the harder it becomes to hide their fatness from the eyes of others. Apparently, weight is not the only beauty standard that matters in relation to body shape and size; there is another, qualitative standard of slimness as well, which can be judged by subjective observers, through looking.

This combination of standards poses questions requiring further research. When do we rely on which standard? What do we do when the two standards conflict—do we trust our scales or our mirrors? Why do we hide our weight if we are convinced that others can see our weight gain (or loss); and if we do not think that others can see our weight loss, why do we measure the effectiveness of our diets by relying on our scales? To address these questions, we first have to be able to ask them. This requires us to separate body weight from body size, fatness and slimness. As this chapter has shown, these may be related, but they are not the same, nor is their relationship self-evident. Body weight, I have argued, is neither a natural nor a neutral standard for a bodily state such as slimness. Stepping onto scales to measure how fat or thin we are is not a necessity, but the contingent outcome of a historical process. Thus, investigating solely the beauty ideals of fatness and slimness does not suffice to understand the role of the scales in our societies. Weight, I have attempted to show, requires and deserves its own historical and cultural analysis to understand better the relationship between beauty and bodily norms.

Acknowledgements This work was supported by the Netherlands Organisation for Scientific Research (NWO) under grant 317-52-010. I would like to thank the editors of this volume, the anonymous reviewers and Filip Herza for their helpful comments during the writing process.

NOTES

1. In this chapter, I follow the convention in the field of fat studies of using 'fat' and 'fatness' to describe larger bodies without judging them. This solution is not ideal (one problem is that the dividing line between fat and thin or larger and smaller bodies is itself historically constructed), but I think it is the best available. For more on this issue, see Lupton (2013, 5–7) and Saguy (2013, 7).

2. The database is freely accessible online at http://kranten.delpher. nl (Delpher; last accessed 3 October 2017). I did not search the database through this website but instead used Texcavator, a digital tool to engage with large text repositories, which has been developed in the digital history project Translantis (http://www.translantis.nl, last accessed 3 October 2017). For a detailed discussion of Texcavator's dataset, see Wevers (2017, 70–85; see also Eijnatten et al. 2014). I did use Delpher to access specific articles and advertisements after locating them with help of Texcavator.

3. Weight is the most prominent quantitative beauty standard in the modern West, but not the only one. Other examples include cup size, dress size and waist-hip ratio.

4. All newspapers cited have been consulted online at http://kranten.delpher.nl (last accessed 3 October 2017). The advertisements tended to appear in multiple newspapers and on multiple dates; for each advertisement, I refer to one instance.

5. I have analysed 1148 Bonkora advertisements; 1100 of these refer explicitly to weight.

6. A Dutch pound (*pond*) is 500 grams, so slightly more than a US pound.

7. For more on how Foucault's work can be used to analyse the emergence and effects of weight as a standard for the healthy body, see, for example, Czerniawski (2007), Kwan and Graves (2013, 43–45, 133–36), Lupton (2013, 38–41) and Wright and Harwood (2009).

REFERENCES

Alsen, Ola. 1935. *Vrouwenspiegel: Lichaamsverzorging als middel tot schoonheid en levensvreugde.* Leiden: Leidsche Uitgeversmaatschappij.

Bacon, Linda. 2010. *Health at Every Size: The Surprising Truth About Your Weight.* 2nd ed. Dallas: BenBella Books.

Bingham, Adrian. 2010. "The Digitization of Newspaper Archives: Opportunities and Challenges for Historians." *Twentieth Century British History* 21 (2): 225–31.

Bivins, Roberta, and Hilary Marland. 2016. "Weighting for Health: Management, Measurement and Self-Surveillance in the Modern Household." *Social History of Medicine* 29 (4): 757–80.

"Bonkora." 1936. *Maandblad van de Vereeniging tegen de Kwakzalverij* 56 (1): 7.

"Bonkora." 1938. *Maandblad van de Vereeniging tegen de Kwakzalverij* 58 (2): 12.

Bordo, Susan. 2003. *Unbearable Weight: Feminism, Western Culture, and the Body.* Tenth Anniversary ed. Berkeley: University of California Press.

Brake, Laurel. 2012. "Half Full and Half Empty." *Journal of Victorian Culture* 17 (2): 222–29.

Bruin, Martine de. 2002. "'Hoepsa! Fibele! Krakeling! De kermis is een aardig ding.' Rolzeilen, liedbladen en het kermislied." In *Kennis, kunstjes en kunnen: Kermis – de wondere wereld van glans en glitter,* edited by Johanna Jacobs, 23–33. Amsterdam: SUN.

Byrdal, Lis. 1939. *Over charme en schoonheid.* Translated by M. Röntgen-Otter. Amsterdam: Van Holkema & Warendorf N.V.

Campos, Paul. 2004. *The Obesity Myth: Why America's Obsession with Weight Is Hazardous to Your Health.* New York: Gotham Books.

Cooper, Charlotte. 2010. "Fat Studies: Mapping the Field." *Sociology Compass* 4 (12): 1020–34.

Czerniawski, Amanda M. 2007. "From Average to Ideal: The Evolution of the Height and Weight Table in the United States, 1836–1943." *Social Science History* 31 (2): 273–96.

Daston, Lorraine, and Peter Galison. 1992. "The Image of Objectivity." *Representations* 40: 81–128.

Daston, Lorraine, and Peter Galison. 2007. *Objectivity.* New York: Zone Books.

Dawes, Laura. 2014. *Childhood Obesity in America: Biography of an Epidemic.* Cambridge: Harvard University Press.

Dumas, Alexander. 2012. "Rejecting the Aging Body." In *Routledge Handbook of Body Studies,* edited by Bryan S. Turner, 375–88. London: Routledge.

Eijnatten, Joris van, Toine Pieters, and Jaap Verheul. 2014. "Using Texcavator to Map Public Discourse." *Tijdschrift voor tijdschriftstudies* 35: 59–65.

Espeland, Wendy Nelson, and Mitchell L. Stevens. 2008. "A Sociology of Quantification." *European Journal of Sociology* 49 (3): 401–36.

Fletcher, Isabel. 2012. "Obesity: A Historical Account of the Construction of a Modern Epidemic." PhD diss., University of Edinburgh.

Fletcher, Isabel. 2014. "Defining an Epidemic: The Body Mass Index in British and US Obesity Research 1960–2000." *Sociology of Health & Illness* 36 (3): 338–53.

Foucault, Michel. 1986. "Of Other Spaces." Translated by Jay Miskowiec. *Diacritics* 16 (Spring): 22–27.

Foucault, Michel. 1990. *The History of Sexuality*. Vol. 1, *An Introduction*. Translated by Robert Hurley. New York: Vintage.

Gard, Michael, and Jan Wright. 2005. *The Obesity Epidemic: Science, Morality, and Ideology*. London: Routledge.

"Gewichtsboekje." 1918. Regional Archive Eindhoven. 10142 Collection Fens, Inventory Number 62 (Documents related to Eindhoven).

Goupy, Hortense de. 1898. *De schoonheid der vrouw: Hoe wordt zij verkregen, bevorderd en onderhouden? Practische gids voor dames van elken leeftijd*. 2nd ed. Amsterdam: Van Klaveren.

Hacking, Ian. 1990. *The Taming of Chance*. Cambridge: Cambridge University Press.

Hemels, Joan. 2002. "Van rarekiek tot bioscoop." In *Kennis, kunstjes en kunnen: Kermis – de wondere wereld van glans en glitter*, edited by Johanna Jacobs, 187–203. Amsterdam: SUN.

Hess, Volker. 2005. "Standardizing Body Temperature: Quantification in Hospitals and Daily Life, 1850–1900." In *Body Counts: Medical Quantification in Historical and Sociological Perspective*, edited by Gérard Jorland, Annick Opinel, and George Weisz, 109–26. Montreal: McGill-Queen's University Press.

"Het wondervermageringsmiddel 'Bonkora'." 1937. *Maandblad van de Vereeniging tegen de Kwakzalverij* 57 (9): 71–72.

Hitchcock, Tim. 2013. "Confronting the Digital: Or How Academic History Writing Lost the Plot." *Cultural and Social History* 10 (1): 9–23.

Horstman, Klasien. 2001. *Public Bodies, Private Lives: The Historical Construction of Life Insurance, Health Risks, and Citizenship in the Netherlands, 1880–1920*. Rotterdam: Erasmus Publishing.

Huistra, Hieke. 2017. "Experts by Experience: Lay Users as Authorities in Slimming Remedy Advertisements, 1918–1939." *BMGN—Low Countries Historical Review* 132 (1): 126–48.

Huizinga, Laurens. [1900?]. "Groninger kermislied." Translated from dialect into standard (present-day) Dutch by Tjaard W. R. de Haan. Cited in translation in "Kermis in Nederland." Special Issue *Neerlands Volksleven* 28 (4): 165.

Jacobs, Johanna, ed. 2002. *Kennis, kunstjes en kunnen – Kermis: De wondere wereld van glans en glitter*. Amsterdam: SUN.

Jansen, Gerrit H. 1987. *Een roes van vrijheid: Kermis in Nederland*. Meppel: Boom.

Jorland, Gerard, Annick Opinel, and George Weisz, eds. 2005. *Body Counts: Medical Quantification in Historical and Sociological Perspectives*. Montreal: McGill-Queen's University Press.

Jutel, Annemarie. 2001. "Does Size Really Matter? Weight and Values in Public Health." *Perspectives in Biology and Medicine* 44 (2): 283–96.

Jutel, Annemarie. 2005. "Weighing Health: The Moral Burden of Obesity." *Social Semiotics* 15 (2): 113–25.

Jutel, Annemarie. 2006. "The Emergence of Overweight as a Disease Entity: Measuring up Normality." *Social Science & Medicine* 63 (9): 2268–76.

Keikes, H. W. 1978. *Kermis en circus in beeld tot 1940*. Zaltbommel: Europese Bibliotheek.

Keyser, Marja Claudine. 1978. "Kermis in Nederland tot het einde van de negentiende eeuw." *Neerlands volksleven* 28 (4): 170–75.

Kockelkoren, Petran. 2003. *Technology: Art, Fairground, and Theatre*. Translated by Peter Mason. Rotterdam: NAi Publishers.

Kwan, Samantha, and Jennifer Graves. 2013. *Framing Fat: Competing Constructions in Contemporary Culture*. New Brunswick: Rutgers University Press.

Lampland, Martha, and Susan Leigh Star. 2009. *Standards and Their Stories: How Quantifying, Classifying, and Formalizing Practices Shape Everyday Life*. Ithaca: Cornell University Press.

Latour, Bruno [Jim Johnson, pseud.]. 1988. "Mixing Humans and Nonhumans Together: The Sociology of a Door-Closer." *Social Problems* 35 (3): 298–310.

Latour, Bruno. 1992. "Where Are the Missing Masses? The Sociology of a Few Mundane Artifacts." In *Shaping Technology/Building Society*, edited by Wiebe E. Bijker and John Law, 225–58. Cambridge: MIT Press.

Lears, Jackson. 1994. *Fables of Abundance: A Cultural History of Advertising in America*. New York: Basic Books.

Lupton, Deborah. 2013. *Fat*. London: Routledge.

Maas, W. 1950. "Een en ander over de Zaandamse kermis." *De Zaende: Maandblad gewijd aan de historie, folklore en genealogie van de Zaanstreek* 5: 11–14.

Marchand, Roland. 1985. *Advertising the American Dream: Making Way for Modernity, 1920–1940*. Berkeley: University of California Press.

Oers, Hennie van, Paul Spapens, and Lauran Wijffels. 1986. *Veel vermaak en weinig wol: De geschiedenis van de Tilburgse kermis*. [S.l.]: [s.n.].

Oliver, J. Eric. 2006. *Fat Politics: The Real Story Behind America's Obesity Epidemic*. Oxford: Oxford University Press.

Olson, Cheri L., Howard D. Schumaker, and Barbara P. Yawn. 1994. "Overweight Women Delay Medical Care." *Archives of Family Medicine* 3 (10): 888–92.

Pater, Ben de, and Tom Sintobin, eds. 2013. *Koninginnen aan de Noordzee: Scheveningen, Oostende en de opkomst van de badcultuur rond 1900*. Hilversum: Verloren.

Pickering, Andrew. 1995. *The Mangle of Practice: Time, Agency, and Science.* Chicago: University of Chicago Press.

Pinkhof, H. 1932. "Weegschaal met hartslagspiegel." *Nederlandsch tijdschrift voor geneeskunde* 76 (45): 5210.

Popenoe, Rebecca. 2005. "Ideal." In *Fat: The Anthropology of an Obsession,* edited by Don Kulick and Anne Meneley, 9–28. New York: Jeremy P. Tarcher/Penguin.

Porter, Theodore. 1995. *Trust in Numbers: The Pursuit of Objectivity in Science and Public Life.* Princeton: Princeton University Press.

Putnam, Lara. 2016. "The Transnational and the Text-Searchable: Digitized Sources and the Shadows They Cast." *The American Historical Review* 121 (2): 377–402.

Rothblum, Esther, and Sondra Solovay, eds. 2009. *The Fat Studies Reader.* New York: New York University Press.

Saguy, Abigail Cope. 2013. *What's Wrong with Fat?* Oxford: Oxford University Press.

Schat, Ellen. 2005. "De ontwikkeling van de Leeuwarder kermis (1850–1920)." *Leeuwarder historische reeks* 8: 85–118.

Schwartz, Hillel. 1990. *Never Satisfied: A Cultural History of Diets, Fantasies, and Fat.* New York: Anchor Books.

Sliggers, Bert. 2002. "Mensen te kijk op de kermis." In *Kennis, kunstjes en kunnen: Kermis – de wondere wereld van glans en glitter,* edited by Johanna Jacobs, 147–68. Amsterdam: SUN.

Stallybrass, Peter, and Allon White. 1986. *The Politics and Poetics of Transgression.* Ithaca: Cornell University Press.

Stearns, Peter N. 2002. *Fat History: Bodies and Beauty in the Modern West, with a New Preface.* New York: New York University Press.

Timmermans, Stefan, and Steven Epstein. 2010. "A World of Standards but Not a Standard World: Toward a Sociology of Standards and Standardization." *Annual Review of Sociology* 36 (1): 69–89.

Tjeertes Sr., J. 1978. "De kermis in Wormerveer." *Neerlands Volksleven* 28 (4): 202–7.

Verbeek, Peter-Paul. 2005. *What Things Do: Philosophical Reflections on Technology, Agency, and Design.* University Park: Pennsylvania State University Press.

Wevers, Melvin. 2017. "Consuming America: A Data-Driven Analysis of the United States as a Reference Culture in Dutch Public Discourse on Consumer Goods, 1890–1990." PhD diss., Utrecht University.

Wright, Jan, and Valerie Harwood, eds. 2009. *Biopolitics and the "Obesity Epidemic": Governing Bodies.* London: Routledge.

Zoonen, Arie van. 1996. *"Stap op en laat je wegen": De geschiedenis van 550 jaar Hoornse kermis.* Hoorn: Gemeente Hoorn.

Zweiniger-Bargielowska, Ina. 2005. "The Culture of the Abdomen: Obesity and Reducing in Britain, Circa 1900–1939." *Journal of British Studies* 44 (2): 239–73.

PART II

Representations of 'Alternative' Beauty

Extraordinarily White: The De/Spectacularization of the Albinotic Body and the Normalization of Its Audience

Christopher Hohl and Matthias Krings

We would like to begin with a comparison of two photographs taken a hundred years apart. Each shows two individuals, one black and one white—or so it seems at first glance. The older photograph (Fig. 4.1) is from around 1910 and, according to its title, depicts a 'white Negress' and her sister from West Africa. Printed on postcards, it was sold as souvenir of a freak show act with the same title. The more recent example is an image from a 2011 fashion editorial in *CHAOS Magazine* (Fig. 4.2) showing two male models. Senegalese Papis Loveday, on the right, is wearing a black jacket and almost black makeup; the African-American Shaun Ross, on the left, is wearing a white shirt and has his pale, hypopigmented skin and blonde hair coloured white. On the one hand, despite the different periods in which they were taken, the two photographs share certain elements. Both play with the contrast of dark and light skin and hair, of black and white garments and makeup, while simultaneously spectacularizing the potential transgression of racial binarism in an

C. Hohl (✉) · M. Krings
Johannes Gutenberg University, Mainz, Germany

© The Author(s) 2019
C. Liebelt et al. (eds.), *Beauty and the Norm*,
Palgrave Studies in Globalization and Embodiment,
https://doi.org/10.1007/978-3-319-91174-8_4

AMAUNA, la Négresse blanche, avec sa Sœur
de la Côte-d'Or (Afrique)

Fig. 4.1 Souvenir card of Amanoua Ankrah Kpapo (right) with another actor as the show act of 'The white Negress and her sister' (From around 1910)

Fig. 4.2 Shaun Ross (right) and Papis Loveday in the fashion editorial 'Out of Circulation' for *CHAOS Magazine* in 2011 (Photographed by Rebecca Litchfield. Courtesy of Reese Larsen and *CHAOS Magazine*)

albinotic body of African descent. On the other hand, they also differ in significant ways. While the fashion editorial frames Ross as 'beauty' personified, the freak show frames the 'white Negress' as an 'oddity'.

Albinism is a contested phenomenon.[1] Biomedicine nowadays regards it as a congenital condition resulting in a lack of pigment in the skin, hair and/or eyes that is sometimes considered a disability because it impairs vision and because of the need to protect the skin from the sun to prevent skin cancer.[2] Many social activists have also taken this stance, not least to oppose an older and competing understanding of albinism as having an other-worldly quality. Around the world, the very humanness of the hypopigmented body was and sometimes still is not fully acknowledged and is even denied. Hollywood films, such as *Powder* in 1995 or *Matrix Reloaded* in 2003, like spiritual beliefs in East Africa, bestow supernatural powers on the albinotic body. As anthropologists, we are social constructivists and treat albinism primarily not as a congenital syndrome but as a socially constructed category, that is, as one of many forms of cultural differentiation. Much like other embodied social categories, such as race and gender, its definitions, conceptual borders and frames vary in place and time. In this chapter, we discuss three such frames, looking at how their representations have gone hand in hand with either spectacularizing or normalizing the albinotic body.[3]

Studying the presentational work that turned disabled bodies—or able ones, for that matter—into the freak figures of the nineteenth- and early twentieth-century side-show business, Robert Bogdan makes the case for a social constructivist understanding of their reality (1988, 2–3). It was not so much their bodily condition as their presentation and interpretative framing that made them freaks: as Rosemarie Garland-Thomson puts it, 'what we assume to be a freak of nature was instead a freak of culture' (1996, 10). By tracing different frames of representing and interpreting the albinotic body, we share this approach, but extend it beyond both the institution of the freak show and the figure of the freak. As in many other fields, critical attention in disability studies has shifted in recent years from deviance to norm, showing how they are not only related but also co-constructed. Indeed, it is argued that society's very understanding of what is normal only came about through certain processes of dissociation and comparison. Lennard Davis elaborates how the norm developed as a concept during the mid-nineteenth century, related to the development of the statistical average and the eugenic aim of normalizing the non-standard population (1995, 23–49). In line with this type of inquiry, Garland-Thomson (1998) probes the conventions of display and the narratives of embodiment

employed in the cultural institutions of the freak show and the beauty pageant. As two public spectacles, these not only produced the figures of the
freak and beauty, they also gave shape to their opposites, namely the spectators, who were allowed to imagine themselves as normal citizens:

> In the freak show, the anomalous body functions similarly to the stand-
> ard body of the beauty queen by working to establish the borders of the
> canonical body. Both exhibitions unify a disparate audience into the fantasy
> of an egalitarian community of citizens and assure them of their status as
> ordinary and normal. (ibid., n.p.)

Charles D. Martin (2002) rejects this binary between the freak and the
normal. On the basis of his study of the presentation and perception of
the 'white Negro' in the United States, he outlines their interpretation
as racially ambivalent, hybrid characters and thus stresses their unsettling
effects on an audience: 'Rather than secure identity for the audience of
the freak show—as previously stipulated in freak show criticism— ... categories are violated and left unresolved. As a result, the audience feels
more unease than reaffirmation' (ibid., 7). For the figure of the African-
American 'albino', this makes for a tragic in-between status in racialized
terms. They are, Martin concludes, caught in a double bind: 'neither
black enough nor white enough, stuck in a violent cultural crossfire in a
world that still demands the security of binary opposition' (ibid., 115).

However, the ambivalence of this perception and its ability to 'encourage
simultaneous identification and differentiation' (Garland-Thomson 1998,
n.p.) is not entirely lost on Garland-Thomson either. She does indeed recognize that 'the freak's and the beauty's cultural function depends upon
their being seen as simultaneously self and other, at once comfortable and
strange, as both alluring and repelling' (ibid., n.p.). This ambivalence makes
them attractive to their viewers. While Martin reminds us of the figure's
double bind, he misses Garland-Thomson's analysis of the institutional
arrangements in their production. It is as much the structured seeing these
shows entail as the exhibited figures themselves to which she attributes the
construction of a normal subject. Because the freak show and beauty pageant positioned a particular, visible and readable object of embodiment
against the undifferentiated, anonymous and disembodied reading subject,
the audience could 'freely assume the egalitarian, anonymous position of the
"common man"' (ibid., n.p.). The ambiguous and racially impure figure up
on stage enabled the spectators down in the auditorium to imagine a proper
place of racial purity—indeed, of normality—for themselves.

Drawing on this perspective, in this chapter we argue that the (re) presentations of people with albinism that range from freaks to carriers of a medical condition to aesthetic beauties help co-produce and negotiate different versions of their spectators' normality. In the following, we present three case studies in which hypopigmented bodies are rendered freaks, photographic subjects and fashion models respectively. In doing so, we discuss the dis/continuities in spectacularizing albinotic bodies and show how they concurrently vest normality in their audience.

White Negress and Ice King: Hypopigmented Bodies as Freak Show Oddities

Freak shows were spectacular exhibitions institutionalized in the mid-nineteenth century. They were based on older practices of displaying 'wonders' and 'monsters' dating back to antiquity and interpreting them as evidence of either the divine or the natural order (Daston and Park 1998; Garland-Thomson 1996). Freak shows fed on the audience's desire to indulge in spectacle. Their heyday was from around the mid-nineteenth century to the early twentieth century. After World War II, freak shows largely disappeared when a medical discourse became dominant and replaced curiosity with treatment, sending 'freaks' off the stage and turning them into medical 'patients'.

Before albinotic bodies were presented in freak shows, they had already had 'careers' in aristocrats' curiosity chambers and under the gaze and assessments of natural historians of the Enlightenment (Krings 2017a, 363–367; Curran 2009). Freak-show managers drew on this history, its concern with racial categories and their relations when crafting their acts. One example is described in Rea Brändle's (2007) history of the Togolese impresario Nayo J. C. Bruce and Amanoua Ankrah Kpapo from Accra, who became a member of Bruce's troupe and later one of his wives. In November 1902, advertisements in Berlin announced her as the latest wonder from Africa for her white skin, white hair and light grey eyes. She was presented in Castan's Panoptikum, a permanent wax museum that also staged changing shows of living 'curiosities'. The size of Bruce's troupe varied, as did its acts and names. Kpapo played the contrasting part in a couple. The postcard (Fig. 4.1) from the early twentieth century, for example, shows her standing next to another woman. Both are roughly the same height, have the same hairstyles and wear the same necklaces and the same patterned, off the shoulder dresses. The caption reads 'AMAUA, la Négresse blanche, avec sa Sœur de la Côte-d'Or (Afrique)', or 'The white Negress with her sister from the Gold Coast (Africa)'.[4] The only difference, aside from all this sameness, is their skin and hair colour—or rather greyness, in the case of this black and white print. While the woman identified as her sister has black hair, Kpapo has light grey hair. Similarly, her skin is lighter and contrasts with her sister's darker skin tones. This contrast is also employed in written presentations. The programme of Bruce's Togomandingo-Truppe, printed on 15 July 1903 in the Swiss newspaper *Berner Tagblatt*, advertises the show as 'das größte Naturwunder der Gegenwart' (Brändle 2007, 59), or 'the greatest natural wonder of our time', and continues:

> The Negro sisters from West Africa. White Negress Amuana and her black sister Ama, born from black parents (Negroes). The only example of its kind, and labelled a phenomenon by the Anthropological and Ethnological Society of Berlin and by Professor Jung from Geneva. Please note, certificates and reports ready to be reviewed by our cherished audience. [our translation]

While in 1896 Bruce initially refused to permit any examinations of the women in his troupe by the anthropologist Felix von Luschan (ibid., 18–19), he obviously allowed them later and used the resulting reports for promotional purposes. These certificates added to Kpapo's sense of novelty. They also testify to the close collaboration between science and the entertainment industry in spectacularizing the albinotic body.

The white Negress's act was apparently so successful that Bruce, though changing the figure's social status or origin, never altered its ambivalent tension. In 1912, a religious dimension was added to the 'sisters' for a new show entitled 'Die heilige weisse Negerin und ihre schwarze Priester-Schwester' (ibid., 81), or 'The holy white Negress and her black priest-sister'. Bruce's other wives alternated in playing the part of the 'sister'. The relationships in the family's private life were sometimes also played out in acts in public shows. Many postcards show images of Kpapo sitting among several of her co-wives—once even supported by more women hired to play additional wives—together with their husband Bruce and their children. The cards are entitled 'Souvenir de la Foire: La famille Amoema de la Négresse blanche' (ibid., 74–75), or 'Souvenir from the fair: Amoema, the white Negress's family'. Later, Congo replaced Togoland as the geographical reference, and Kpapo was elevated to royalty when the act was advertised as 'Kongolesen mit ihrer weissen Königin' (ibid., 83), or 'Congolese with their white queen'. In 1905 and 1906, when Bruce collaborated with Fritz Geissler's 'The American Living Novelty and Curiosity Compagnie', Kpapo was presented next to other freak figures (ibid., 66). A poster shows her as a shining light figure with a spear in her hand and rays of sunshine beaming out from behind her, hovering over a caricatured group of terrified Africans (ibid., 68).

The staging of sameness and difference just described deliberately played with the racial categories that were so prominent in the minds of European audiences at the turn of the century. The displayed contrast between relatively light and dark skin on bodies otherwise presented as of the same kind defied the audiences' expectations in view of the emphasis on inheritance in racial theories. It is exactly this potentially unsettling confusion and ambiguity which Bruce used to try and capture his customers' attention. Here the white Negress is in exactly the double-bind position that Martin (2002) describes in relation to similar cases in the United States. On the one hand, she is both black and white; on the other hand, she is neither one nor the other. Her similarity vis-à-vis her white European spectators in terms of skin colour had an unsettling and irritating effect on them. Medical doctors and physical anthropologists writing around 1900 on albinotic Africans display considerable zeal in their reports in rejecting any similarity between their objects of study and themselves. An article written by J. Frédéric, who was given an opportunity to 'examine' Kpapo in Berlin in 1907 or sometime before, is revealing in this regard. While he begins by observing the similarity of her skin tone, eye and hair colour to that of European 'blondes', after examining her in somewhat closer detail, he concludes:

> However, there can be no doubt that she is a true negress; apart from the typically ulotric nature of the scalp hair, this is sufficiently proved by the proportions of the face, the width of the nose, which is characterized by large nostrils …, the strongly bulging lips, the saggy conical breasts. (Frédéric 1907, 221, our translation)

A similar deprecatory rhetoric can be found in many other reports of this genre, which usually end by expelling any doubt that the person in question could be anything but a 'veritable *nègre* blanc' (Atgier 1910, 455, emphasis added). Such examinations and the subsequent reports constituted acts of 'cleansing' and, therefore, of restoring the social order (Douglas 1966). They served to stabilize pre-existing 'racial' categories and the overall construct of 'race' challenged by Kpapo and other 'white Africans' who had been brought to Europe before her (Krings 2017a).

However, it was not only persons with albinism of African or African-American origin that were presented in freak shows. Karl Breu, born 1884 in Dubiau, Bohemia, was one of several Europeans with albinism who worked as a show character. In his late teens, he joined a travelling circus and eventually became an escape artist. Reportedly, his otherwise pale face turned bright red from the strenuous task of stretching his body in order to remove his shackles (Böhmerwald Heimatkreis Prachatitz, n.d.). Legend has it that he nearly died when he struggled to free himself from his restraints after letting himself be thrown into the Thames at London. Such legends were, of course, part of the act. Breu worked under the stage name of Tom Jack, but he was also known by the epithets 'Weißschädl' (Marschall 2016), meaning 'White Skull', and 'The Ice King' (Pednaud 2008). Cabinet cards and posters show him with hair in the form of a white-grey fuzzy bush (Fig. 4.3), a trademark of many European performers with albinism. Like his beard and eyebrows, his hair seems to have been retouched and made even whiter than the rest of the black and white photograph. Breu later married Wally Paradise, a woman with albinism. Together, they established an exotic act entitled 'To-Ya and his Ice Family' (Illugadóttir 2015, 30; Vilhálmsson 2013). According to the act's storyline, they were the representatives of the last truly indigenous population of extremely pale Icelanders. Non-albinotic members wore white wigs to pass themselves off as Icelanders. The same dark dress with lighter coloured zigzag patterns on the collar, cuff and hem hinted at a specific ethnic background and contrasted with their light skin and white hair. So, although Breu started out as a 'novelty act' presenting an unusual ability (escapology), he incorporated his paleness into his 'Ice King' and later 'To-Ya' acts.

As the examples of Kpapo and Breu show, and similar to the staging of other so-called freaks (see Herza, this volume), having an extraordinary body was not sufficient in itself to be exhibited in a freak show. In the case of the albinotic body, it had to be contrasted with darker colours and woven into symbolic references that re-contextualized it into a human or not so human oddity. Freak-show managers relied on extensive presentational work to achieve this kind of re-contextualization in the eyes of the audience. In his landmark study, Bogdan (1988)

Fig. 4.3   Karl Breu on a postcard as 'Tom Jack the Ice King' (Date unknown)

elaborates on the techniques, strategies and styles of exoticization and aggrandizement used to construct freaks. To lure potential visitors, the show's ads, handbills, banners, talkers and press releases not only exaggerated the exhibit to grab their customers' attention (ibid., 98–104), they also aroused the expectation that one would be seeing something spectacular, thus framing the audience's interpretation beforehand. Scientific assessments, as in the case of Kpapo, were used to authenticate the claims made regarding the alleged freaks. At the time, Europeans and North Americans were preoccupied not only with the relations of what they considered distinct races towards each other and their possible miscegenation, but also with the limits of humanness and of crossbreeding with beasts (ibid., 106). The figure of the freak was used to negotiate the symbolic boundaries of who counts as an ordinary human. As the examples of Kpapo and Breu show, the exhibit was presented with a fabricated biography and title suited to their role in the act. George and Willie Muse, two African-American brothers with albinism, were even staged as extraterrestrials who had allegedly been found beside their spaceship in the Mojave Desert in the southwestern United States, and they were hailed as Eko and Iko, two ambassadors from Mars (ibid., 105; Macy 2016). During and after the show, visitors could buy postcards or cabinet cards of the exhibited 'freaks'. The photographs on these cards were taken in professional studios against various painted backdrops and with additional props to fit the act. Negatives were doctored to hide, add or accentuate specific features. Show managers and exhibits would review the photographer's work and give instructions for printing. Bogdan found the note: 'Make half length and have the hair show as white as possible' (1988, 13) on the back of a photo of a woman with albinism. To sum up, merely having particularly light-coloured skin and hair was not spectacular enough to qualify as a freak.

Conversely, the audience's normality was not an essential quality of the freak figures' viewers either. Instead, it is co-constructed by the very presentations of albinotic bodies as oddities. In the same move, as the scientific reports grapple with Kpapo's racial ambiguity and certify her 'proper' distance from her European audience, they construe this audience as her opposite, that is, unambiguous whites occupying their 'proper' place in the popular racial order. Breu's presentation, by accentuating his pale skin, exoticizing his origins and displaying his extraordinary skills, turns its audience into normal locals. It is the spatial and symbolic distance created by the show's stage, props, ads and artificial biographies that keeps the albinotic freak figure's unsettling potential at bay. While they turned albinotic bodies into extraordinary spectacles, they constituted their viewers as ordinary beings: 'The freak confirms the viewer as bounded, belonging to a "proper" social category' (Grosz 1996, 65). It is by externalizing an ambiguous, particular Other that the common Self comes into existence and gains meaning as homogenous, whole and normal.

BEAUTIFUL INDIVIDUALS: PERSONS WITH ALBINISM AND A PHOTOGRAPHER'S QUEST TO REDEFINE BEAUTY

By the mid-twentieth century, freak shows had gone out of fashion, and another institution came to dominate the representation of the hypopig-mented body. Since around 1800, when biomedicine began framing it as a case of a pathological lack of pigment, as analysed elsewhere by Krings, the stereotypical 'red eyes' of 'the albino' have become the pathogno-monic sign of the condition (2017a, 368–372). Images of people with albinism circulating in medical textbooks conceptualize 'the albino' as pathological. It is this portrayal against which activists' criticisms turned in the 1990s. Former fashion photographer Rick Guidotti, for example, deliberately parted from what he deemed a negative, even dehumanizing portrayal of persons with albinism. His approach, which was intended 'to transform public perceptions of people living with genetic, physical, intellectual and behavioral differences,'[5] is epitomized in the name of his charity, 'Positive Exposure'. His first breakthrough came in 1998 with a five-page article in *Life Magazine* mostly filled with portraits of persons with albinism.

On the first page, we see a side view of Charla McMillan, the then president of the US-based National Organization of Albinism and Hypopigmentation (NOAH), a support group for people with albinism and their families. Her long white hair contrasts even more sharply with the black background than the yellowed paper of the old, second-hand magazine copy that we bought online. Blown slightly behind her head and shoulders, her hair extends her upward gaze. In this side view, she reminds the viewer of depictions of the Goddess of Liberty, like that in Eugène Delacroix's famous painting, 'Liberty Leading the People', from 1830. This association resonates well with the article's title, 'Redefining Beauty'. The subheading further proclaims its progressive agenda: 'Photographer Rick Guidotti opens our eyes to the beauty of albinism'.

The *Life* article features ten photographs of persons with albinism. All are photographed in front of a black or dark blue background that accentuates their nearly white or very light cream-coloured skin and hair. The spotlight directed on them from the side or back intensifies this effect. They are wearing fashionable clothes and adopt a model pose that signals the self-reflexive nature of the situation. They smile, laugh, spread out their arms, pose with their hands on their hips, look into the camera, etc. They all seem to be aware of what they are partaking in and present themselves in an apparently comfortable, even proud manner.

But, as with the presentation in freak shows, the visual does not seem to be sufficient in itself. Again, a textual narrative accompanies it. We find the respective subjects' names and some quotes next to their images. A brief text informs the reader about Guidotti's project, as well as the intended connection between visual and textual representation:

> Marshaling [sic!] his [Guidotti's] industry's standard resources – hair, make-up and great clothes – he made each person see how beautiful he or she is. To help others see it as well, he asked NOAH members to tell their stories. Their words – some belonging to the people pictured, some not – are unattributed on these pages because the message, says Guidotti, is universal: 'Nothing is uglier than ignorance.' (Guidotti 1998, 67)

After his article in *Life Magazine*, Guidotti elaborated and developed his narrative further through a series of reiterations in interviews and public talks. The narrative now contained several elements. First, Guidotti was discontented with the fashion industry's narrow definition of beauty. Second, he had an encounter with a young girl with albinism that revealed her beauty to him. Third, he was discontented with the standards of depiction in medical representations. Fourth, he formed an alliance with the represented, and fifth, their self-perception changed through his portraits of them. He uses this account of his own and his photographic subjects' change in perception as examples of what he hopes to achieve for his audience, as well as for those he has photographed.

A good example of this narrative is a lecture Guidotti (2011) gave at the TEDxPhoenix conference in 2011. A video recording of the speech available online had been viewed over 160,000 times at the time of our writing in May 2017. Guidotti delivers his story in a lively style, accompanied by a slideshow of images and videos. It begins with his own frustration, despite a successful career as a fashion photographer in New York City: 'I was always told, every single day, who was beautiful. I was forced to work within certain parameters of the beauty standard. ... It was kind of really crazy, because I'm an artist, I see beauty everywhere' (Guidotti 2011). Then, to prove his point, he gives an account of the chance encounter that, he claims, changed his whole life. On a street corner in Manhattan, he ran into 'this gorgeous kid. She had long white, beautiful hair, pale, pale skin. ... she was stunning and I never met a model like this before' (ibid.). This revelation contrasted with the visual representations of people with albinism that Guidotti found in medical sources. This discrepancy led to his critique of their standard representation, and ultimately, of representations of beauty:

> I started seeing images from ... cancer wards and clinics, where [people with albinism] are just in bed. Images of illness, of sadness, of sickness. ... I sort of found these typical images of kids and adults in their underwear up against the walls in doctors' offices, with the black bar across their eyes, saying disease. This is a disease. Defined by a disease. I was like, 'This is crazy!' (ibid.)

After outlining the problem, Guidotti presents his solution and its effects. His first project was the aforementioned article in *Life Magazine*. On stage, Guidotti retells and plays a scene from the photoshoot to illustrate the effects his portrayals had:

> So, in walks the first person we're about to photograph, her name is Christine. And Christine is a knockout, long white hair, really tall, she is stunning. She walks into my studio. The way she walks in, though, instead of this gorgeous girl, she walks in like this [*Guidotti walks along the stage in small steps, his head hanging down, his shoulders bend forward, speaking in a low and sad voice*], her head down, shoulders hunched, one word answer, no eye contact. [*Guidotti returns to his upright posture and normal voice, turning to the audience with frowns on his forehead*] ... I said no, out of respect for this gorgeous kid, I wanna photograph her like I would anybody else. So, the fan went on, the music went on, and I grabbed a mirror that was next to the set. I held it up to her and said, Christine, look at yourself, you're magnificent. And she got it, and she went from this [*Guidotti returns to the hunched pose for a second*] to that [*he strikes an upright posture, hands on hips, elbows out, the head thrown back a bit and smiling*]. ... She was unbelievable. And I saw this transformation right in front of the lens,

through photography, that she was now transformed, with a powerful and positive sense of who she is. The next day she goes to school, she's gonna change the way her community sees her difference. Instead of walking in like this [*he hunches down again*], she's walking in like this [*he walks upright again*]. So, it's all about ambassadors for change. (2011)

In one form or another, this narrative is featured in most of the articles about Guidotti and the activities of his Positive Exposure charity. Like the quotes in the *Life* article, it gives the visual images additional meaning, thus enhancing the impact on the viewer, as well as directing the viewer's interpretation towards a certain reading.

Since the 1998 article in *Life Magazine*, Positive Exposure has expanded its activities. Guidotti has travelled the globe to photograph persons with albinism from all over the world. He has organized photo exhibitions and been featured in documentaries. His charity offers educational material, lectures and workshops. Guidotti also began photographing people with other impairments and disabilities. Nowadays, he travels the United States to attend conferences by organizations of people with rare genetic syndromes (cf. Guidotti 2016).

Guidotti's approach deliberately and literally puts his subjects into the spotlight. He photographs and exposes them. What distinguishes his approach from that of medical representations is not the medium, but the presentational techniques and the context in which they are published. The message thus created differs through these presentational techniques. The images speak a different language of sorts. Unlike those depicted in medical textbooks, his photographic subjects smile, laugh and strike a pose like fashion models. They are not anonymized with black bars across their eyes, but instead have their names printed on or next to the images. They show positive emotions, comfort, a certain control and thus agency. They are not placed in backgrounds or settings that are coded as medical, scientific and 'sad'. Instead they are shot in the very same locale—a fashion photographer's studio—where some of society's most admired figures, the supermodels, are created. These technical differences result not in reduction to a medical condition but in a focus on the exhibit's personality and beauty. Indeed, one article quotes Guidotti claiming that 'I have never photographed a genetic disease, ... I have always photographed people' (Lecci and Peterson 2014). It is exactly through this contrasting opposition to medical depictions that Guidotti casts his photographs as personal and beautiful. The stares to which these photographic exposures invite their viewers thus have a generative potential. In her more recent work on staring, Garland-Thomson discusses its ability to create more even relationships and 'revalue devalued people' (2009, 83) in the context of painted portraits of people with disability. Intervening between those staring and those stared at—whom Garland-Thomson calls the starers and the starees—such depictions 'grant us more than permission to stare; they use the clout of high art to transform our staring from a breach of etiquette or an offensive intrusion into an act of appreciation' (ibid., 83–84). What this hinges on, however, is the visual depiction of personality, of resemblance, of vesting the portrayed subjects with a respectful dignity that generates approachability. By achieving this, Guidotti's carefully arranged opportunity to stare allows starers to establish an interpersonal relationship and eventually recognize a mutual humanity with the exposed subjects.

This project, to fight the 'sadness' of pathologizing medical representations, is not directed at altering the supposedly problematic and deviant body. Rather, it addresses how their viewers make such assessments. It is not the so-called anomalous body that is supposed to change, but the audience's perception of it. As Guidotti's first model Christine's example shows, this audience is made up of non-albinotic beholders, as well as those with albinism. Confronting society's negative perceptions of the albinotic body, Guidotti also tries to convince those with albinism who have internalized this negative perception of their own beauty. Positive Exposure's slogan and the title of its book, accordingly, speaks to a generalized audience: 'Change how you see, see how you change'.[6] Many journalists testify to this change in their reports. After a visit to one of Positive Exposure's exhibitions, one of them wrote under the title *Exhibit purely 'Positive' experience*:

> The photographer's mission to force people to expand their perceptions of beauty seems ludicrous at first. But the utter lack of pity one feels when looking at the pictures reinforces Guidotti's aim: one sees the subjects as people, and not as subjects to their conditions. (*Yale Daily News* 2004)

Guidotti thus begins to blur the distinction that his declared opponent—modern medicine—draws between a pathological, deviant condition and healthy norm. He portrays a so-called deviant body exhibiting the same personality that is expected of the so-called normal body. At the same time, he finds a moral lack in the latter, thus implying that it is deviant in another sense. Both can experience themselves as similar or the same on another level by focusing on their shared human qualities. In this way, Guidotti urges his audience to see something more significant beyond the bodily condition. Indeed, a newspaper quotes him saying this about his photographic subjects: 'They should be seen how their parents see them and how people who love them see them' (Tress 2015).

However, this rhetoric of beauty, personality and change in perception aside, some aspects of Guidotti's work still bind his subjects to the condition that he is trying to make the viewers overlook. Thus, his work is more ambivalent than we have shown it to be so far. One aspect is the constant written and spoken-word reference. For example, Guidotti's 1998 article for *Life Magazine* still explicitly declares the photographed subjects to be persons with albinism. In the same manner, Guidotti describes the girl he saw and the people he photographs as persons with albinism. Discursively, the category is not left aside but remains part of the narrative. The second aspect that binds his subjects to the medical category of albinism is a visual one. By presenting his subjects in a photo series where the images of several individuals are arranged next to one another, Guidotti shows them as 'of the same kind'. In combination, these linguistic and visual techniques create categories of people. Like those used in medical representations, these techniques are still elements of the process that Ian Hacking (2007) terms 'making up people', that is, the ways in which the demarcation, sorting and classifying of humans by social actors and institutions generate and reproduce 'kinds of people' (ibid.) as ways to be a person. So, while Guidotti's subjects are shown in a more positive light, and even with a personal touch to them, they are still portrayed as members of a specific medical category. Guidotti's claim that he portrays individuals rather than the representatives of a medical condition, quoted above, is not wrong, it is just incomplete. He has indeed always photographed people, but people of a specific sort, namely people with albinism.

Guidotti's visual language resembles the linguistic, people-first language that has been common in the disability rights movement since the 1980s. In a critique of what many considered dehumanizing, discriminative and derogatory terminology, activists stressed that 'the disabled' are not just defined by their medical diagnosis. Instead, they proposed using a terminology that instead puts the person before the condition, hoping thus to emphasize that 'people with disabilities' are individuals with a multitude of personal characteristics to which their disability is secondary. In people-first language, terms like 'albino' are replaced by expressions like 'person with albinism.' Not only does Guidotti adhere to this linguistic practice in his printed and auditory materials, his visual presentations work in a similar way. While he does not conceal his subjects' conditions deliberately, he does not make them the sole focus of his photographs. Rather, the photographed person is allowed and encouraged to express her or his personality. The crux of the matter is that, just as the person-first language still contains the category of disability—even by rendering it secondary—Guidotti does not part completely with the category he is seeking to de-spectacularize. Paradoxically, his approach to working with a photo series, as well as with references to medical portrayals, even while dissociating his approach from the latter, again conjures up the category of albinism and thus reconstructs his subjects as a certain kind of person. The differentiation between bodily deviance and norm is problematized, but not completely removed. On the one hand, Guidotti's ongoing, albeit attenuated differentiation of albinotic bodies implicitly still constitutes the non-albinotic audience as a norm. On the other hand, this difference now only carries little meaning.

Fashion Models: The Aesthetic Economy of Albinism in the Twenty-First Century

While Guidotti quit the fashion industry to lend his services as a photographer to disability rights activism, a number of persons with albinism entered the very same industry he had left to become professional fashion models. Connie Chiu was the first so-called 'albino model' to grace the catwalk in 1994 for Jean-Paul Gaultier in Paris, followed by Stephen Thompson in New York City in 1999. Refilwe Modiselle began modelling in Johannesburg around the same time. But it was not until ten years later that models with albinism gained wider media attention beyond the confines of fashion journalism. Shaun Ross and Diandra Forrest, two African-American natives of New York, both began modelling in 2008, and they appeared together on Tyra Bank's talk show on 21 April 2010. Since then, they have become the most famous and successful models with albinism, walking on numerous runway shows, shooting dozens of editorials and starring in a few films and music videos. Around the world others have followed, among them Sanele Xaba and Thando Hopa in South Africa, Anastasija Zhidkova in Russia, Jessica Langlois in Canada, Jewel Jeffrey in France and Justin Bullock in the United States.

This recent success of persons with albinism as fashion models corresponds to larger trends in the modelling business and fashion industry. Constantly craving for novel 'looks', these industries have begun to valorize extraordinary bodies, at least to a certain degree, and they play deliberately with the transgression of standardized beauty norms. So-called 'quirk models', for example, conform to the bodily norm of modelling in an overall sense (in terms of height and seize) while transgressing it in individual details (for example, freckles, a tooth gap, flappy ears). This trend can be linked to the 'regime of the blink' (Wissinger 2015, 18), the imaging regime of the present-day digital culture, which is characterized by ever-shrinking attention spans. Fashion journalists have labelled the 'New Quirk' 'an adjustment of sorts to an Instagram world, where amateur images of beauty fly fast, and editors and advertisers are looking for something to make the viewer linger longer than a nanosecond' (Meltzer 2013). The valorization of unusual bodies like those of models with albinism can be read along the same lines. They are employed as eye-catchers and as such have become valuable resources for grabbing the beholder's attention (Krings 2017b).

Apart from models with albinism, transgender persons like Andrea—earlier Andrej—Pejic have also made it into modelling. Other examples include Daphne Selfe, who is over 80 years old and seems to defy age, and Tess Holliday (formerly known as Tess Munster), who, with a US size 22 (that is UK size 24) at 5 feet 5 inches and vital statistics of 52-49-56 inches (Holliday, n.d.), transgresses the frequently criticized size restrictions. Jillian Mercado models in a wheelchair, Alex Minsky with a prosthetic leg. While this trend has already been labelled 'freak chic' (Mackinney-Valentin 2014, 18), the most explicit continuity with the nineteenth-century freak show is perhaps Rick Genest. Like the nineteenth-century tattooed ladies and gentlemen, his entire body is covered with tattoos. Most motifs make him look like a living skeleton, and he models under the epithet 'Zombie Boy'.

Playful references to the freak show can also be found among editorials featuring models with albinism. Ross thus appears with Genest in a 'Marvel'—titled fashion spread in *TRAFFIC News-to-go* magazine (Baldauf 2012), which clearly draws on the aesthetics of awe and wonder peculiar to the freak show. A much more striking, though perhaps not even deliberate reference to past constructions of albinotic Africans as ambivalent figures in racialized terms is Ross and Loveday's aforementioned editorial for *CHAOS Magazine* (2011; see Fig. 4.2). Its visual language resembles the aesthetics of difference and sameness that was already at play a 100 years earlier in the images of Kpapo and her 'sister'. In the fashion editorial, Ross personifies the white part, contrasting with Loveday's black role. This oppositional character plays up the difference, which is further intensified by several other techniques. First, both models are covered in make-up. Ross's otherwise light pink skin tones are covered with cream-white paint, which also covers his blonde hair and pink lips; Loveday, by contrast, is partly covered in black paint. Second, both wear black and white—and only black and white—garments. While they appear in different clothes on other images throughout the editorial, this colour contrast is maintained. Third, the two models also exhibit similarities. Both are roughly the same height and pose in several matching combinations that signal affiliation. These serve to direct the viewer's attention to the differences between them. In the racially conscious eyes of their beholders, they also share the facial features of black people. While this similarity lets their contrasting colours stand out even more, it epitomizes the editorial's ambiguity.

Sometime after the editorial was published, its cover image depicting the two models facing each other went viral and was shared online under the headline 'The Lightest and Darkest skin colour. Human Diversity is amazing.'[7] Interestingly, this interpretation totally neglects the fact that the bodies have been painted to suit the photographer's aesthetic intentions. Instead, it takes the makeup as skin colours and translates them within the framework of diversity language. This mirrors Ross's very own self-fashioning as a symbol of diversity. Early on in his career, he began to present himself as role model for all those whose bodies in one way or another fall outside the contested spectrum of corporeal normality. His appearance on Tyra Banks's TV show is a good example of this kind of self-presentation. Banks leads the interview into the transformative tale of victim turned hero, from bullied outsider to successful model.

> *Banks:* Explain some of the pain you went through as a child.
> *Ross:* It was kinda rough growing up for the simple fact that I was the – I grew up in the Bronx – I was the only light-skinned child, not alone with albinism, out of a school of 600 African American and Hispanic kids. So, it's almost like being the only Caucasian inside of an all-black school.
> *Banks:* Tell me what happened in seventh grade.

Ross: When I was in seventh grade, I used to get antagonized a lot. There was this boy one day who was calling me names, and we got sent down to the detention room. He starts calling me Powder, white, bread, paper, all these things. ... I said to him, 'Whatever, who cares.' ... He pushes me. All of a sudden, I feel something going into my back. And he sticks the pen... he stabs me six times in my back. Each wound was six inches deep. ...

Banks: So how do you go from there to being now, strong man, in demand? ... How do you go from being such a victim to now doing this?

Ross: I put it this way, it's just like anybody. You can be black, you can be white, you can be fat, you can be skinny. If it's you, you know how to work around that area. Let no one tell you no different. You are yourself. No one can sit there and tell you you're bad, you look different. ... I might have a big left leg. Well, you know what? I'm gonna make that leg look like it's from a Givenchy ad.

Banks: That's what I say: work it. Work with what you got. (*The CW* 2010)

Another transformation is also being told here, that of a stigma turned into an aesthetic quality. It becomes more explicit in the following blog post about Diandra Forrest, Ross's female counterpart:

Being different often carries the risk of discrimination. Modern Western medicine views albinism as a genetic condition, where a body cannot produce the pigment melanin – hence we tend to label it as an illness. But model Diandra Forrest, who has albinism, proves that a rare, remarkable beauty can be found in her unique look. It's like a fragile material in an unusual form. Scouted by young photographer Shameer Khan, Diandra soon joined leading agency Elite Models NY. Her distinct look is her trademark and it drew the attention of avant garde fashion designers. (*Sons and Daughters Magazine* 2014)

In repudiating the medical framing as the only valid perception, proponents of this narrative stress the beauty of exceptionally pale skin and hair. While this bears some similarities to Guidotti's aim of 'redefining beauty'—indeed, the same phrase is found in many articles about models with albinism—the focus here is not so much on the personality as on the outward appearance, the surface of the body. Whereas at the heart of Guidotti's campaign, at least discursively, was the valorization of the victimized self, now it is the aesthetic valorization of the alternative model. While this instance of aestheticization clearly involves an act of appreciation, too, it also exposes the limits of artistic presentations. In that the presentation focuses on the aesthetic dimensions of pale skin and hair and thus likens the model to a piece of art, the potential of staring to establish a social relationship between starer and staree—the potential that Garland-Thomson (2009) stresses so much—is somewhat lost here.

During his interview on *The Tyra Banks Show* mentioned above, Ross's name, together with the information 'first male model with albinism,' is shown at the bottom of the screen. While this information is only partly true—it was corrected in later reports to 'first African-American male model with albinism,' since Stephen Thompson entered the profession almost ten years before Ross—it nonetheless shows a first-comer narrative at work. It testifies to the uniqueness and novelty of the model, an important good in an industry that sells exclusivity. At the same time, the first-comer narrative resembles the strategies of freak show managers to enhance their exhibit's rarity.

What emerges from these examples and others is a set of recurring elements that forms a narrative in which models with albinism are commonly presented. There is, first, the biographical experience of stigmatization and discrimination. A reference to it, even in faraway places or times, is something we find in nearly every interview. So far, albinism seems unthinkable without a reference to its stigmatization by hostile outsiders. Second, there is a critique of medicine and genetics as only valid framings of albinism. This hints at the success of disability rights activism as it has begun to inform public discourse beyond its immediate domain. Third, we find the recoding of albinism as a valuable aesthetic quality, which is also a recoding from stigma to asset. Instead of being something for which persons with albinism are ostracized, ridiculed or persecuted, their bodily features become something for which they are praised and celebrated. Fourth, there are helping hands from within the fashion world, who introduce and embrace models with albinism. The presentation of persons with albinism in this narrative thus also constitutes a unique chance to shed some positive light on an industrial complex whose body politics are frequently subjected to heavy criticism. Finally, these discursive elements boil down to a story of success and fame, not despite albinism, but because of it.

This narrative and its iterations, whether by the models themselves or by faithful commentators such as fashion journalists, supporters and fans, is essential for making meaning out of 'albino models'. As such, it fulfils a function similar to that of the side-show talkers' introductory 'lectures', which were a constitutive element of the 'enfreakment' (Garland-Thomson 1998, n.p.) of persons with albinism who worked as freak-show performers around 1900. Paradoxically, perhaps, in both cases a hypopigmented body is treated as not being spectacular enough in itself and therefore needing discursive and artefactual enhancement to be turned into a real attraction. In the case of the 'models with albinism', it is therefore only consistent that overcoming stigmatization has become as much part of their 'brand' as their unique look itself. Ross and Forrest's social media campaigns labelled 'In-my-skin-I-win' and 'Beyond the skin' mirror this fact.

By re-spectacularizing the albinotic body, the fashion industry has re-established a sharp distinction that construes models with albinism as extraordinary beings while conferring on their viewers the status of normality. Against 'The Lightest and the Darkest skin colour', the audience is confirmed in its ordinary appearance. While the fashion industry sometimes, whether unintentionally or deliberately, plays with practices of depiction that refer to the freak show, it does not resurrect the figure of the 'albino freak'. Instead, the albinotic body is constructed as having an edgy and unsettling beauty. Its peculiarity makes for its attraction in fashion circles: it promises to confer distinction and glamour on those who are associated with it. This is a valuable promise that functions not only as an aesthetic, but also as an economic valorization in what is a multi-billion-dollar industry. While the construction as a figure of beauty is indisputably a much more positive conception for people with albinism when compared to that of an 'oddity', it nevertheless produces distance once more. Models with albinism, like models in general, are nearly unattainable icons detached from everyday life. To those who aspire to become like them, but never quite manage to do so, is left the uniformity of the normal, lacking their glamour, attractiveness and distinction. Thus, as potential customers of the fashion industry, viewers are treated as incomplete figures with as yet unfinished identity projects. As such, they are left the promise to buy themselves into completion through the acquisition of fashionable garments.

Conclusion: The Co-Production of a Norm Vis-à-Vis the De/Spectacularization of the Albinotic Body

The three cultural institutions outlined above—freak show, art photography and fashion modelling—produce hypopigmented bodies as markedly different figures. By turning these figures into spectacles or rendering them quite ordinary, these institutions also position their audiences differently. As Garland-Thomson (1998) has argued, the construction of freakness and beauty goes hand in hand with the co-production of their viewers. The former's staging as an extraordinary spectacle positions the latter as normal. Taking up Garland-Thomson's argument, we now discuss the spectator's co-production in the above cases.

Freak shows differentiated exhibits from their audiences both figuratively and literally. The first were spectacularized as extraordinary, whereas the latter, in turn, came to represent an unspectacular norm. As we have shown, this differentiation is not at all essential, but was constructed through the technical means of a particular cultural institution. Stage, props and fictional characters produced physical space as well as symbolic distance between an illuminated and embellished exhibit and a secure and anonymous auditorium. The figures produced by Kpapo's and Breu's show acts, conversely, co-construct their viewers' position. While the ambiguity of these figures potentially challenged their audiences' ideas about racial differences or human capabilities, their exposure on stage also kept these challenges at bay. Functioning like a photographic negative for their viewers, the displays of the white Negress, Ice King and To-Ya thus provided their spectators with an opportunity to appear as 'proper' and 'pure' categorical cases themselves. Against the white Negress's racial ambiguity—an African origin, but a skin colour read by contemporaries as white/European—the spectators appeared racially normal enough not to be displayed on stage. Against the Ice King's almost superhuman abilities or To-Ya's folkloristic demeanour and origin as an indigenous Icelander from Europe's civilizatory rim, the audience appeared equipped with average capabilities and constituted a part of modernity. Representing the liminal space or the borders between 'proper' categories, these performances thus enabled and reproduced the classificatory order. Against these extraordinary differences on stage, the everyday flaws or talents of members of the audience are rendered minor and nullified. In this way, the viewer's particularity is dissolved, and he or she becomes part of the undifferentiated mass of onlookers, bestowed with normality by the figure of the freak on stage (see also Herza, this volume).

The work of Guidotti, by contrast, tones down the sharp distinction between albinotic and normal bodies. Portraying both in the same way and shifting the focus from the body and medical condition to signifiers of personality—although still exhibited visually via the body—Guidotti stresses the similarity between people with albinism and those without. Furthermore, unlike freak shows or medical textbooks, Guidotti's art and activism do not constitute a unilateral address directed at the viewers by cancelling out the exhibits. Instead, his work speaks to both his pigmented and his hypopigmented viewers, both of whom are supposed to change their perceptions. Through these techniques, Guidotti attains a blurring of the distinction between so-called bodily deviance and the standard norm of beauty, especially with regard to pigmentation. If anything, he distinguishes between those who have come to embrace his celebration of diversity and uniqueness and those who are not (yet) willing to do so—but this is yet another differentiation. While the albinotic body is thus de-spectacularized, its 'positive exposure' does not aim to completely end its sense of difference. Working with photo series and retaining discursive categorization, Guidotti still frames his subjects as persons with albinism. Instead of constructing the figure of the 'freak', the photographer produces relatable persons of a specific kind. In doing so, he implicitly continues to distinguish between a specific and deviant Other and a norm of non-albinotic bodies. Despite and because of this, Guidotti's positive exposure approach can be considered an experiment of inclusion. Those who formerly fell outside the dominant beauty norm are now supposed to be embraced as the same, yet a different part of it. Following the current discourse of diversity, Guidotti hopes for an expansion of the norm to include one more phenomenon. He does not want to assimilate or dissolve deviance per se, but to redefine the norm by broadening it.

In the contemporary world of fashion-modelling, designers, photographers, journalists and fashion magazines are once again spectacularizing the albinotic body. In a field that sells glamour and exclusivity, such spectacularized distinctions are indeed a valuable good. Along with differentiating albinotic bodies as extraordinary, these representations relegate non-albinotic bodies to a normality that needs to be transcended in order to become truly glamorous. While both the freak show and the fashion industry construct albinotic bodies as unsettling figures, they position them and their audience quite differently. Presenting the 'albino freak' as a 'racially impure' or 'superhuman' Other, the freak show provided viewers with a negative example against which they could elevate and lull themselves into a sense of 'proper completeness'. The fashion industry, by contrast, presents 'albino models' as possessing an edgy beauty of artistic vigour. This sought-after quality turns them into shining examples against which their viewers are left wanting. Their normality is not a desired goal but a lack to be surmounted. Hardly surprisingly, it is the fashion industry and its products that hold out the promise of 'completing' them. Thus, over the course of the past 100 years or so, and in terms of their hierarchical positioning in relation to each other, the pigmented beholder and the albinotic beholden shift places: while the beholden is looked down upon during the era of the freak show, both beholder and beholden are allowed to experience sameness through Guidotti's photographs before switching positions yet again in fashion modelling—this time, however, in favour of the beholden, who is looked up to and admired.

Albinism activists we spoke to have lauded Guidotti's attempts at inclusion and, despite its sometimes playful references to the freak show, they have also welcomed the fashion industry's embracing of models with albinism. What they approve of is the effect that these positive representations habituate viewers to seeing albinotic bodies. Despite the continuous differentiation, the steady public attention that art photography and the fashion industry bring to their respective albinotic figures accustoms society to people with albinism. While the freak show reproduced and reinforced the stigmatization of hypopigmented bodies, art photography and the fashion industry are partly challenging this stigma. It remains to be seen if this is indeed the beginning of its dismantling.

NOTES

1. This article presents the first findings of a research project, *Un/Doing Albinism: Recodings of a Bodily Difference Through Historically Shifting Frames*, which forms part of DFG Research Group 1939, *Un/Doing Differences: Practices in Human Differentiation*, at the Johannes Gutenberg University Mainz. We would like to thank Hieke Huistra and the editors for their helpful comments on earlier versions of this chapter.
2. The medical framing of completely hypopigmented bodies became dominant in the natural sciences at the end of the eighteenth century and among most lay people in the twentieth century. For reasons of space, we cannot go into detail regarding this development here. For an overview of the historical genealogy, different framings and eventual medicalization of completely hypopigmented bodies, see Krings (2017a).

3. 'Albinism' and its derivations 'albino' and 'albinotic body' not only carry connotations of a pathology, they also denote completely hypopigmented bodies as a medical phenomenon, i.e. medicalize them. The same actually holds for terms like 'hypopigmentation'. By using these words as descriptive terms or categories of analysis, we risk not only reproducing pejorative connotations, but also foreclosing the contingency of meanings and differentiations that our social constructivist approach emphasizes. For lack of a better alternative, we feel compelled to continue with this ambivalent practice for the time being.
4. Note that Kpapo's first name, Amanoua, is misrepresented on this postcard, as in most of the contemporary printed material.
5. See: https://positiveexposure.org/about-the-program-2/. Accessed 3 November 2017.
6. The slogan is also the title of Positive Exposure's first book, published in 2016 (see Guidotti 2016).
7. Headline and image seem to have appeared together for the first time on the online image-hosting service Imgur on 26 March 2013; see: http://imgur.com/uB49E3V. Accessed 28 July 2017. From there it was linked to numerous other websites like Reddit and Pinterest.

REFERENCES

Atgier, Paul. 1910. "Un nègre blanc. Étude d'albinisme comparé dans la race noire et la race blanche." *Bulletins et Mémoires de la Société d'anthropologie de Paris* 6 (1): 451–55.

Baldauf, Joachim. 2012. "Marvel." *TRAFFIC News to-go* 25 (June/July): 13–20.

Bogdan, Robert. 1988. *Freak Show. Presenting Human Oddities for Amusement and Profit*. Chicago: University of Chicago Press.

Böhmerwald Heimatkreis Prachatitz e.V. n.d. "Berühmte Persönlichkeiten aus dem Böhmerwald: Karl Breu - genannt Tom Jack." Böhmerwaldheimatkreis Prachatitz e.V. Accessed 13 May 2017. http://www.bhk-prachatitz.de/beruehmte-persoenlichkeiten/ [German].

Brändle, Rea. 2007. *Nayo Bruce: Geschichte einer afrikanischen Familie in Europa*. Zürich: Chronos-Verlag [German].

CHAOS Magazine. 2011. "Out of Circulation." *CHAOS Magazine* 13 (The Wicket Issue, End of Winter 2011–12): 304–13.

Curran, Andrew. 2009. "Rethinking Race History: The Role of the Albino in the French Enlightenment Life Sciences." *History and Theory* 48: 151–79.

Daston, Lorraine, and Katharine Park. 1998. *Wonders and the Order of Nature, 1150–1750*. New York: Zone Books.

Davis, Lennard J. 1995. *Enforcing Normalcy. Disability, Deafness, and the Body.* London and New York: Verso.

Douglas, Mary. 1966. *Purity and Danger: An Analysis of Concepts of Pollution and Taboo.* London: Routledge and Kegan Paul.

Frédéric, J. 1907. "Beiträge zur Frage des Albinismus." *Zeitschrift für Morphologie und Anthropologie* 10 (2): 216–39 [German].

Garland-Thomson, Rosemarie. 1996. "Introduction: From Wonder to Error—A Genealogy of Freak Discourse in Modernity." In *Freakery: Cultural Spectacles of the Extraordinary Body*, edited by Rosemarie Garland-Thomson, 1–19. New York and London: New York University Press.

Garland-Thomson, Rosemarie. 1998. "The Beauty and the Freak." *Michigan Quarterly Review* XXXVII (3). Accessed 1 March 2017. http://hdl.handle.net/2027/spo.act2080.0037.312.

Garland-Thomson, Rosemarie. 2009. *Staring: How We Look.* Oxford and New York: Oxford University Press.

Grosz, Elizabeth. 1996. "Intolerable Ambiguity: Freaks as/at the Limit." In *Freakery: Cultural Spectacles of the Extraordinary Body*, edited by Rosemarie Garland-Thomson, 55–66. New York and London: New York University Press.

Guidotti, Rick. 1998. "Redefining Beauty." *Life Magazine* (June): 65–69.

Guidotti, Rick. 2011. "From Stigma to Supermodel." *TED.* Accessed 18 May 2017. http://www.ted.com/talks/rick_guidotti_from_stigma_to_supermodel.

Guidotti, Rick. 2016. *Change How You See, See How You Change.* New York: Positive Exposure Productions.

Hacking, Ian. 2007. "Kinds of People: Moving Targets." *Proceedings of the British Academy* 151: 285–318.

Holliday, Tess. n.d. "FAQ." *Tess Holliday Official.* Accessed 29 April 2017. http://tesshollidayofficial.tumblr.com/FAQ.

Illugadóttir, Vera. 2015. "The Invasion of the Ice Family: That Time a Group of Albinos Drove Icelanders Crazy." *The Reykjavik Grapevine* (15): 30.

Krings, Matthias. 2017a. "Albinismus. Rekodierungen einer Humankategorie in historisch variablen Rahmungen." In *Un/Doing Differences: Praktiken der Humandifferenzierung*, edited by Stefan Hirschauer, 358–90. Weilerswist: Velbrück [German].

Krings, Matthias. 2017b. "Ein Model mit 'Makel.' Shaun Ross und die Produktion besonderer Berühmtheit in der Modewelt." *Zeitschrift für Medienwissenschaft* 16: 37–48 [German].

Lecci, Stephanie, and Eleanor Peterson. 2014. "Former Fashion Photographer Aims to Create 'New Standard of Beauty' Beyond Physical Differences." *WUWM Milwaukee Public Radio*, 4 April. Accessed 8 March 2017. http://wuwm.com/post/former-fashion-photographer-aims-create-new-standard-beauty-beyond-physical-differences.

Mackinney-Valentin, Maria. 2014. "Face Value: Subversive Beauty Ideals in Contemporary Fashion Marketing." *Fashion, Style and Popular Culture* 1 (1): 13–27.

Macy, Beth. 2016. *Truvine. Two Brothers, a Kidnapping, and a Mother's Quest: A True Story of the Jim Crow South.* New York: Little, Brown.

Marschall, Clemens. 2016. "Ausgestellte Wundermenschen: 250 Jahre Wiener Prater." *Wiener Zeitung Online,* 30 June. Accessed 13 May 2017. http://www.wienerzeitung.at/nachrichten/wien/stadtleben/828697_Ausgestellte-Wundermenschen.html [German].

Martin, Charles D. 2002. *The White African American Body: A Cultural and Literary Exploration.* New Brunswick: Rutgers University Press.

Meltzer, Marisa. 2013. "For Fashion Models, Quirk Is In." *The New York Times,* September 9. Accessed 26 May 2017. http://www.nytimes.com/2013/09/05/fashion/for-fashion-models-quirk-is-in.html.

Pednaud, J. Tithonus. 2008. "TOM JACK—The Albino Ice King." *The Human Marvels,* September 24. Accessed 13 May 2017. http://www.thehumanmarvels.com/tom-jack-the-ice-king/.

Sons and Daughters Magazine. 2014. "The Lightest Shade of Beauty." *Sons and Daughters,* December 14. Accessed 16 March 2017. http://sonsanddaughtersmag.com/diandra-forrest-by-hana-knizova/.

The CW. 2010. "The Tyra Banks Show." *The CW Television Network,* April 21. Accessed 17 May 2017. https://www.youtube.com/watch?v=OQoaF6t5QH0.

Tress, Luke. 2015. "Photographer Zooms in on the Beauty of People with Albinism." *The Times of Israel,* July 16. Accessed 14 August 2017. http://www.timesofisrael.com/a-photographers-lens-zooms-in-on-the-beauty-of-the-disabled/.

Vilhálmsson, Vilhjálmur Örn. 2013. "To-Ya and His Ice Family." *Fornleifur,* June 14. Accessed 13 May 2017. http://fornleifur.blog.is/blog/fornleifur/entry/1301961/.

Wissinger, Elizabeth A. 2015. *This Year's Model: Fashion, Media, and the Making of Glamour.* New York: New York University Press.

Yale Daily News. 2004. "Exhibit Purely 'Positive' Experience." *Yale Daily News,* September 24. Accessed 7 March 2017. http://yaledailynews.com/blog/2004/09/24/exhibit-purely-positive-experience/.

CHAPTER 5

'Disability Gain' and the Limits of Representing Alternative Beauty

Ann M. Fox, Matthias Krings and Ulf Vierke

Sarah Böllinger: Drawing on the notion of 'deaf gain' (Bauman and Murray 2014), Rosemarie Garland-Thomson coined the term 'disability gain' to ask what would happen if we reframed disability as a source of gain, rather than a loss. Behind this is the demand to regard disability inclusion as a resource gain, instead of a resource drain. While this approach complicates, and indeed questions, the social definition and devaluation of 'disability,' it also raises a number of debatable issues. For example, what happens when 'disabled' bodies are commodified in an attempt to represent 'alternative beauty'?

When Patrick Mohr, a German fashion designer, launched his *Human* line at the 2013 Berlin Fashion Week, he filled the catwalk with bouncers, bodybuilders, people of colour and people with disabilities all

A. M. Fox (✉)
Davidson College, Davidson, NC, USA

M. Krings
Johannes Gutenberg University, Mainz, Germany

U. Vierke
University of Bayreuth, Bayreuth, Germany

© The Author(s) 2019
C. Liebelt et al. (eds.), *Beauty and the Norm*,
Palgrave Studies in Globalization and Embodiment,
https://doi.org/10.1007/978-3-319-91174-8_5

wearing his haute couture. They were put on little white pedestals and obliged not to move. With *Human*, Mohr explained ahead of the opening,[1] he wanted to proclaim that to him all humans were equal, that is, of equivalent value, and that the society he lives in should regard them as such. This, of course, is a contradiction in terms in that he was singling out social minorities singled out for presentation by way of sheer otherness, confronting those Mohr termed the 'normal,' yet rhetorically negating their alterity.

Four years later, seeing models with disabilities on international catwalks is no longer perceived a 'shocker', but rather as a designer's commitment to 'alternative beauty'. So, to repeat, what happens when 'disabled' bodies are commodified in an attempt to represent 'alternative beauty'? What would you argue is the 'gain' involved?

Ann Fox: Thank you for this thoughtful and nuanced question! I had not heard of Mohr's work, so I was intrigued to see the layout in *Vogue* (2013). I guess I would start by saying that not every example of inclusion is equal, and that visibility is not necessarily the same thing as 'disability gain.' When I think of 'disability gain,' I think of the ways in which disability shows itself to be a source of new knowledge, innovative ways of looking at the world and creativity that moves us past old conceptions of the normate. When I look at Mohr's work in *Human*, those things don't jump off the page at me. Instead, I see a strange, and familiar, hybridity at work. For example, as you suggest in your question, it strikes me as telling that social and racial 'others' were all lumped together in one mass Exhibit of Others as though they had no individuation. Paradoxically, in another sense, they did have individuation: as specimens of different kinds of Otherness. To put them on plinths and oblige them not to move may have suggested to Mohr they were artworks, although it makes me think of them being displayed as museum oddities and freak shows.

I'm further struck by the strange and disturbing disability impersonation I saw in the photos of the show. In several of the photos, women who are clearly otherwise normate, i.e. conventionally beautiful models, have been enfreaked. A Frida Kahlo-esque unibrow has been affixed to their foreheads, and their hair has been drawn up in severe buns (perhaps a reference to microcephaly or so-called 'pinheads'); their jaws are slack, their eyes are dull. But as if these attempts to replicate intellectual disability were not enough, some of them have prosthetic eyes protruding from their mouths, which are circled by growths of hair (mouth brows?

mouth lashes?). Suddenly, Mohr has tipped his hand. *Human* is ultimately about exoticism, even a nightmarish landscape, and what could be more exotic or fearsome than 'disfiguring' his models? Mohr is using the grotesque and monstrous in what is actually a fairly conventional manner, to shock and disgust. This is the opposite of disability gain; rather, it reinforces the idea that disability is something appalling and disturbing. As they drape themselves lethargically over banisters and other bodies, these models have no agency and are interchangeable. Which is perhaps the one thing disabled people as they are commonly imagined and the models trying to portray them have in common: that their bodies are not meant to signify their own meanings, but rather, those that others project on to them. So in this case, the use of disability by high fashion is not only not disability gain—it's the same old ableist stereotypes of intellectual disability dressed up and laid out in *Vogue*. I don't know the circumstances of this collection, but I would be very willing to bet it was conceived and assembled without any input from disabled people themselves.

But disabled bodies are moving to the fore on other fashion fronts. As you say, the inclusion of models with diverse embodiments in fashion shows and layouts is on the upswing in recent years. Can disability gain exist in such places? Consider, by contrast to Mohr, American model Jillian Mercado. Mercado is a wheelchair user and a Dominican-American model who has appeared in campaigns for the Italian clothing company Diesel and the American discount store chain Target. What do we gain by Mercado's presence in these campaigns? To begin with, Mercado has agency and knowledge: as someone who has lived in a disabled body, she is presenting her experience and embodiment, rather than assuming it as an exoticized mask. But I think there's more at work here than just including Mercado—after all, a disabled body is perfectly able to portray an ableist image if inserted into visual rhetorics that don't challenge conventional stereotypes. Whereas Mohr seemed to check off boxes of different exoticized types, Mercado's identity is intersectional as a disabled Latinx woman. Furthermore, Mercado's body is not simply an idealized type pretending to assume a kind of disability simulation.

In one Diesel ad, for example, there is a lot that is familiar in terms of how we read the semiotics of fashion: Mercado's somewhat androgynous and stylish pixie haircut, implicitly echoing that of the male model sitting next to her; her elegant lipstick; and her piercing eyes grab the viewer's attention.[2] Her body is also pleasingly draped in the soft denim Diesel is trying to sell us. It's not a body that looks like a typical fashion model's; she is smaller, her limbs are shorter, and it is clear she has some impairment and limb difference. But her body is also presented as one that has agency and energy: she seems poised in her aptly-named power chair, seemingly ready to speed away from our presence once she has fixed us in her fierce gaze. She does not look away, vacuously, in the manner of Mohr's faux-disabled models; her very particular size and shape challenges our understanding of who has agency, intelligence and what constitutes bodily beauty. Mercado faces away from the nondisabled male model, her image being in the foreground and larger than his. Her chair is not hidden, but rather presented as a part of this rewritten landscape of beauty. Diesel may gain more sales in its attempt to be inclusive, but that inclusivity also forms a sharp retort to old conceptions of beauty, femininity, and disability, conceptions that Mohr's work simply reinscribes under the aegis of universal humanism.

The short answer, then, is that we need to consider these campaigns on their own terms. What we can gain from disability, when deployed with care and thought, is an understanding of human agency, a redirection of typical power relationships between the viewer and the viewed, and an appreciation of bodily difference as a source of beauty that catalyses further creativity, rather than rehashes unoriginal stereotypes.

Matthias Krings: Let me jump in here. I wish to thank Ann for juxtaposing these two examples because this serves well to illustrate the extremes we find on two opposing ends of a broad spectrum of deploying models with extraordinary bodies in the fashion world. I would like to complicate the notion of disability gain by urging us to ask who exactly gains what? There is a material ring to the word 'gain,' and though I am perfectly aware of the fact that its original coining as 'deaf gain' (vs. 'hear loss') and its conceptual extension as 'disability gain' refer to the rather immaterial gains for society at large–the 'we' that Ann mentions in the paragraph above. Let us stick to the more mundane material gain for a moment.

For models with albinism like Shaun Ross and Diandra Forrest, whose presentational work I have been following for some time now, their unconventional appearance has become an asset that translates into a source of income. So, the baseline of 'disability gain' might very well be some form of financial profit on the level of the disabled model. Which is a great thing in and of itself. Because jobs for models with albinism are still rare, and since most models don't have a say in how they are deployed in campaigns anyway, it is easy to understand why even someone like Shaun Ross—who is otherwise very outspoken and activist-minded about raising awareness of albinism and the expansion of conventional notions of beauty—has also taken part in campaigns clearly located on the exploitative end of the spectrum mentioned above. While this is perfectly understandable on an individual level—wo/men must eat, and models in general can't be too picky if they want to stay in the game—this is of course problematic on a political level.

For designers and art directors, 'disability gain' first and foremost translates into increased attention for their collection or label. How this 'attention gain' translates into sales is somewhat difficult to predict, though. However, models with unconventional bodies not only serve as mere eyecatchers, their bodies are also attributed meanings that depend on whatever frame of reference the designer or art director choses. While some, like Patrick Mohr, draw on exploitative traditions in an attempt to lend their couture some kind of 'freak chic', others rather opt for crafting their labels with an image of social responsibility by fostering inclusion and diversity. This strategy, however, often employs a rhetoric that Sandra Umathum (2015, 102, quoted from Wihstutz 2017, 71) has called the 'logic of despite'. Ann's example of the Diesel ad with Jillian Mercado, at least to my reading, operates along these lines. It asks the beholder to acknowledge Mercado's beauty, despite her unconventional body and her sitting in a wheelchair. The problem I have with this mode of presentation is the 'despite'.

Other designers, yet, use models with unconventional bodies as inspirations for their couture. In my opinion, this comes closer to Rosemarie Garland-Thomson's notion of 'disability gain'. In this case, the model's role is somewhat similar to that of an artist's muse. Nina Athanasiou, a German designer who has worked with Shaun Ross several times, may serve to illustrate this point. In 2015, she presented a collection which featured Ross's face printed in a collage-like manner on the fabric itself and thus literally transformed the model into fashion. In an interview (Roth 2015), she explained her fascination with Ross by referring to his 'incredible presence.'

Lastly, there is the gain for the audience or society at large, which needs to be discussed: the expansion of aesthetic norms, the plurality of beauty, the mainstreaming of diversity and the stakes the fashion industry has in all of this.

Ann Fox: Matthias, I really like that you're reminding us that disability gain is not just a reception issue, but also a practical, material one for the disabled people who themselves are pictured in the images we are discussing here.

I think our discussion here interestingly echoes debates that have happened around historical entertainments like freak shows, popular in the US in the late nineteenth and early twentieth centuries. Is the freak show problematic in how it reproduced racist, ableist and/or sexist views of extraordinary bodies? Or is it to be lauded for the ways in which it gave agency—starting with economic independence, which opens up other kinds of freedoms—to disabled people at a time when they otherwise might not have been able to gain it? The answer is not so obvious, either then or now. I certainly can laud the fact that models with albinism like the ones you discuss are able to earn a living. This is 'disability gain' in terms of individual accomplishment, a kind of material gain that, certainly, it would be hypocritical at best and paternalistic at worst for me to say the models in question do not have a right to move toward accessing. And yet, to me, this is still not 'disability gain' in the sense I'm talking about it. In fact, to laud individual gain without trying to look beyond it and its repercussions for cultural values seems to me to be akin to those kinds of feminism that, while laudably trying to get more women represented in boardrooms and other positions of power, don't question the very structures of power that are being infiltrated. Such gain, then, will always—inevitably if not intentionally—be premised on someone else losing out. This is why I think the representations that exoticize are dangerous: they promote individual gain for the models, and make a viewer believe their conceptions of beauty have been changed, but at the end of the day, they can also be easily reproduced as familiar enfreakment.

I can understand why you see my citation of Mercado as a potentially more conservative one. I don't totally agree with your interpretation of Mercado as a 'despite' image, though I understand your point. Perhaps this is a personal sense of degrees of difference in what makes an image part of the 'in spite of' school of thought. I like the way you challenge the 'in spite of' school of thinking, but wouldn't models who are considered physically beautiful and proportionate in every other way but albinism also fit into this way of thinking? For me, Mercado disrupts gender binaries, the notion that a model must be ambulatory and perfectly proportioned, and presents disability as intersectional. I see these elements as pushing past 'despite,' though I grant you there are still enough of those more typical ways of framing her used in conventional fashion advertisements to make this image familiar and appealing to a viewer expecting typical beauty. Maybe the answer is less about which model is more or less successful as a kind of representation of disability, and more about what each kind of representation does to draw on disability embodiment to challenge the conventions of typical beauty and the norm.

Let me throw in a different wrinkle here, one that removes the idea that a disabled person has to be present in the image for disability gain to happen. There need not always be disabled bodies included for there to be disability gain in fashion design. In summer 2017 I saw the Rei Kawakubo retrospective *Comme des Garçons: Art of the In-Between* at the Metropolitan Museum of Art in New York City. I was alternately frustrated and fascinated: Kawakubo is clearly inspired by bodily variation in her sculptural—and not always comfortably wearable—dress designs, though she walks a fine line between gain and exploitation.[3] The 'tumour-like' quality of the bumps in the dresses seems to evoke grotesquery. Some of these designs as presented on the dress forms in the exhibition are a potentially dangerous flirtation with old racist stereotypes, given the rough hair and their excessive posteriors. And yet, there's still something pleasing to me about the dress designs. They're not recognizable in conventional ways as beautiful, yet they don't fit completely into old archetypes of disability stereotype, either. Rather than presenting us with a ready-to-wear version of beauty, is Kawakubo compelling us to take our own flight of fancy as we imagine the body beyond its typical, but not really so fixed, borders? Her work is also interesting because it's clearly not meant to be mass-produced as is. What, then, I wonder, is the line between art object and consumable? These objects, which we're not sure if we can wear or not, defy such easy categorization, and in so doing, offer us a way past easy binaries. Here, individual gain becomes kind of beside the point.

Ulf Vierke: I am tempted to add more examples to our repository with beauty-freaky-art samples. But let me try to give this debate another twist.

My first of two thoughts on this is as follows. The first examples, Mohr's fashion show and the Diesel campaign with Mercado, are both images strongly related to, or even coming from within, the fashion industry and advertisement, and as such can be understood alongside an analysis of the logics of the economic sphere. They are manoeuvring within the logics of a capitalist market. Furthermore, fashion is *the* example of distinction in the sense that Bourdieu (1996) used it. First, we have to understand that Mohr and others draw upon an idea of diversity that has its origin in Anglo- or US-American culture and that is almost incongruent with the German-European idea of inclusion. Whereas the idea of inclusion aims at creating a society that allocates conditions in which the ability, opportunity and dignity of people are safeguarded so that any disadvantage on the basis that their identity is neutralized and that they thoroughly can take part in society. The idea of diversity picks up the thread at the opposite end by first identifying the differences and disadvantages on the side of the individual, trying to balance them in an affirmative way. The idea of an inclusive society might be more utopian in that regard. I think that the critique transcending the system (*systemtranszendente Kritik* in German) is more inherent in inclusion than it is in most diversity approaches.

This labelling and distinction according to gender, race, religion, etc. is very much bound to ideas of modernity in an early twentieth-century sense and the ideological basis for all kinds of Marxist affirmative attempts to change society—I will come back to this in a moment. Let's first look at the possible inter-iconicity that links the images to which Ann and Mathias refer to others. I propose that one can see Mohr's images in a tradition that goes back to the images of the early United Colors of Benneton campaigns. By highlighting distinction, wrapped in an ideology of diversity, one can claim the following line of argumentation: Look at how diverse human bodies can be!—You may think you see the 'other', the un-normal, the freak; it is visible and even tangible in front of you, but we can bear it because we all subscribe to the claim of universal humanism that Ann already pointed at. Following this line of thought, we experience difference, being confronted with difference, because it is (morally) good: at least we claim it to be 'Human,' and I don't think that Mohr is being ironic here. To sum up, difference is an empirical fact. Mohr's moral claim is that we are united as humans. Such an approach is still about othering, and I am not willing to buy into the logic that othering can be whitewashed of the hegemonies fuelled by it, simply by claiming that othering can be morally good and is always already a part of universal humanism. The representation of Mercado is not that different, I think, even though the Diesel campaign plays with rather antagonistic concepts and images.

The second layer is the capitalist logic. There is hardly any social field in which one can experience social distinction in a blunter way than fashion: it is about money, profit and taste in a directly visible way. Now, market logics push towards distinction. For example, why does one not find any unisex fashion or toys for children anymore? As we all know, it is not as if girls only like pink and boys blue, but the more you are able to segment a market, the more you are able to sell—if both boys and girls wear the same, you sell, say 100 pieces, but if they don't, or if they are not allowed to, the demand is remarkably higher, it is 100 plus X. I am not trying to explain capitalist market logics here, but I would like to point at the interdependence of diversity, difference and the making of profit in our times. If diversity is understood as an ideology or moral category, the first two examples in our debate both point at a vicious amalgam of market logics and diversity—indeed, they illustrate this in a prototypical way. What do they tell us about disability gain? There surely is a gain involved, but from my point of view in the end, this gain is more or less about profit—and thus leading us in the wrong direction. By focusing on material and financial gains, we will not get closer to the incredible potential implicit in the idea of 'disability gain'.

If we now turn our lens by 180 degrees and start from the economic and social conditions of our society, different kind of subjects and identities come into view. The truly interesting question regarding disability is under what conditions would any given disability become irrelevant? How would the street in front of my office look if it was free of any barriers for someone with sensual impairment, with physical, mental or whatever other impairment? From this perspective, we are not at all interested in the gain of the wheelchair user or the blind person.

To refer to what Matthias wrote on the economic 'disability gain' by models with Albinism, I am not sure about this and perhaps one could rather understand it as a form of the biblical 'hire of a whore' that a capitalist system is offering to pay as a kind of compensation for what Stella Young, in a recent Tex-X conference in Australia, termed 'inspiration porn.'[4] One could even juxtapose 'disability gain' and 'disability porn' here. First of all, it becomes true disability gain in the case that the wider society expands its intelligence; thus, the barrier-free street in front of my office is less a question of money than of clever ideas. And secondly, in the event that all kinds of potential barriers and discriminations are identified beforehand, this means that we really have to take a close look at all kinds of disabling conditions in our society, and we have to develop a high degree of awareness. Thus, we have to take into consideration not only the street in front of our office and home, or computer software, tools, legal processes, or anything really for that matter, but always and at the same time the human being with all plurals possibly included in this general idea, in order to adopt a truly humanistic perspective.

That was my rather lengthy attempt to shift the debate from a micro-Marxist, empirical perspective to a fundamental humanistic-philosophical one. To sum up, I would like to define 'disability gain' as an increasingly intelligent and human society and form of conviviality. We only get there if we know and understand the human being and her environment perfectly well in all its capacities. We are talking about a utopian project here, and thus it is less about a finite social or physical condition but about shifting perspective and the creation of political consciousness.

Finally, though very briefly, on the example that Ann gave us of the model sitting in a wheelchair in the Diesel ad: the depiction of her with her technical device may be subtle here, but it is still striking, and I think it's an important element of the campaign. It reminds me of the triple amputee and Iraq War veteran Brian Anderson. Mass-mediated images of his half-naked body proudly displaying multiple prostheses are as much about twentieth-century cyborg fantasies as they are about a fascinatingly blunt belief in what technology can do. They send out the message that engineers and technology can solve almost everything and can almost replace the biological human body. If you combine technology and the right attitude or mindset, everything is possible—and perhaps, with this, we are back to Stella Young's 'inspiration porn'. So perhaps, what I just tried to say in a rather complicated way is that the idea of 'disability gain' might be a close relative to that of 'inspiration porn'. Maybe I also tried to say that 'disability gain' only makes sense within a capitalist logic and thus is bound up with a certain neoliberal dispositive. Can we even think of 'disability gain' beyond that?

Ann Foxn: Ulf, I love the layers to your answer here! Let me respond to some of them. First, I'm with you on Mohr. I like how you're reminding us that 'diversity' per se is neither inherently good nor bad; Mohr's use of it suggests, as you say, that there is an inherent benefit to diversity when, in the case of his construction of it, that is certainly not a given. I would add that his naiveté is also based in the fact that the images aren't as diverse as he thinks they are, even though they startle. But here, I'm thinking particularly of the images of the models with a fake unibrow, sewn mouths and so on; such representations still fit into a lineage of the monstrous or deviant, or that against which the normate can and has defined itself in both high art and popular culture.

I also like your critique of these images as disability gain because they are profit-driven. I return to the idea that is a slogan of the US disability rights movement: 'Nothing About Us, Without Us' (cf. Charlton 1998). One way of reading the notion of 'gain' in these images is as financial profit; another is to see the cultural capital accruing to someone like Mohr for being 'diverse.' But when I think of disability gain, I also think about how the kind of knowledge and embodiment disabled people themselves have contributes a kind of more capacious knowledge about humanity—not just one that is profit-driven for a particular individual or corporation. Indeed, because disabled people have been erased, murdered, incarcerated, and excluded from citizenship worldwide because they are not 'useful' or 'productive,' we can see that a utilitarian concept of disability gain can get pretty dangerous pretty fast if thought of solely in economic terms: i.e. if you're not 'gaining' financially, for yourself or for society, you're a non-valid citizen. Disability gain—stemming from disability experience and embodiment—might well even challenge our notion of what it means for something to be useful or a contribution. For example, I'm thinking here of Ellen Samuels's (2017) excellent essay on 'Six Ways of Looking at Crip Time.' 'Crip time' is a term many disability studies scholars, activists and artists use to distinguish the different daily rhythms that result from living in a disabled body. In the essay, Samuels draws on her experience with chronic illness to invite us to see her temporal and emotional reality. One of the ways she defines crip time is as 'broken time,' about which she says:

> It requires us to break in our bodies and minds to new rhythms, new patterns of thinking and feeling and moving through the world. It forces us to take breaks, even when we don't want to, even when we want to keep going, to move ahead. It insists that we listen to our bodyminds *so* closely, *so* attentively, in a culture that tells us to divide the two and push the body away from us while also pushing it beyond its limits. Crip time means listening to the broken languages of our bodies, translating them, honoring their words. (ibid., n.p.)

What would it mean to extend out our understandings of how our bodies and minds exist in the world informed by this new understanding of crip time? Could somehow adopting the rhythms and realities of disability experience shift what we think of as normative ways of being in the world? Could it shift the way we design the world for all bodies, moving us toward true inclusion, rather than simply a nod to diversity? I think this last question is something you very much get at in your comments, Ulf.

Here's a totally different question: is it always necessarily bad if disability gain and profit are intertwined? I'm not trying to be an apologist for large corporations, particularly those that profit from cripwashing, that is, of masking their more troubling or oppressive functions under the guise of doing good for disability. Yet, I'm also mindful that market forces can often drive change in representation in interesting ways. When companies recognize disabled demographics and markets, they represent those communities into being. Paul Longmore (2003) writes about the fact that some of the first ads to feature disabled people in the United States were by McDonald's and General Motors. While I know those two companies can also certainly represent a kind of cultural imperialism, I have to ask, What might it mean to a disabled person to see themselves represented as part of the human landscape? What might it mean for their friends and family? If disability representation is tied in any way to profit, does that completely negate the potential good it can do? (Which is a very American question for me to ask, I suppose, and also somewhat contradicts my earlier stance on Mohr. Still, it's a question worth asking.)

Another interesting layer is when you discuss the possibility of a world in which disability would become irrelevant. I think this is indeed an interesting concept; it suggests a world in which the social model has come to reign supreme, a world in which bodies in their variations are accommodated so well and so thoughtfully that those who have impairments are not 'disabled.' However, I don't think a world in which 'disability is irrelevant' is one we could or even should seek. First, I think it suggests a world in which perfect accommodations could exist everywhere for everyone. But is it really possible to account for such infinite variety? The utopian ideal is laudable, but the needs for accommodations can compete, conflict, and shift depending on their context. Second, disability is not just extant as physical appearance or emotional or psychological affect. What of the feelings and sensations particular to certain embodiments? What of the pain? What of the experiential quality of being a non-visual learner versus a visual learner? Even if we took away disabling conditions, there is still a range of diverse experiences particular to disability that I would want to claim for our world, that makes our understanding of embodiment more nuanced and rich. These are experiences others claim as part of their identity; to assume all disabled people would feel fine ceding them to irrelevance, were the world sufficiently accessible, seems a kind of back door to compulsory able-bodiedness.

Because of this, I take issue with the proposition that 'disability gain' can be construed to be the same as 'inspiration porn.' Inspiration porn, by its very nature, attempts to flatten our understanding of disability as an identity. It does not ask about the embodied experience of the disabled person; it asks about the affective experience of the (I assume) nondisabled spectator. This suggests the disabled person's worth exists in the extent to which they serve as an example to nondisabled people—and that they should stand as inspiration for feats no more remarkable than living their lives in the best way they know, in a way that works for them. Such a response presumes incompetence as the baseline nature of disability existence, and therefore, even the most mundane movements are to be seen as wondrous.

By contrast, when I speak of disability gain, I do not speak of being inspired by the fact that a disabled person has a job, falls in love, brushes their teeth, has sex, takes a bus, or buys groceries. Rather, I speak of appreciating their ways of knowing and moving through the world as a kind of knowledge that benefits all of us, not simply inspires. Let me give an example from a recent experience I had here in Charlotte, North Carolina, where I live. Blind Canadian artist Carmen Papalia, in residence at a local arts centre, led what he calls a 'blind field shuttle walk.'[5] He has led such walks all over the world; when he does so, he leads the walk with his cane, and others follow him in a chain, their hands on the shoulders of the person in front of them, eyes closed (although they are free to open them at any point they wish). The point here is not to suggest this as a one-to-one simulation of blindness, but rather, to emphasize non-visual learning. What does it mean to navigate a space when we do not privilege eyesight? What other senses must we rely upon and appreciate, what ways of knowing can we explore?

For me, someone who relies primarily on sight to orient myself in the world, the walk was scary at first. But once I started to let go of my emphasis on the visual, I could appreciate how the surfaces under my feet and at my fingertips, the Doppler effect of ambient sound, and the warmth of the sun on my face, served to situate and guide me. This made me experience the hierarchy of my senses differently, defamiliarizing the ways in which the world ranks them, rather than simply making me believe I had had some complete, simulated experience of blindness. Even so, it was interesting in the discussion afterward to see how others on the walk (including some curators) were more interested in asking Papalia about when and how he lost his sight, thus reinscribing ableist voyeurism. In that instance, they shunted the experience of disability gain back into the much more comfortable and familiar patterns of inspiration porn. Old habits die hard, even (and maybe especially) among those who work with the visual arts.

Finally, I really love that you engaged the question of the cyborg, referring to the images of Brian Anderson. I am totally on board with the idea that cyborg fantasies are quite problematic. The idea that technology can fix everything feeds a kind of disability avoidance: we can talk about the sexiness of the human–machine combination, but do we talk about the realities of life with a disability as well? To claim identity as a 'cyborg' rather than 'disabled'—is that itself a kind of disability avoidance, or an implicit suggestion that disability is not a legitimate identity? Regan Brashear's movie *Fixed: The Science/Fiction of Human Enhancement* (2013) takes up this question: when we talk about the cyborg and transhumanism, do we risk ignoring important ideas about disability? I would not, however, equate the depiction of Mercado's wheelchair with the cyborgian image of Anderson; Mercado's wheelchair as included in her ad, and presented as part of her embodiment. That is a radical act in itself, given the stigma against wheelchairs in our culture.

Here in the United States, media coverage tends to privilege images of the latest advancement in artificial limb development as sexy and cool; their treatment of wheelchairs never ventures into similar territory, despite the fact that wheelchairs are also a form of technology that can be extremely sexy and cool. News outlets regularly use language like 'wheelchair bound' to describe wheelchair users when in fact wheelchairs are a device for movement, freedom, and energy conservation for disabled people. Disabled writers from Simi Linton to Harriet McBryde Johnson have pointed out that how disabled people imagine themselves in their wheelchairs does not at all align with how ableist culture sees them. Therefore, to imagine the wheelchair as a meaningful and alluring part of Mercado's selfhood, and not as something she is 'trapped' in, is a powerful way to claim disability. This is why disability activists fought so hard to have an image of a wheelchair-using Franklin Delano Roosevelt added after the fact to his national monument in Washington, DC: the monument as originally designed had tried to erase this image, hiding his wheelchair as something implicitly shameful.

Transhumanism is somewhat different than valuing the image of the wheelchair—it aims to 'transcend' disability, and even arguably embraces a kind of quasi-eugenic mindset, suggesting the human body needs to be radically improved generally, and most particularly when it is disabled.

Matthias Krings: The cyborgian modes of representing disabled people in popular culture are indeed a fascinating topic. While I can see the problematic side of it, which both of you have pointed out already, I have at least one example in mind that is more progressive: Viktoria Modesta, a Latvian model and performance artist. At the age of twenty, Modesta had a voluntary below-the-knee amputation of her left leg which since birth had severely limited her mobility despite numerous surgeries. This voluntary amputation is dramatized at the beginning of her music video 'Prototype' (Saam Farahmand, 2014), which also shows her sporting several fancy-looking prostheses. What is interesting about this re-enactment and the subsequent portrayal of her screen character is the considerable amount of agency she gains, which is associated with the iconic prostheses. The amputation and the subsequent missing leg are not portrayed as loss but as quite the opposite—as a conscious act of resistance and symbol of positive difference. In the story, which is set in a dystopian world governed by a junta of uniformed Nazi-looking men, Modesta's character becomes a role model for all those who are unwilling to succumb to the regime of normalcy. Her followers get themselves tattoos of her iconic likeness or even attempt to become like her by having one of their own legs amputated. So, unlike the more typical cyborgian representations of disabled people, which either draw on the 'logic of despite' or on the notion of repair or transcendence of the impaired body–which, by the way, is also very much present in the award-winning trailer 'We're the Superhumans' for the 2016 Paralympics (Channel 4, 2016)—Modesta's music video represents disability as something which not only has its own beauty, but can also become the source of feeling cool and different in a positive sense.

This is far from 'inspiration porn'. It addresses able-bodied and disabled audiences alike, and it can only be called inspirational in a yet different sense, as it urges its viewers—irrespective of the 'nature' of their bodies—to become like her: cool, sexy and proud, even if this would imply *exchanging* a limb for a prosthesis. What the music video suggests is a kind of symbolic barter which reminds me of the initial reconceptualization intended by Bauman and Murray's 'deaf gain' vs. 'loss of hearing' (2014); and this symbolic barter has its seat in the real life of Viktoria Modesta herself, who didn't *lose* a leg but *gained* mobility.

So, here we have a representation of 'alternative beauty' that has been produced by someone who is disabled and therefore actually can claim to *represent* a larger group of people with similar embodiments. It is progressive in the sense that it doesn't privilege an ableist perspective. How much it also allows its audience to claim some of the feelings and sensations particular to this kind of embodiment and to thus make our understanding of embodiment in general more nuanced and rich—i.e. Ann's and Rosemarie Garland-Thomson's conceptualization of 'disability gain' proper—remains debatable, though. But this is not so much a question of this particular music video, but a more basic one: How can we apply the concept of 'disability gain' to various forms of visual representation?

The answer depends on how we conceptualize disability gain. So far, our discussion has touched on two different, perhaps related notions of the concept. If we (1) conceptualize disability gain by claiming for all of us 'a range of diverse experiences particular to disability' 'that makes our understanding of embodiment more nuanced and richer' (I am quoting Ann here, again), we need to tackle the task of translating Ann's example of the 'blind field shuttle walk' into the field of visual representations. And I am thinking not so much of works of art and artsy performances here, but rather of the more mundane world of advertising because it is here in the everyday where the visual politics that effect society at large are made. What would be an equivalent of the blind walk for TV commercials, billboard or magazine ads? Blurring images to enable the seeing to experience the world like the visually impaired? TV commercials without sound to enable the hearing experience its absence? I don't think this would be the right approach, because for one thing it would run counter to the very job advertising is supposed to do, and for another it would only *simulate* disability without *enabling* the fully sighted and the hearing to appreciate their other senses, let alone explore different ways of knowing, such as communicating by sign language, for example. So, unless someone can point out an example to me, which works, I suggest we take a different approach in exploring the notion of 'disability gain' in combination with visual culture. This would imply that we allow ourselves, i.e. society at large, able-bodied and disabled alike, to gain from disability by (2) conceptualizing it as an epistemological instrument to deconstruct normalcy. This dialectic is not new, of course, but it has been discussed in disability studies for at least 20 years, and it is somewhat like the role anthropology's other assumes in providing a chance to cast a new ('estranged') look back at the self.

My point is that, if appropriate strategies of visual representation are employed, images of people with extraordinary bodies can be very powerful tools to help bring to light the unconscious and unchallenged modes of constructing normalcy. Of course, this is not an easy task, neither for the disabled models, nor for any other of the many people involved in the production of any form of image-based advertising; and the danger of falling back into conventional, exploitative forms of representing the disabled is always at hand. However, I think we have already discussed two examples that point in the right direction: first, the Diesel Ad with Jillian Mercado, which—I have to admit despite my initial reservation—challenges expectations about the 'normal order of things' quite a bit, as we see a kind of symbolic role reversal that turns the able-bodied model into the sidekick of the disabled model. And second, the music video by Viktoria Modesta, which I just discussed.

Ulf Vierke: Viktoria Modesta's story as represented in her video work 'Prototype' is the story of how the marginalized and oppressed subject stands up to fight back. The question is whom are they fighting back against? I see a strong iconographic filiation line for Modesta's 'prototype', linking it to Andrew Nicol's 1997 science-fiction film *Gattaca*. Vincent Freeman, the main character in the dystopian society of Gattaca, is able to live his dream against all norms and the genetic selection that would have prevented him from doing so. He is overcoming the inhuman norms of a dystopian society, and he may be challenging these norms by his own example, but in the end he is neither changing norms nor society as such.

Modesta's prototype is more about the anger of someone who resists an evil system. The idea again is not that the protagonist tries to change hegemonic norms as such. The angry subject becomes a role model, a prototype, that inspires other subjects to follow her. This is the whole idea of diversity, isn't it? It is all based on the same old US-American story of the good guy fighting the bad guy. The extraordinary bodies become not just angry and powerful bodies but morally good individual bodies. But how can these images of people with extraordinary bodies become powerful tools to help bring to light the unconscious and unchallenged modes of constructing normalcy? It is perhaps the American New Man we are talking about in this case and not a utopian new society? I have my doubts that these images are challenging modes of constructing normalcy at all—we create heroes, but we do not touch the normative frame in this black and white, evil and good, set of metaphors.

Ann, you are certainly right that 'disability gain' cannot be construed to be the same as 'inspiration porn'. The latter is not much good as an analytical category here. I also see your point in stating that a world in which 'disability is irrelevant' is not one we could or even should seek. In as much as I see it as an un-realizable utopia, I still would claim that it is worth 'seeking'—in as much as it can be an encompassing thought. In the end there is quite a substantial consensus about 'disability gain' shared by us in appreciating disabled subjects and their ways of knowing and moving through the world as a kind of knowledge that benefits all of us, as Ann stated above. By pointing at the utopian dimensions, I tried to regard the political and cultural dimension. Disability gain might lead us to an intelligent and human society and form of conviviality.

Ann Fox: I love ending on a note of conviviality, Ulf. To me, that's really the spirit of disability gain: it is a space of generosity, imagination and playful creation. Indeed, your final sentence above reminds me of a talk I heard by American artist and designer researcher, Sara Hendren (2017), who explores the intersections between technology and a wide range of disabled embodiments. In that talk, she called for 'spaces of conviviality' in which disability and technology can be brought into conversation in a way that is generative, imaginative and fun. Such a spirit of conviviality ignores neither material realities nor utopian ideals, but lets them bump up against each other without shame or stigma.

It seems to me that Viktoria Modesta is a perfect convivial image with which to end, Matthias. I love her work, and my students have been very taken with her as an in-your-face example of disability creativity. I think everything you say is true here; her image posits a powerful challenge to normalcy, particularly in the ways her music videos and photographs incorporate a range of prostheses from The Alternative Limb Project,[6] from the amazing cone-shaped, pointed limb upon which Modesta pivots, to the dazzling, high-fashion leg containing Swarovski crystals and a stereo speaker perched above a high-heeled foot. (The Project, by the way, is a powerful challenge in its own right to ableism, with a range of bespoke prostheses that also seem to flout the notion that being a cyborg means having to be superhuman or an overcomer. Instead, the prostheses play with how we might expand the boundaries of human beauty and form in whimsical, delightful ways). I find myself in strong agreement with your call, Matthias, for understanding disability gain as 'an epistemological instrument to deconstruct normalcy.' As you say, we must always be aware that, as with any representation, when we subvert some normate expectations, we can inadvertently reinforce others. A fair critique of Modesta might be, for example, that, other than her limb, she reinforces the normate, sexualized views of women already enshrined in popular music (we don't, after all, have an older, or more obviously disabled, or fat woman in Modesta).

Yet I don't think that erases the powerful good her representational work does. The way of knowing/seeing disability she represents is an incredibly powerful retort to old ideas about ableism, also inscribing disability as sexy and cool, associations culture generally rejects. So we need this conviviality: the ability to imagine representations about disability that dance (as Modesta does) away from old normate ideas, even as we understand the flirtation with more conventional images of femininity she engages. This doesn't mean we reject her example; it means we engage it (as I have with my undergraduates) in a lively, excited interrogation. (The trailer mentioned above, 'We're the Superhumans,' is another such example: is it a representation of nonnormate bodies that challenges who can participate in exuberant dance and high-level sport, or another example of the overcoming narrative, in that our focus is on so-called 'supercrips' in a video that privileges movement and agility? My students have also hotly debated this question.) At the end of the day, maybe this is as good as it gets for now: better an imperfect visual representation we can debate and query that teaches others about disability stereotype *and* gain, and that can further catalyse our imagination around disability, than the continued cultural erasure of the extraordinary body.

To me, our conversation has been such an expansive 'convivial space'; the concerns and challenges that Ulf and Matthias have articulated about disability gain are significant ones from which I have learned a lot about the very concept I have been championing. Their questions, as well as the questions of others who might well find the concept of 'disability gain' radical and provocative, must be embraced if we want to bring a 'convivial space' around which curators, scholars, artists and activists can more deeply exchange ideas about disability, beauty, and the norm into being. My radical hope is that the result will be a society that is more inclusive generally, but also a mindset within which people can embrace their own variable embodiments (because we *all* live in contingent, changeable bodies) with more appreciation, even gusto. Thank you all!

Sarah Böllinger: Indeed, thank you all for this thought-provoking and I hope ongoing conversation on 'disability gain' and the representation of alternative beauty.

NOTES

1. Quoted in http://www.vogue.de/mode/mode-news/berlin-fashion-week-patrick-mohr-human-kollektion-fruehjahr-sommer-2014/(bild)/813685#-galerie/17 (19 December 2017).
2. The ad can be viewed online at http://www.huffingtonpost.com/2014/01/22/jillian-mercado-diesel-blog_n_4643574.html (7 January 2018).
3. Exhibition images can be seen online at https://www.nytimes.com/2017/05/04/arts/design/the-mets-rei-kawakubo-show-dressed-for-defiance.html (7 January 2018).
4. Young, S. (2014). 'I'm Not Your Inspiration, Thank You Very Much'. *TED*. Online at: http://www.ted.com/talks/stella_young_i_m_not_your_inspiration_thank_you_very_much?language=en (19 December 2017).
5. Images of Carmen Papalia can be seen online at https://mccollcenter.org/artists-in-residence/carmen-papalia; his 'An Accessibility Manifesto for the Arts' can be read at https://canadianart.ca/features/access-revived/ (7 January 2018).
6. See http://www.thealternativelimbproject.com/ (7 January 2018).

References

Bauman, H-Dirksen L., and Joseph J. Murray, eds. 2014. *Deaf Gain: Raising the Stakes for Human Diversity*. Minneapolis and London: University of Minnesota Press.

Bourdieu, Pierre. 1996. *Distinction: A Social Critique of the Judgement of Taste*. London: Routledge.

Charlton, James I. 1998. *Nothing About Us Without Us*. Berkeley and Los Angeles: University of California Press.

Hendren, Sara. 2017. "Public Is Plural: Disability, Design, and Audiences for Our Work." Keynote Address Presented During DisArt Symposium, ArtPrize Hub, Grand Rapids, MI, 7 April.

Longmore, Paul. 2003. "Screening Stereotypes: Images of Disabled People in Television and Motion Pictures." In *Why I Burned My Book and Other Essays on Disability*, 131–46. Philadelphia: Temple University Press.

Roth, Anna-Lena. 2015. "Albino-Model Shaun Ross. Makel? Marke!" *Spiegel-Online*, 8 July. Online at: www.spiegel.de/panorama/leute/shaun-ross-albino-model-laeuft-fuer-nina-athanasiou-in-berlin-a-1042478.html (21 September 2016) [German].

Samuels, Ellen. 2017. "Six Ways of Looking at Crip Time." *Disability Studies Quarterly* 37 (3). Online at: http://dsq-sds.org/article/view/5824/4684 (19 December 2017).

Umathum, Sandra. 2015. "Actors Nonetheless." In *Disabled Theater*, edited by S. Umathum and B. Wihstutz, 99–112. Zürich: Diaphanes [German].

Vogue. 2013. "Patrick Mohr: HUMAN-Kollektion Frühjahr/Sommer 2014." *Vogue*, 27 June. Online at: http://www.vogue.de/mode/mode-news/berlin-fashion-week-patrick-mohr-human-kollektion-fruehjahr-sommer-2014/ (bild)/813685#galerie/17 (19 December 2017) [German].

Wihstutz, Benjamin. 2017. "Nichtkönnen, Nichtverstehen: Zur politischen Bedeutung einer Disability Aesthetics in den Darstellenden Künsten." In *Re/produktionsmaschine Kunst*, edited by F. Kreuder, E. Koban, and H. Voss, 61–74. Bielefeld: Transcript [German].

CHAPTER 6

Broken Beauty, Broken Cups: Disabled Bodies in Contemporary African Art

Sarah Böllinger

This chapter is a homage to Tobin Siebers' theory of 'broken beauty.' It is not a philosophical treatise on 'the beautiful,' but rather an exemplary description and discussion of the varieties of the inventive, which allow the broken beautiful to come into being.

Siebers (2009, 8) defines disability aesthetics as '[a] program, which should carve out the strong presence of disability in the tradition of aesthetic representation and which denies that aesthetics is represented sufficiently, through only representations of the healthy body and our associations of the body with terms like harmony, wholeness and beauty.'[1] Like all the contributions to this book, in invoking Siebers' argument in this chapter, I am interested in the relationship between beauty and processes of normalisation or standardisation. Siebers calls this relationship a tradition of aesthetic representation and suggests that the idea of beauty always goes hand in hand with harmony and

S. Böllinger (✉)
University of Bayreuth, Bayreuth, Germany

© The Author(s) 2019
C. Liebelt et al. (eds.), *Beauty and the Norm*,
Palgrave Studies in Globalization and Embodiment,
https://doi.org/10.1007/978-3-319-91174-8_6

127

wholeness. Standardised beauty distinguishes itself through uniformity, even though the founder of the philosophical discipline of 'aesthetics,' Alexander Gottlieb Baumgarten (Baumgarten 1986), does not evoke this idea (see Baumgarten and Schweizer 1983).

According to Baumgarten, aesthetics is the relationship between bodies and their affective space; they are simultaneously the subject and the object of their creation, irrespective of whether they are viewed as beautiful, normalised, good or ugly, non-conformist or bad. Siebers writes that '[a]esthetics follows the sensory perception of bodies in the presence of other bodies' (2009, 7). Of course, given that not everything that is beautiful is art, how to appreciate art as something beautiful, something enriching, whether ideal or non-conformist, is the basis for my subsequent deliberations. In this chapter, I will discuss two 'broken beauties,' that is, two works of art, which I will investigate in respect of the relationship between disabled bodies and beauty that they evoke. I begin, however, with a brief history of the Museum of Contemporary African Art in Bayreuth, the so-called Iwalewahaus, and its collection, to which they both belong. I will then focus on the artworks themselves in order to ask the following questions: What do we gain if we consider the body as a variant of the form? Where is the 'disability gain' involved in this form of disabled art? What is the potential of the formal-aesthetic utilisation of disability? What do these transnational works of art achieve that the representation of disabled bodies cannot? The 'brokenness' of artworks, as Siebers calls it, aims at the diversification of their materialisation. He tries to embrace disability as one relevant factor for aesthetic encounters with artworks. Therefore, 'broken beauty' concentrates first of all on the artwork in production and on its methods of production, like montage, assemblage, sculpting, etc. Siebers tries to establish that all these artworks—and there are plenty of them—are beautiful only through their brokenness. This brokenness can be found, for example, in antique statues or cubist works, which are considered perfect and beautiful in their brokenness. Yet, their potential for re-forming the standardisation of the human body has not been explored, nor have broken artworks been brought into a relationship with the broken human body at all. This means that 'disabled artworks,' as I call them, may have a positive identity which is not yet labelled 'disabled,' while a human body that is called 'disabled' is commonly not, or not yet, granted a positive identity. By analysing artworks as disabled, I argue, a disability gain can be made that may also be able to help transform the image of a negative disabled identity and the stigmatisation from which non-normative human bodies tend to suffer.

'Disablity gain,' as discussed in this volume (see Fox, Krings and Vierke), describes the idea that a society can gain added value through disability and its engagement. The term 'disability gain' is derived from the notion of 'deaf gain' (see Bauman and Murray 2014), which refers to the added knowledge that is generated and passed on to society as a whole by the deaf community. 'Disability gain,' analogously, refers to the diversity of people with disabilities and attempts to get rid of the stigma that is often anticipated in association with disabled bodies. This special knowledge can only be produced in the presence of disabled people, meaning that 'disability gain' does not constitute a goal-oriented promise of a future society without disabled bodies; but rather the opposite.

In this chapter, I argue that the representation of disability in African artworks, among others, need not be investigated solely through the representation of disabled bodies, but can also appear as a formal aesthetic quality. Within the Iwalewahaus collection, the works of Hezbon Owiti and Yassine Balbzioui especially lend themselves to this possibility. While Owiti's work takes the form of a bold and simple representation of a disabled body, in Balbzioui's work disabled art bodies are only hinted at. This different formal visibility of disabled bodies is the starting point for my argument. Moreover, I consider the view of art by these two African artists to represent a 'disability gain,' that is, they are a chance to make the disabled body accessible to artistic representation and thus to point out its beauty. I argue that this can be understood as a form of gain, even if it happens in a rather privileged and inaccessible context like a museum.[2] The art works under discussion in this chapter are 'Porcellanographie: Future Traces' by Yassine Balbzioui (see Figs. 6.1 and 6.2) and 'The Lame Beggar' by Hezbon Owiti (Fig. 6.3). They were created under different geographical circumstances and in different times. Balbzioui is from Morocco, and his work was created in Bayreuth in 2016, whereas Hezbon Owiti, from

Fig. 6.1   Cover of the catalogue 'Glücklose Köpfe – Luckless Heads,' 1982.
Scanned by DEVA

Kenya, painted 'The Lame Beggar' in Oshogbo, Nigeria, in 1966.
What, then, connects these two works, which are not only separated
by half a century, but at first glance by their forms and the themes they
deal with?

Fig. 6.2 'Lame beggar,' Hezbon Owiti, 1966. Photographed by DEVA

Fig. 6.3 'Porcellanographie: Future Traces,' Yassine Balbzioui, 2016, installation shot. Photographed by Katharina Greven

BROKEN BEAUTIES IN THE COLLECTION
OF THE IWALEWAHAUS

First of all, these two artworks have a place in the exhibitions and the collection of the Iwalewahaus respectively. The Museum of Contemporary African Art, founded in the small German town of Bayreuth in 1981 by Ulli Beier, himself an art patron, today also accommodates the Research Centre for African Studies of the University of Bayreuth. The modern, contemporary and popular art collection of the Iwalewahaus is derived from Beier's private collection, whose beginnings can be traced back to his fascination with so-called 'outsider art' or *l'art brut* (Rhodes 2000; Krajewski 2004). According to Nadine Siegert (2014, 1), Ulli Beier and his wife Georgina started their collection 'with non-academic artworks, primarily with autodidactic and "raw" art, known as Art Brut and Outsider Art'. This collection, which started in Nigeria with a couple of outsider artworks, has today grown into a diverse and rich depot of modern and contemporary artworks, not only from the African continent and its diaspora, but also from Papua New Guinea, India and Australia. It is the largest institutional collection of transnational modern and contemporary African artworks within Europe.

While living in Oshogbo (Nigeria) with his wife and artist Georgina Beier, Ulli Beier collected pieces by residents of the Lantoro Mental Hospital.[3] His fascination for artworks produced by those with psychological disabilities started when, as an English teacher in Ibadan, he visited a patient at Lantoro Mental Hospital in the guise of a friend.[4] He was seemingly fascinated by the place and its residents, most of them convicts who had been institutionalised for regular crimes, rather than for any mental disorder. From then on he visited them once a week over a period of eighteen months.[5] When he visited he took painting materials with him, which a group of twenty people regularly made use of as an opportunity to paint. When, later on, he was relocated to Oshogbo, his fascination with the artworks of the residents of the institution and their life stories remained. Accordingly he collected some of the works produced during his painting workshops and brought them to Bayreuth. This particular part of the collection was later augmented by works produced in workshops hosted by Georgina in Oshogbo, including some by the artists Muraina Oyelami, Twins 77, Jimoh Buraimoh, Bisi Fabunmi and Jacob Afolabi from the period between 1964 and 1966. Presently, the collection contains modern and contemporary artworks and ethnographic objects, as well as pop cultural pieces from Africa, its diasporas, Australia and Papua New Guinea.

The themes of disability and impairment, which so strongly influenced the beginning of the Iwalewahaus's now well-known and qualitatively outstanding collection, were further boosted by Ulli Beier during his time in Bayreuth. For example, in 1982 he curated an exhibition on *l'art brut* objects in the former Brunnenhaus together with Heike Schulz. This led to the exhibition 'Glücklose Köpfe – Malerei von Ver-rückten – aus Nigeria' (Luckless Heads—Paintings of the Mentally Dis-Placed from Nigeria),[6] which showcased 170 works of art by the so-called Abeokuta Group (see Fig. 6.4).

Beier kept the works of these fourteen patient-artists from Nigeria and Benin for at least thirty years. In the bilingual catalogue, each artist is given an introduction of roughly one page detailing aspects of their lives before they were institutionalised, their lives in the mental hospital and their assumed impairment. Beier writes from his own perspective,

Fig. 6.4 'Porcellanographie: Future Traces,' Yassine Balbzioui, 2016, detail. Photographed by Katharina Greven

analysing the paintings according to the references available to him. These brief reports and assessments are accompanied by figures showing the artworks. In a brief final excursion, Beier explains his affection for *l'art brut*. During his childhood, his father gave him a volume of the collected drawings from the Prinzhorn Collection as a present, which enchanted him. The impressions he derived from them continued to accompany him in Bayreuth for half a century (see Beier 1982).[7]

It is thus not surprising that Beier chose a word that grapples with the concept of beauty when he named the university's Museum for Contemporary African Art, namely 'Iwalewa,' a Yoruba expression roughly translated as 'character is beauty' (Abiodun 1983, 13–18). Beier's vision for the Iwalewahaus was that it should be a space in which artists would come together, live together, work together and produce art contrary to European ideals of beauty and art (see Greven, Forthcoming). Even though Beier did not explicitly design the project to deal with the aesthetics of disability, he still saw these new connotations of beauty as an act of resistance against established norms in the art world, just as Siebers does with his concept of disability aesthetics.

Ulli Beier's successors, Ronald Rupprecht (1985–1989), Till Förster (1997–2001), and Tobias Wendl (2001–2010), did not follow-up on the aspect of disability or impairment while the collection was being increased. They did not share Beier's love of outsider art and did not place any emphasis on the idea of inclusion. However, Beier's legacy and the circumstances in which he started the collection became a guiding principle again under the directorship of Dr. Ulf Vierke. Vierke has been the director of the Iwalewahaus since 2010, and since 2012 he has been the representative for disabled and chronically ill students at the University of Bayreuth. He combines an interest in disability and art in both his research and his teaching. Even though he does not draw on *l'art brut* when discussing disability, the theme of inclusion has nonetheless received a new impetus under his directorship. This interest is not only visible in the research projects and the design of the exhibitions, as the collection now also includes more recent artworks that deal with the topic of disability. Beside the works by *l'art brut* artists from Nigeria, Papua New Guinea, and India mentioned above (the Schulz collection), the collection also contains objects of representational disabled bodies. Next to the works labelled 'outsider art,' these are the works that make the most explicit reference to disability.

The two works of art that I discuss in the following, 'Porcellanographie' and 'The Lame Beggar,' thus stand for two different forms of 'disability gain' in the collection of the Iwalewahaus. 'The Lame Beggar' can be compared to a person in a wheelchair in front of a flight of steps: it seems obvious that, in order for the person to be able to overcome the physical obstacle, the environment has to be adjusted. In contrast, the porcelain installation in 'Porcellanographie' goes beyond this structural approach and asks rather what does not seem so obvious. It is beautiful, it is gentle, but how can that possibly be, given that its design deviates from the standard? The works by Owiti and Balbzioui both clarify the approach enshrined in the idea of 'disability gain,' not only through the content of disability, but also by being on the look-out for disabled forms.

HEZBON OWITI'S 'THE LAME BEGGAR': DISABLED CONTENT

Reflecting on art works such as 'The Lame Beggar' under the aspect of disability is a rather classic approach that has frequently been adopted in disability studies (see Siebers 2008; Waldschmidt 2007; Garland-Thomson 2007). Representations of disabled bodies in images, texts or music are analysed, and their stereotypical depictions in medical images of disability are contrasted with the social model of disability. Even though it is obvious that this is not an avant-garde approach, it does have its merits. It is only through the analysis of disabled bodies that these can become visible beyond the artwork itself. In respect of art by African artists, however, this approach has only rarely been adopted, just like reflections on and analyses of disabled art and 'disability aesthetics.'

Hezbon Owiti was born in Central Nyanza (Kenya) in 1946. Very little is known about him, apart from the fact that he had his most productive period in the 1960s and 1970s. In his introductory volume *Contemporary Art in Africa* (1968), Ulli Beier writes that '[t]he career of Hezbon Owiti, a young Luo from Kenya, is full of promise' (ibid., 68). He relates how the young Kenyan was discovered by the South African Es'kia Mphalele, received a bursary to go to Nigeria to work there, and later returned to Kenya with fine works of art in order to try his luck as an artist (see also Kennedy 1992). Beier's wish, however, was never fulfilled, as Owiti only continued to produce until the 1970s (Agathe 1990, 376). Overall, only a few of Owiti's artworks are known.

Owiti worked at the University of Ibadan,[8] earned a bursary from the Fairfield Foundation in New York (USA) and was artist in residence at the University of Sussex (England). During his time in Oshogbo, Owiti crafted prints and oil paintings, such as 'The Lame Beggar' discussed above, which is dated to 1966. Like many artists of his generation, Owiti was an autodidact,[9] who, using water colours, pencil and clay, taught himself methods of artistic production. Like so many aspiring artists, young Owiti was unable to live off his art and therefore took work as a caretaker at the Chemichemi Cultural Centre in Nairobi. There he was discovered by Es'kia Mphalele, a South African writer and art lover, who procured the Fairfield bursary for him, which allowed him to travel to Nigeria. Hezbon was inspired by the atmosphere in the workshops, and for the first time he used oil paint with very strong colours, as in 'The Lame Beggar.' He held his first exhibition at the legendary Mbari Mbayo Gallery in Lagos (Nigeria) in 1965 (Kennedy 1992), located in the upper section of the Mbari Club, which was housed in a market hall. The club and the gallery were accessible spaces, as their names indicate. Thus, the club was named after the Igbo word *mbari*,[10] and '[i]ts core members clearly wished to situate their work, even if only rhetorically and philosophically, within the paradigm of communal rather than elite art practice' (Okeke-Agulu 2015, 150).

'The Lame Beggar' was painted in one of the Beiers' workshops, in an environment that was quite accessible in itself. The workshops organised by the Beiers foregrounded the artistic ability of each person and rejected didactic learning from the outside. The policy of giving freedom to the artists' creative vein, ideally without Western influences, leaned on Ulli's fascination for outsider art. Besides providing spaces for independent works, the Mbari Mbayo Club offered a social and cultural framework in which the participation of its members was considered a core aspect. It was in this innovative and liberal framework that Ulli Beier developed his aspiration to create an art space that would not bow down to the elitist norms he saw at work in European institutions. Such a space would also respect the beauty of art production and its discourse. This wish was realised in 1961 through the formation of the Mbari Mbayo Club. Even today his approach can be described as the creation of an open, participatory and diverse space, similar to what James Clifford (1997) describes in his 'Museum as Contact Zone'. The Mbari Mbayo Gallery was intended to be 'a place for the living and the dead, the sane and insane, the rich and the poor' (Okeke-Agulu 2015, 149). Therefore, it should come as no surprise that, within such an environment, an artist should create a piece denoting disability, one that welcomes 'insanity' and that also elicits an ethical appraisal from its viewers. Jean Kennedy, an expert on contemporary African Art at the time and a friend of Beier's and many artists', clearly describes Owiti's work when she writes: 'One painting depicting a crippled person with large crutches and whose head is bent at a right angle to the body is especially touching' (1992, 149).

'The Lame Beggar' is a colourful painting, dominated by orange, red and blue. The faded wooden frame encasing the canvas looks as though it will crush the figure of the Black beggar from head to toe at any moment. Propped up on his crutches, the beggar depicted is wearing shorts and a torn shirt, and his head is resting on his right shoulder, looking directly at the viewer with slightly hanging eyelids. His left leg has been amputated below the knee (or perhaps has been short from birth), and his right leg and right arm show what appear to be open, inflamed, saucer-sized wounds. His mouth is not distorted, even though he appears pitiful, but is shut, giving his countenance a sober feel, with a neutral facial expression. The beggar takes up most of the space in the painting. He stands in front of a dark blue background on a yellow-orange ground, enhancing the impression of his crutches. The brush strokes are broad and alternate between short and long movements, giving the background a restless feel, while making the beggar appear static. Through the hinted at movement towards the viewer, the painting arouses the feeling of address: the beggar has moved toward the viewer, looking expectantly at the latter. His gaze seems to evoke the questions with which Rosemarie Garland-Thomson begins her excellent work, *Staring—How We Look* (2009), namely 'Who stares? Why do we stare? When do we stare? What do we stare at? Why can't we stop staring? What do we do when we are stared at? Should we stare?' (ibid., 3). Garland-Thomson defines 'staring' as a social relationship that stimulates dialogue and is not just a form of 'domination.'

Usually we stare at someone or something when normal habits of looking are not sufficient to comprehend the person or object being stared at. Staring and being stared at begin when normality becomes somewhat distorted, when the usual, the standard of what is habitual, becomes troubled. 'The Lame Beggar' encourages staring on a number of levels.[11] Perhaps first of all the bright colours, chosen by Owiti to portray the begging man, draw our attention. The narrowness of the painting within a frame that seems too small for its subject leads us to wonder why the man is bent over so painfully and is looking at us in such an unmediated fashion. Just at the last moment, we see his amputated leg and the open wounds on his left arm and remaining leg. All of these dispositions, of course, deviate from bodily normality and the representation of beauty. They are neither standardised beauty nor standardised normality; rather, they invite us to look voyeuristically at the begging man to start a dialogue. Yet he is subject to our power to define this dialogue. We make a judgement about him, be it ethical or aesthetic. We decide whether to continue facing him or to turn our back on him (in disgust, maybe). Like Garland-Thomson, W. J. T. Mitchell sees the dialogue between the one doing the staring and the one being stared at as productive, claiming that '[t]he picture wants you to stare' (Mitchell 2005, 7, quoted in Garland-Thomson 2009). According to Mitchell (ibid.), pictures have their own agenda and should be understood as 'animated beings' with an independent existence.

Yassine Balbzioui shares this conception of art, which plays a decisive role in his work 'Porcellanographie: Future Traces' and its interpretation as an image of disability. The idea that every piece of art has a life of its own supports Garland-Thomson's concept of staring as an animated dialogue marking disabled bodies that are defined by their deviation from the norm. The same can be said about artworks: 'To a certain extent, art objects are themselves living bodies, and as such mark a field, that keeps in flux the spectrum of acceptable, human forms of appearance' (Siebers 2009, 11). We look at people and artworks from the perspective of 'broken' bodies because they are different and do not, or cannot, hide their visible difference. Thus, they invite us to stare and to increase the visibility of disabled bodies. 'The Lame Beggar' invites us to stare, not only because it is a painting and we are only able to encounter it through our gaze, but also because of its main protagonist's direct, provocative facial expression. In contrast to other representations of disability in which those depicted are stared at, beggar actually returns the gaze. A moment of anticipatory pressure is created: what do I, as a viewer, do with this obviously vulnerable begging man? Do I allow myself to be addressed? Is the aesthetic of Owiti's painting so affective that it triggers an aesthetic response in me? And am I able to move away from staring to attentive reflection?

It seems as if Owiti has already made a judgement about the person he painted. The attribute 'lame' marks the latter as disabled and makes him a seemingly pitiable character. Even if the unknown beggar were not standing in front of us with a distorted face, he would still seem to be suffering, as is visible not in his facial expression, nor in his general appearance, but in his contextualisation through external factors, namely the frame that surrounds and nearly squashes him, which he seems hardly able to bear. He is depicted as reliant on support, not least because he is begging. In many ways he seems to be the perfect embodiment of the pitiful beggar, a figure overdetermined by the stereotypical perception that poverty follows from disability and vice versa.[12]

'The Lame Beggar' does not tell us a new story about disability or disabled identities, but entrenches existing stigmas (see Goffman 1983). This becomes most apparent in the depiction of the crutches, which are placed and coloured in such a way that they strike the eye at first sight. Through them, the representation of disability and the focus on the beggar's physical deviance are made central. A favourable reading would emphasise the movement of his crutches in the sand, which reveals that the almost squashed man is not completely helpless, but can move independently. However, this moment of recognition is only possible once the process of staring has been overcome and been transformed to an inner discourse. If one accepts disability as a discursive construction, and not as a matter of personal misfortune, it becomes an analytical category and a moral question (see Quayson 2007, 1–30). Even though 'The Lame Beggar' suggests an interpretation of his arguably restricted freedom of independent movement, it is still a quite classic representation of disability. It does not inspire or offer new perspectives on disabled identities, nor does it expand our canon of normative beauty. Classic representations of disability are static allegories, in which the viewer does not fear that they will touch or change reality. The viewer passes the test of (Kantian) indifference by not wishing to embrace the painting (Siebers 2009, 53). By foregrounding a tormented body on oversized crutches, this is exactly what Owiti's 'Lame Beggar' achieves: the man depicted disappears behind his disability. Even when we gaze at him, we only gaze upon his disability and not on himself as a person. His disabled identity appears central. It almost seems as if Owiti himself was affectively overwhelmed by the impact of the man's disability. Garland-Thomson has written on the affectivity of the extraordinary body in contrast to the ordinary: '[T]he extraordinary excites but alarms us; the ordinary assures but bores us' (Garland-Thomson 2009, 19).

Although the disabled and injured body of the beggar appears extraordinary, it is in no way necessarily so. A begging black man in tattered clothes, with crooked sticks under his arms, standing on a somewhat sandy surface, begging on the margins of society, coming towards the viewer and indeed staring at him or her, would certainly have been a daily occurrence in the urban Oshogbo of the 1960s. The reason for Owiti's painting not being boring at all, but rather being a representation of disability that relies on the extraordinariness of the depicted, is its direct approach in format and colour. 'The Lame Beggar' and other representations of this format expect their viewers to assume an ethical position, one they decide with regard to disability, as well as their discursive stance. Owiti's work demands this decision precisely because his beggar's stare is directed unmediated into the eyes of the person standing in front of him, so that they have to either return it or avert it. 'In other words,' Garland-Thomson writes, 'things happen when people stare' (2009, 4).

When such a decision is made and 'things happen,' we can say that a decisive step in the direction of 'disability gain' has been made. The viewer has provided the beggar with a disabled identity, even if this means also stigmatising him because of his disability. The direct nature of his representation creates the conditions for this stigmatisation, which forces the viewer to make a judgement. The beggar is thus a pathetic creature, who must have experienced severe adversity.

In order to fully appreciate the full force of 'disability gain,' it becomes the task of the context—for example, of the museum, the curator or the researcher—to formulate and embed disabled identities in such a way that they are perceived as strong. This can be achieved by providing accessible exhibition space, as well as content (see Russell 1998). The choice and analysis of different kinds of artworks by the curator and viewer become crucial.

If pieces that depict a fractured beauty or a disabled aesthetic—that is, works on fragmented identities that concern themselves with the question of beauty—are placed next to 'classic' representations of disabled persons, they help to change the beggar's identity and similar representations of disability. In this context, the canon of images of disability and the range of disabled identities and disabled bodies can be expanded on significantly. The affective experience of art, its underlying stories and practices of staring, will become more diverse and possibly remove the stigma of the disabled body as ugly. One felicitous example of such a new story of disabled bodies is depicted in Yassine Balbzioui's installation, to be discussed in the next section. Balbzioui understands his works as objects with histories which only become beautiful through their biographies.

YASSINE BALBZIOUI'S: PORCELLANOGRAPHIE: FUTURE TRACES— THE DISABLED FORM/BEAUTY AS A CHALLENGE

Aristotle was the first to formulate the idea that beauty is connected to its imitative representation in art. Referring to corpses and disfigured animals, he claims that what matters is the familiarity with what is represented, which makes it appear beautiful. The unfamiliar, on the other hand, is commonly considered ugly (Aristoteles 2012, 11, quoted in Fuhrmann). However, not all artworks depict their objects in mimetic terms, as does 'The Lame Beggar'. Since the beginning of the twentieth century, artistic practices have more or less dissociated themselves from concrete imitations, and the form of an artwork has become at least as important as its content, capable of being used as a frame of reference, referring to an object or a phenomenon, which only develops upon closer inspection. In Baumgarten's sense (see Baumgarten and Schweizer 1988), this inspection must involve bodily awareness. How, then, can the cups and pots of Balbzioui's installation possibly be considered beautiful if they do not reproduce 'the natural' according to Aristotle? What is the aesthetic awareness of an artwork? And what contribution can it offer to 'disability gain'?

According to Balbzioui himself, the question he pursues in his eclectic project is the question of 'what is beautiful'.[13] Balbzioui was born in Morocco in 1972, and his artistic career began in the 1990s. He followed a number of artistic directions and schools, and acquired two diplomas of fine art from the Universities of Casablanca and Bordeaux, followed by an art and media diploma from the University of California at Berkeley at the beginning of the 2000s.

Balbzioui describes his work as 'Fluxus proximal.' It is multidimensional, though quantitatively speaking most of his artworks are paintings. His paintings are often streaked with neo-expressionist mythical creatures, human bodies with animal heads or masks, or vivid animalistic representations. This involvement with derision and the grotesque extends to his performances, in which he tries to challenge his audience. His performance work scratches the surface of general perceptions of the insane. Marie Dèparis-Jafil states that, in his activity as a performer, 'we can observe the full extent of his madness!' (2017). Balbzioui's work, whether in performance or painting, is never restrained. It is always theatrical and capricious, obviously led by the question asked above: 'What is beautiful?'

The work under discussion comes from the exhibition 'Porcellanographie: Future Traces,' which was showcased in the Iwalewahaus in the spring of 2016. The exhibition was the result of Balbzioui's first contact with porcelain and was developed in collaboration with the long-standing Bayreuth porcelain manufacturer Walküre. For the exhibition, Balbzioui created objects that, according to its accompanying text, 'contradict the imagination of beauty as being pure and uniform' (quoted from Fink and Igabe 2016, n.p.).

The beautiful and the symmetrical, the beautiful and the uniform, the beautiful and the pure, are conceptual pairings, which Balbzioui resists throughout his work. For example, in the accompanying text, he describes the exhibition as '[a]n installation of dramatic objects with their very own history' (quoted from Fink and Igabe 2016, n.p.). According to Balbzioui, it is the object's history that makes it beautiful, a history of, as we shall see below, performed production failure, which has led to 'deformed' bodies. Tobin Siebers likewise argues that it is in fact the asymmetrical in art that may be regarded as beautiful (2009, 5–30), a notion I will return to discuss in more detail below. Moreover, Poe argues that '[t]here is no extraordinary beauty without a certain strangeness of proportion' (1922, quoted in Siebers 2009, 9). With reference to Balbzioui's porcelain, one could say that exactly the opposite is true: it is only the deviation from symmetry that creates art from kitsch and makes it beautiful.

The installation 'Porcellanographie: Future Traces' was made up of a number of different parts.[14] It included sketches of porcelain plates that Balbzioui developed together with Walküre, a video in which he interprets the Arabic Kalila wa-Dimna collection of tales while wearing a jackal mask, and a sound installation of breaking porcelain. At the centre of the exhibition was a shelf filled with objects from Walküre's shop floor consisting of cups, pots and saucers created by Balbzioui. Together with Katharina Fink, during the exhibition in Bayreuth he offered an accompanying workshop for adults and children that dealt with questions of beauty.[15]

At first glance, something seems amiss when looking at Balbzioui's porcelain. It has a pure white quality with a high degree of lustre, yet its form is unsettling. The dishes Balbzioui produced have nothing in common with Walküre's usual products except for its material. The pots look squashed and crooked, the cups lie sideways instead of standing upright on their bases and the saucers appear folded up like tulip blossoms.

Altogether they look pretty in the way they are exhibited on the rustic, wooden shelf, yet the loss of their (alleged) functionality makes them appear broken. This 'broken beauty,' I argue, functions in the sense of Tobin Siebers' 'disability aesthetic.' From a perfectly crafted object, the crockery becomes an art object through its asymmetrical distortion. The collaboration between the multi-disciplinary artist from Morocco and the porcelain producer steeped in the Franconian regional tradition challenges the idea of beauty as being perfect in shape and functionality. It was the pristine material that attracted Balbzioui, along with its connection to local middle-class status and its complicated production process. Drawing on his methodology of drama and performance, mentioned above, Balbzioui wanted to 'conquer' the new material artistically, and accordingly spent three weeks on Walküre's shop floor together with the curator. In that time, he strove to understand the perfection of porcelain production as much as possible to appropriate it for his artistic production and then destroy it. For Balbzioui, the beauty he seeks to achieve is what becomes beautiful through his performance.

According to our ordinary everyday routine and aesthetics, a porcelain pot should be pristine: it should be beautiful to look at and should pour tea or coffee out through a perfect spout into a perfect cup in order to produce the perfect tea-drinking occasion. In contrast, the pots that Balbzioui produced in his performances, by intervening in the logic of production and by staging a dramatic performance with the crockery in dialogue with them, are no longer perfect: instead they are deviations from the norm as well as the standard, and from this they acquire a new aesthetic quality. What may be seen as flawed from the perspective of the logic of production becomes beautiful within the logic of performance.

This beauty of deviation is located in the ensoulment of the objects, which have a recognisable story of deformation and destruction, even a history. This (hi)story is inscribed in their material bodies. It cannot be overlooked but instead invites the viewer to stare at them, as with 'The Lame Beggar'; yet, in contrast to the latter, their histories and identities are not so obviously disabled. They might be called dysfunctional, but they are nonetheless beautiful. The material has lost none of its charm, and the porcelain bodies are not marked with the stigma of the 'disabled,' but can be seen as modern, conceptual or aesthetic. Nevertheless, Balbzioui calls his cups 'handicapped' and 'misshaped' objects. According to curator Fink, this is not meant as a form of devaluation, nor to connote negativity, but rather to describe their quality. Bynum expresses the link between bodily formation and personal history as follows:

[S]hape or body is crucial, not incidental, to story. It carries story; it makes story visible; in a sense, it is story. Shape (or visible body) is in space what story is in time. [...] Identity is finally shape carrying story. (2009, 7, quoted in Garland-Thomson 2009, 167)

Through its personal story—its biography, so to speak—the porcelain becomes animated. Through this ensoulment its disability can be developed, and this in turn makes it beautiful. It is from here that Balbzioui understands beauty as a challenge. By means of the material, with its own long-standing history within European aesthetics, and the forms he gives to his art objects, Balbzioui comes to discuss beauty in his art. Rather than reproducing classic bodily norms of beauty, whether in his paintings, sculptures or performances, he deforms them by pushing them a step further, thereby giving them a positively connoted 'disabled' identity.

In this respect, Balbzioui can be seen as opposing Rosemarie Garland-Thomson's explanation that the hideous is always identifiable in the misshapen: '[v]iolations in shape give us figures such as giants and dwarfs, violations in shape give us monsters. Monsters are unusually formed beings; whose bodies are simultaneously ordinary and extra ordinary' (2009, 163). But Balbzioui is not creating monsters by deforming porcelain, and this is where one can recognise the 'disability gain' involved in his art practice. Balbzioui thus employs his talent and uses the context of the museum to present these deformed bodies, which become beautiful to us through their de-normalisation, thereby acquiring additional value.

To repeat, the object's biography is crucial in this process. Certainly it is easy to argue that all objects have a biography or social history, and indeed, entire research projects deliberate on this point, provenance studies having been borne out of this idea. However, the moments of biography that Balbzioui reveals are created from the form of the objects, which refers to their content. The beauty of the disabled objects, in contrast to non-disabled objects, is that they give the viewer no other option than to notice their disability without depicting a human body. Like 'The Lame Beggar,' Balbzioui's disabled objects demand an aesthetic judgement. However, the material that he uses—perfectly pristine porcelain, whose faulty production usually ends up being sold as second-rate quality—as well as its presentation during a performance in a museum, encourages a different verdict. Unlike Owiti's beggar, their imperfections let them appear beautiful rather than pitiful. The perception of one of Balbzioui's cups as a cup is prone to change our perception of cups more generally, provoking an aesthetic act triggered by art.

To sum up, Balbzioui's cups are not images of disability, but they are themselves disabled, another contrast with the disability art of 'The Lame Beggar.' In this process, the (formal) experience of disability is changed. From disabled content emerges disabled form. If manipulated and 'abnormal' bodies were considered 'freaks' when they appeared as performers before the twentieth century, then Balbzioui twists this perception. It is only through his performance that his porcelain 'bodies' become disabled. The added value, the 'disability gain' of his work, lies precisely in this conscious negotiation of beauty. In this sense, Balbzioui does not produce 'trauma art' in which he changes and traumatises already existing porcelain works, but instead connotes physical trauma not as a negative, but as a positive shattering, thus giving disability a positive identity.

CONCLUSION

What we can learn from those being stared at is the following: the visibility of their non-normate bodies in public space is of immense importance because society will learn to see and think differently only by being confronted with them, whether this concerns human bodies or artworks. In disability studies, this learning process has recently been labelled 'disability gain' (see Fox, Krings, Vierke, this volume). Only if 'abnormal' bodies pretend to be 'normal,' as Rosemarie Garland-Thomson (2009, 9) puts it, and do not let themselves be discouraged by being stared at, will society acquire a more inclusive image of the body. The dialogue between staring and being stared at therefore has enormous social potential in that '[s]taring makes meaning' (ibid.). From this perspective, staring does not produce culprits and victims, but creates identity in social relationships. The quality of the moral verdict that the staring makes about the stared is of high importance. Fine art is the perfect subject with which to encounter the relationship between the one who stares and the thing being stared at. The 'thing' the artwork is therefore able to refer to, namely the human and in this context disabled body, opens up a new spectrum of understanding. The surplus of art being perceived as elite and exceptional helps the disabled body regenerate itself from its stigmatisation as flaw. If 'The Lame Beggar' only triggers a stare because he is so unexpected in his directness, the 'Porcellanographie' unfolds its frame of reference only indirectly. The beauty of Balbzioui's work lies in its form, as well as in its placidity. The material, the presentation and the haptic of the cups and pots appear fragile. Although they are later broken and disabled during

Balbzioui's performance encounter, in their disfigured production state they do not seem useless or even worthless. Rather, their 'brokenness' before actually being broken embeds their quality.

In this chapter, I have emphasised the importance of the form and materiality of artworks in order to add value to the concept of the disabled body. By not reflecting on classical representations of human disabled bodies, but rather looking instead at the disabled bodies of artworks, which are already considered beautiful, we can broaden the perception of the disabled body as such. To repeat, if we know where to look for it, we can see disability everywhere. Therefore, the disabled bodies of artworks and their broken beauty can help us understand the bodily inscriptions of society.

This chapter has also shown that art that works with disabled forms may contribute to countering victimising representations of the disabled body, as well as social stigmatisation more generally. The disabled bodies of artworks or 'disabled artworks' create a positive identity by being classified as artworks of high value. Not least, these artworks—even if they rely on rather different notions of beauty and disability, such as the two works I have discussed above—trigger critical reflections on otherwise unquestioned assumptions about the disabled body among their audience. Staring, then, Garland-Thomson reminds us, 'shows us something about how we look at each other and how we look to each other. Appearances [...] are enactments' (2009, 17). However, the difference in the 'staring relationship' between persons and that between persons and artworks is the one-sided character of the latter. People who have had life-long experience in dealing with being stared at can be markedly more active in their interaction with the staring subject than artworks could ever possibly be. Artworks likewise demand an aesthetic experience, but they do so silently. As objects of the stare, they do not have to counter the pressure of being stared at, thus offering a non-personal and therefore less painful expansion of our understanding of disabled bodies. Analysing artworks as something worth staring at is crucial, as they do not relinquish the potential of disabled bodies all by themselves.

Siebers (2009) asks that the understanding of the disabled body be expanded from the classic representations of disability. According to him, one cannot separate political and aesthetic judgements from persons and subjects. The analysis of disabled bodies must therefore be expanded to include other bodies, such as the body politic, buildings and artworks, to strive against political and aesthetic uniformity. Like Siebers, Rosemarie

Garland-Thomson notes that '[d]isability appears everywhere in culture, once the critic knows where to look for it – from Oedipus to the Human Genome Project' (quoted in Lutz 2003, 421).

As early as 1935, Marcel Mauss (1973 [1935]) explained that society inscribes itself on to the human body. Even though bodily inscription has been extensively discussed, it is still surprising that, in the age of mass media and image saturation, the disabled body takes up little space in art criticism, especially in relation to the efficacy of the human body. Yet, the disabled body is omnipresent in art. Collages, assemblages, fractures, installations, sculptures, statues, paintings and a number of performance artworks can all be seen as disabled bodies in the way described above. In particular, modern and contemporary art, each genre partially represented by one of the artworks discussed above, has appropriated disability as a variety of the beautiful. Thus, it is remarkable that, while in modern art we may deem disfigured facial forms beautiful, we hardly do so when we encounter them in real persons. The inclusivity of disability aesthetics in art therefore still needs to be translated into inclusivity in real life. Artworks such as Balbzioui's broken cups in 'Porcellanographie,' discussed at length in this chapter, can certainly expand our understanding of the disabled body as a modern and beautiful one. From this perspective, these artworks can be seen as heroes and heroines—or rather, they can be turned into heroes and heroines for embodying inclusive ideals of beauty.

NOTES

1. All quotes from German and French have been translated by the author.
2. As historically evolving cultural entities (art), museums are not easily accessible spaces. They mediate an exclusionary principle, which is limited to the knowledge of the connoisseur. The underlying cultural message is that, if you do not belong to the inner circle, you will not understand the museum and its exhibition. Since Clifford's (1997) publication on the 'Museum as Contact Zone,' most (anthropological) museums have opened their collections to the public and have adopted a participatory approach to exhibition making and curating.
3. Lantoro Mental Hospital is located approximately 90 km (55 miles) southwest of Ibadan.
4. Beier is said to have worked already with children with disabilities during his studies abroad at the University of London. Unfortunately, there are no further details of this phase of his life (Greven, Forthcoming).

5. This initial foundation of the collection was undertaken by Ulli Beier together with his first wife, Susanne Wenger in about 1950 (Greven, Forthcoming).

6. In his exhibition title, Beier plays with the German word *verrückt*, meaning 'crazy', by inserting a dash to produce *ver-rückt*. This makes the mentally disabled not only 'crazy' but also displaced, a way of referring to the marginalized position of people with a disability.

7. In 1997, 2001 and 2003, having moved to Sydney, Ulli Beier organised two further exhibitions on outsider art together with the Brunnenhaus and held various talks on the topic (see Bartylla 1997a, 2001). Upon emigrating he gave the social psychiatric clinic of Bayreuth, under the directorship of Dr. Heike Schulz, his private collection of *l'art brut*, including works from Australia, India and Papua New Guinea (see Bartylla, 3 February 1997b). This collection has since been given to Iwalewahaus.

8. I assume that Owiti took part in seminars and workshops as a student, but not much more is known than that. In *Wegzeichen – Kunst aus Ostafrika 1974–89* (Sign Posts—Art from East Africa 1974–89), Johanna Agthe (1990) gives the 'University of Ibadan' as his affiliation but does not specify in what capacity. In a slightly later article, Jean Kennedy (1992) states that, thanks to the bursary from the Fairfield Foundation, Owiti went to Oshogbo for six months and worked at the university and in Oshogbo itself. But even here, there are no further details as to what that work might have looked like.

9. For example, Valente Malangatana, Muraina Oyelami, Twins 77, Jimoh Buraimoh, Bisi Fabunmi and Jacob Afolabi were taxi-drivers, cooks or electricians before they became artists.

10. The Idbo expression *mbari* refers to an artistic art practice in communal spaces, which are filled with statues, figurines and sometimes houses constantly under construction. New works are added until, at one point, everything is torn down and the *mbari* is rebuilt again (see Okeke-Agulu 2015).

11. The fact that the Black body of 'The Lame Beggar' today is part of a collection of modern African art stored in Germany and stared at by a mostly white, western European audience, raises interesting questions that deserve further analysis. However, due to limited space, this chapter focuses on the beggar's identity as a disabled person.

12. A proposal for further reading would include the research pertaining to the so-called Community-based Rehabilitation Programs (CBR programs) that attempt to integrate people with disabilities better into their societies and push forward the co-operation between those with disabilities and those without, such as works by Sally Hartley (2002),

Heike Tüschenbönner (2001) and Peter Coleridge (2001). A unifying factor for all these works and similar studies is that the authors consider disability to be a flaw resulting from poverty. In *Aesthetic Nervousness*, Ato Quayson (2007) also speaks about the link between polio and poverty in Africa.

13. These and subsequent pieces of information come from an interview with the curator of 'Porcellanographie: Future Traces' and close friend of Yassine Balbzioui, Dr. Katharina Fink, held on 4 December 2017.

14. The image on the cover on this volume is a detail from this installation.

15. Similar to 'The Lame Beggar,' 'Porcellanographie' is more than a reference to disability 'only.' Balbzioui's work is also a reflection about his postcolonial ethnic identify, a theme that cannot be elaborated further here.

REFERENCES

Abiodun, Rowland. 1983. "Identity and the Artistic Process in Yorúbà Aesthetic Concept of Ìwà." *Journal of Culture and Ideas* 1: 13–31.

Agthe, Johanna. 1990. *Wegzeichen: Kunst aus Ostafrika 1974–89*. Museum für Völkerkunde. Sammlungs-Kataloge des Museums für Völkerkunde 5: Afrika. Frankfurt am Main: Museum für Völkerkunde.

Aristoteles, and Manfred Fuhrmann, eds. 2012. *Poetik: Griechisch/deutsch*. Bibliogr. erg. Ausg. 1994 [Nachdr.]. Universal-Bibliothek Griechische Literatur 7828. Stuttgart: Reclam.

Bartylla, Eva. 1997a. "Grenzen selbst ausloten: Ulli Beier und die Psychatrie beim Volk der Yoruba in Nigeria." *Nordbayerischer Kurier*, 13 January.

Bartylla, Eva. 1997b. "'Rohe Kunst' zum Abschied: Ulli Beiers Sammlung für den Sozialpsychatrischen Dienst." *Nordbayerischer Kurier*, 3 February.

Bartylla, Eva. 2001. "L'Art Brut: Auf dem Weg zur öffentlichen Anerkennung: Uli (sic) Beier bringt Buch und Bilder ins Brunnenhaus: Eine Kunst in Australien." *Nordbayerischer Kurier*, 8 June.

Bauman, H-Dirksen L., and Joseph J. Murray, eds. 2014. *Deaf Gain: Raising the Stakes for Human Diversity*. Minneapolis: University of Minnesota Press.

Baumgarten, Alexander Gottlieb. 1986. *Aesthetica*. 31750th ed. Hildesheim: Olms.

Baumgarten, Alexander Gottlieb, and Hans Rudolf Schweizer, eds. 1983. *Theoretische Ästhetik: Die grundlegenden Abschnitte aus der "Aesthetica" (1750/58); latein.-dt*. Philosophische Bibliothek 355. Hamburg: Meiner.

Baumgarten, Alexander Gottlieb, and Hans Rudolf Schweizer, eds. 1988. *Theoretische Ästhetik: Die grundlegenden Abschnitte aus der "Aesthetica" (1750/58); lateinisch-deutsch*. 2nd ed. Philosophische Bibliothek 355. Hamburg: Meiner.

Beier, Ulli. 1968. *Contemporary Art in Africa*. London: Pall Mall Press.

Beier, Ulli. 1982. *Glücklose Köpfe: Malerei Von Ver-Rückten Aus Nigeria*. Bremen: Ed. CON.

Clifford, James. 1997. *Routes: Travel and Translation in the Late Twentieth Century.* Cambridge, MA: Harvard University Press.

Coleridge, Peter. 2001. *Disability, Liberation, and Development.* An Oxfam Publication. Oxford: Oxfam.

Déparis-Jafil, Marie. 2017. "Yassine Balbzioui: Biographie." Accessed 18 December 2017. http://yassinebalbzioui.com/cv/.

Fink, Katharina, and Gloria Igabe. 2016. "Yassine Balbzioui - Porcellanographie: Future Traces: Eine Rauminstallation mit Arbeiten von Yassine Balbzioui." Accessed 9 March 2017. http://www.iwalewahaus.uni-bayreuth.de/de/program/archive/2016/20160324_Yassine-Balbzioui/index.html.

Garland-Thomson, Rosemarie. 2007. *Extraordinary Bodies: Figuring Physical Disability in American Culture and Literature* [Nachdr.]. New York: Columbia University Press.

Garland-Thomson, Rosemarie. 2009. *Staring: How We Look.* Oxford and New York: Oxford University Press.

Goffman, Erving. 1983. *Stigma: Über Techniken d. Bewältigung beschädigter Identität.* 15th ed. Suhrkamp Taschenbuch / Wissenschaft 140. Frankfurt am Main: Suhrkamp.

Greven, Katharina. 2020. *Das Archiv als konstruierte Heimat – Die 'Fantasie Afrika' der Kunstpatrone Ulli und Georgina Beier.* Berlin: Lit. Forthcoming.

Hartley, Sally. 2002. *CBR: A Participatory Strategy in Africa: Based on the Proceedings of a Conference, Uganda, September 2001.* 1st ed. London: University College London [U.A.].

Kennedy, Jean. 1992. "Between the Natural and Supernatural." In *New Currents, Ancient Rivers: Contemporary African Artists in a Generation of Change,* 143–54. http://www.africa.upenn.edu/Smithsonian_GIFS/Ken_text.html.

Krajewski, Michael. 2004. *Jean Dubuffet: Studien zu seinem Frühwerk und zur Vorgeschichte des Art brut.* Osnabrück: Der Andere Verlag.

Lutz, Petra, ed. 2003. *Der [im-]perfekte Mensch: Metamorphosen von Normalität und Abweichung.* Schriften des Deutschen Hygiene-Museums Dresden 2. Köln: Böhlau.

Mauss, Marcel. 1973. "Techniques of the Body." *Economy and Society* 2 (1): 70–88. https://doi.org/10.1080/03085147300000003.

Mitchell, W. J. T. 2005. *What Do Pictures Want? The Lives and Loves of Images.* Chicago: University of Chicago Press.

Okeke-Agulu, Chika. 2015. *Postcolonial Modernism: Art and Decolonization in Twentieth-Century Nigeria.* Durham: Duke University Press.

Poe, Edgar Allen. 1922. *Werke.* Edited by Theodor Etzel, 272–97. Berlin: Propyläen-Verlag.

Quayson, Ato. 2007. *Aesthetic Nervousness: Disability and the Crisis of Representation.* New York: Columbia University Press.

Rhodes, Colin. 2000. *Outsider Art: Spontaneous Alternatives.* 1st ed. World of Art. London: Thames & Hudson.

Russell, Marta. 1998. *Beyond Ramps: Disability at the End of the Social Contract: A Warning from an Uppity Crip.* 1. Printing. Monroe, ME: Common Courage Press.

Siebers, Tobin. 2008. "Disability Aesthetics and the Body Beautiful: Signposts in the History of Art." Edited by Henri-Jacques Stikker. *ALTER—European Journal for Disability Studies* 2: 329–36.

Siebers, Tobin. 2009. *Zerbrochene Schönheit: Essays über Kunst, Ästhetik und Behinderung.* Disability Studies 3. Bielefeld: Transcript. 2014. African Art History and the Formation of a Modern Aesthetic. African Modernism in Institutional Art Collections Related to German Collecting Activities. With the Assistance of Greven Katharina, K. Klaphake-Perters, L. Naumann and S. Salmanian. Universität Bayreuth.

Siegert, Nadine. 2014. *African Art History and the Formation of a Modern Aesthetic. African Modernism in Institutional Art Collections Related to German Collecting Activities.* With the Assistance of Greven Katharina, K. Klaphake-Perters, L. Naumann, and S. Salmanian. Universität Bayreuth.

Tüschenbönner, Heike. 2001. *Behinderung in Afrika: Zur Situation und Rehabilitation behinderter Menschen im östlichen und südlichen Afrika mit besonderem Schwerpunkt der Community-Based Rehabilitation (CBR).* Denken & Handeln 42. Bochum: Evang. Fachhochsch. Rheinland-Westfalen-Lippe.

Waldschmidt, Anne. 2007. "Behinderte Körper: Stigmatheorie Diskurstheorie und Disability Studies im Vergleich." In *Marginalisierte Körper - Zur Soziologie und Geschichte des anderen Körpers,* edited by Torsten Junge and Imke Schminke, 27–43. Münster: Unrast.

PART III

Fashioning the Muslim Female Body

Reshaping 'Turkish' Breasts and Noses: On Cosmetic Surgery, Gendered Norms and the 'Right to Look Normal'

Claudia Liebelt

With a large number of reconstructive plastic and cosmetic surgeons, Turkey now ranks among the top ten countries worldwide with the highest number of cosmetic surgeons per capita (ISAPS 2017), and its cultural capital Istanbul has become a regional centre for the beauty and fashion industries. Against the background of neoliberal urban restructuring, the feminization of the urban service sector and an expansion of the urban middle classes, aesthetic body modification and surgery have become ever more normalized forms of consumption. There are specific bodily concerns in Turkey that are the product of history and that tie a particular bodily appearance to imaginations of modernity, femininity and urban citizenship. 'Heavy' female breasts and 'large' or 'hooked' noses, whose surgical treatment is the focus of this chapter, are clearly among these.

C. Liebelt (✉)
University of Bayreuth, Bayreuth, Germany

© The Author(s) 2019
C. Liebelt et al. (eds.), *Beauty and the Norm*,
Palgrave Studies in Globalization and Embodiment,
https://doi.org/10.1007/978-3-319-91174-8_7

In the language of medical experts in Turkey, heavy female breasts and large or hooked noses are national bodily defects, and their treatment is commonly labelled 'ethnic plastic surgery.' Developed by US-based cosmetic and plastic surgeons, the notion of ethnic plastic surgery is commonly employed to account for the specific physical characteristics and different anatomic features of 'minority patients,' that is, non-Caucasian plastic surgery patients (cf. Mann 2014; Slupchynskyj 2005). In societies in which ethnic features are tied to marginalized minorities, the correction of these features has been characterized as a major motivation for cosmetic surgery. For example, in his comprehensive cultural history of cosmetic surgery, Sander Gilman (1999) foregrounds 'racial passing,' that is, the desire to pass visibly from a negative category to a positive one, as 'the basic motivation for aesthetic surgery' (ibid., xvii). According to Gilman, the rise of cosmetic surgery at the end of the sixteenth century in Europe thus rested on attempts by those constructed as dangerous, namely the syphilitic, 'no longer to be identified as different' (ibid., xxi), in this particular case by reconstructing a nose lost from illness. Gilman shows that, with the emergence of ideologies of race and racial science, passing meant primarily racial passing, with patients turning their deviant 'Jewish,' 'Irish' or 'Black' noses into normative 'Aryan,' 'English' or 'White' ones (ibid., 23).

This chapter seeks to contribute to the debate on the standardization of bodily appearances by probing an understanding of cosmetic surgery, in particular nose and female breast (reduction) surgery, as a classed, gendered and racialized desire for a 'normal' body image in urban Turkey. Labelling specific cosmetic surgery procedures ethnic, I argue, is problematic not only because it sets a norm, namely Caucasian physical features, while labelling looks that deviate from this norm 'ethnic.' Also, as the following account will show, it pays little attention to the complexities of local meanings of and motivations for surgery within particular social, urban and cultural settings. Drawing on surgeons' and religious experts' accounts of what constitutes a 'normal' appearance with regard to nose and breast surgery practices on the one hand and female patients' accounts on the other, this chapter analyses the multiple and changing meanings of nose and breast surgeries for women in contemporary urban Turkey.

As sexualized and prominent personal features, large breasts and noses are not problematic for women as racial or ethnic features per se, but they may become so in some cases and in particular social settings. Not least, female breasts and noses are scrutinized by a patriarchal society that seeks control over the sexual female body. Against this background, my ethnographic data suggest that surgery may also be a tool for women hoping to reduce 'dominating stares' on their bodies by 'normalizing' them (cf. Garland-Thomson 2009) in an attempt to regain control. This, I argue, complicates the 'negative hermeneutics' (Felsky 2006, 273) of feminist approaches to beauty practices that focus on the oppressive, painful and harmful aspects of cosmetic surgeries that these certainly also involve. In line with recent approaches to beauty and cosmetic surgery (Coleman and Figueroa 2010; Elias et al. 2017; Jarrín 2017), I argue for an understanding of these as affective processes embedded in particular biopolitical histories as well as a transnational beauty economy.

In the following, I will discuss feminine beauty and normative body images in Turkey along four major lines, first, in respect of the histori-cal relationship with hegemonic norms of femininity and citizenship in Turkey, where the 'Western' and secular woman has long been a norma-tive ideal, including beauty, one that has been subject to heated debates and transformations in Turkey's recent past. Secondly, as a relationship that cosmetic surgeons and religious experts claim can be 'objectively' determined and treated. Thirdly, as a normative and affective practice engaged in by women to create 'normal-' and 'natural-looking' bodies that no longer defy the norm or, by refraining from aesthetic body mod-ification, that actively violate the norm. Finally, this chapter documents the normalization of aesthetic body modification in urban Turkey, where an increasing number of (young) women, in spite of its risks and possible violation of religious norms, have come to regard cosmetic surgery as a standard practice of bodily grooming and proper self-care.

RESEARCH AND METHODOLOGY

This chapter is part of ongoing research into femininity, beauty work, and aesthetic body modification in Istanbul,[1] drawing on fifteen months of anthropological field research, including five short field trips since 2011 and an uninterrupted period of eleven months of fieldwork in 2013 and 2014. I conducted some one hundred ethnographic guideline interviews, mostly scheduled and recorded, with customers and patients of hair and beauty salons and clinics; beauty salon owners and workers; cosmetic surgeons and other experts, among them tattoo artists; activists in various feminist organizations; a fashion photographer; and an Islamic scholar who rules on the permissibility of beauty treatments. Moreover, the project employs media analysis, including the systematic analysis of newspaper archives, online forums (*Kadinlar Kulübü* and *Fetva Meclisi*), and so-called makeover shows on private television. In 2013 and 2014, I attended the annual Istanbul Beauty and Care Fair and distributed questionnaires among its visitors. I also distributed questionnaires among participants in two municipal training courses on make-up and facial care. The interlocutors selected for presentation in the following are not representative, but they do draw attention to some common themes and issues with regard to aesthetic practices in Istanbul, Turkey.

In focusing on the manufacture of beautiful, feminine, and more generally proper bodies in a particular urban setting, I seek to contribute to a fast-growing body of feminist literature on the politics of beauty. Women's involvement in beauty work has long been criticized as the effect of disciplinary power (Bartky 1990; Bordo 1993; Sawicki 1991) and indeed, as functioning as a pervasive 'beauty myth' that has triggered a feminist backlash in patriarchal societies (Wolf 1991). More recently, however, there has been what Elias et al. (2017, Pos. 366) call a feminist '(re)turn to beauty.' Recent studies have now come to re-centre the affective and future-oriented 'aspiration to normalcy' that is also involved in women's beauty work (Coleman and Figueroa 2010). My research contributes to this debate and is rooted in an inter-sectional critique of earlier feminist approaches to beauty that tended to assume the existence of a generalized female subject who is a 'racially unmarked, implicitly heterosexual woman, of unspecified class' (Craig 2006, 162). Instead, Craig suggests we conceive of individuals and groups as differently located in fields that promote 'particular ways of seeing beauty' (ibid.). Such an approach underlines the importance of ethnographic research on particular economies and cultures of beauty in relation to gendered subjectivities.

Body Aesthetics and Normative Femininity in Urban Turkey

As elsewhere, in urban Turkey the construction of femininity, and with it bodily beauty, is highly normative and excludes certain bodies or else creates pressure to modify them visually. It has long been tied to disciplinary practices that are a prerequisite for achieving what is considered 'the right look.' Being involved in beauty work and bodily self-care is widely expected, and women's failure to do so is commonly associated with a lack of discipline, cleanliness and, more generally, moral degeneration. An oft-quoted saying in beauty salons and clinics is that 'there are no ugly women, just careless ones' (in Turkish, '*çirkin kadın yoktur, bakımsız kadın vardır*'). Urban middle-class women's standard routines of bodily grooming are increasingly relegated to professional beauty service workers and include regular manicures, pedicures, complete body and facial hair removal, eyebrow shaping, the dying or highlighting of hair and, for middle-aged to younger elderly women especially, various anti-ageing treatments. Most importantly, as I will show in what follows, cosmetic surgery has become an ever more normalized technique for (re) shaping bodies so that they correspond to dominant ideals of gender.

However, the visible manufacturing of normative femininities in urban Turkey includes not just beauty (service) work, but also processes of identity politics and self-fashioning. Thus, it is the secular, modern and 'Western' feminine body that has long been the unmarked category in urban Turkey, against which other women have been measured and found wanting as a deviance from the norm. This normative ideal has to be seen within the context of Turkey's nation-building process as a young republic seeking to replace and modernize a supposedly 'degenerate' Ottoman elite, one that nevertheless already regarded itself as a part of European cosmopolitan society based on civilizational principles and the desire for modernity (Aydin 2007). In her analysis of beauty contests in early republican Turkey, A. Holly Shissler (2004, 117) shows the pivotal role of the public presentation of feminine bodily beauty in republicans' attempts to project images of just such a modern and 'civilized' nation. The public presentation of uncovered, yet 'honourable' (in Turkish, *namuslu*) women in state-sponsored beauty contests redefined patriarchal concepts of honour and shame to 'secularize Islam' and 'normalize the female body' (ibid.). The outcome was an imaginary ideal of the secular Republican woman that one pious interlocutor in Jenny White's ethnography on the pious new middle class described as 'blond and modern, also honourable (*namuslu*), clean, sexually honourable (*iffetli*). ... [and wearing] her skirt below the knees' (quoted from White 2013, 141). In recent decades, this hegemonic ideal has been subject to change due to the increased importance of hyper-femininity in contemporary consumer capitalism, with its emphasis on youth and sexual attractiveness in women on the one hand and political changes towards more pious gendered norms on the other.

Much has been written on the role of Islamic dress and sartorial styles in creating new Islamic (elite) lifestyles and feminine subjectivities following the banning of the head scarf in the public sector during the 1980s and 1990s.[2] In an atmosphere of 'hyper-politicization' (Kandiyoti 2015, 8) and ongoing public debate and conflict about gendered roles and norms after the consolidation of power by the conservative and pro-Islamic Justice and Development Party (*Adalet ve Kalkınma Partisi*, AKP) and its increasingly authoritarian rule, women's bodies have recently become a battleground once more between imaginations of modernity and tradition, secularism and Islamism. Today, a new Islamic urban middle class is questioning the taken for granted-ness of the earlier feminine ideal by promoting more pious modes of outer appearance and public behaviour for women. Defying common assumptions, and despite the problematic nature of aesthetic body modification from a religious perspective, upwardly mobile pious women often share a willingness to engage in forms of hyper-feminine beautification and actively negotiate the boundaries of moral permissiveness and bodily appearance (Liebelt 2016). Perhaps as an outcome of these dynamics, as what follows will show, the narrative focus in cosmetic surgery is on the 'right to look normal,' rather than the 'right to be beautiful.'

During the 1990s and early 2000s women in Islamic dress who ventured into the more 'secular' neighbourhoods of Istanbul's upper (middle) classes were commonly subject to verbal abuse and harassment as space intruders (Turam 2013). More recently, an increasing number of stories of attacks on women for dressing 'provocatively' in shorts or miniskirts, sporting 'un-Islamic' tattoos, make-up or piercings and more generally behaving 'loosely'—for example, by kissing or consuming alcohol in public—have gone viral in the social media and the wider public.[3] To varying degrees, however, *all* women are subject to dominant stares that, according to Garland-Thomson (2009, 42), function to regulate looks and may lead those stared at to employ strategies of 'gender and racial passing.' As one interlocutor, Esma,[4] a veteran beauty service worker and beauty school teacher in her early thirties observed:

> [In Turkey today,] there's no one who dresses in a really extravagant way, really. ... If you go to Spain, for example, you see girls dressed in miniskirts, coloured tights and Converse [shoes]. Also in Britain. They might even go to work like this, dressed in sneakers. ... In Turkey, you won't see this. You won't even see young women cutting their hair very short.

The maximum is like this (points to her chin), and they will go to have blow-outs all the time to look presentable. ... People pay much attention to what others might think of them, [wondering:] 'If I do this, what will they think?'; 'If I do this or that, what are they going to say?'; 'How will they look at me?'[5]

The quote illustrates the strong normative ideals of gendered identities and body images in urban Turkey and shows that 'people', as Esma puts it, take great care of what others might think or say or how they might look at them. While she quotes long hair and 'presentable' looks as gendered ideals for women, adherence to such norms, as what follows will show, now prominently includes cosmetic surgery which promises not only to 'beautify,' but also to 'normalize' the body.

BODY AESTHETICS AND THE 'RIGHT TO LOOK NORMAL'

In the past two decades, cosmetic surgery in Turkey has developed from an elite phenomenon associated with the urban *sosiyété* (high society) to an increasingly common procedure among younger and middle-aged women especially. The most common cosmetic surgery procedures in Turkey—in descending order and according to the statistics gathered by the International Society of Aesthetic and Plastic Surgeons (ISAPS 2017)—are rhinoplasty or nose surgery, breast augmentation, liposuction or fat removal surgery, eyelid surgery, and until recently, breast reduction for women. While this list resonates with the global average, as well as with the ISAPS listings for the US, Brazil, Japan, Russia and India, who currently top the list of countries with the highest number of plastic surgery procedures worldwide (ISAPS 2017), nose and breast reduction surgeries are more frequent in Turkey than in any of the countries just listed. As mentioned above, these procedures are commonly called 'ethnic plastic surgery' by cosmetic surgeons in Turkey and associated with particular national or even 'racial' bodily defects. By utilizing 'standard' measures of beauty, cosmetic surgery promises not only to beautify bodies, but also to normalize them.

In contrast to Brazil, where Alex Edmonds (2007) reports cosmetic surgeons proclaiming the 'right to be beautiful,' in Turkey, where the High Commission on Religious Affairs and other religious experts regularly warn that aesthetic body modifications are a 'sin' (*günah*) for both men and women, cosmetic surgeons and their patients more usually champion the 'right to look normal,' framing cosmetic surgery within a discourse of health rather than aesthetics. Religious experts commonly emphasize *inner* beauty in contrast to outer appearance and frequently quote the well-known saying that beauty and ugliness lie in the eye of the beholder. In Sunni Islam and the Hanafi school of thought and jurisdiction, which are dominant in Turkey, changing one's features as created by God and, following a particular hadith, shaping one's eyebrows and tattooing are prohibited (*haram*), an interdiction that has been confirmed by a number of religious commissions and individual clerics.[6] However, even the most staunchly conservative religious experts are prepared to consider exceptions to this rule, for example, if the surgery is predominantly a matter of health or is intended to correct 'inferiority complexes' or bodily 'abnormality,' according to the High Commission on Religious Affairs.[7] In prototypical fashion, Ahmed Şahin, a chaplain at the Istanbul Süleymaniye Mosque, who regularly contributed to and provided advice on cosmetic surgery in the popular conservative daily *Zaman* (1986–2016), differentiates between two cases in response to a reader's query about the permissibility of cosmetic surgery. In the first case, a person looks 'normal' but desires to become more attractive, for example, by changing their nose. In such a case, cosmetic surgery is 'absolutely not permitted' (*haram*) because it means changing 'God's creation' for no good reason. In the second case, an 'extraordinarily ugly' person desires the same surgery because they feel 'disabled' or 'anxious' due to their appearance. In this case, cosmetic surgery is permissible (*caiz*) because it is a 'medical treatment' to 'correct an abnormality.'[8]

This raises the question of how religious experts establish criteria for scrutinizing bodies and measuring bodily 'normality' or 'abnormality.' To this question, another religious scholar and advisor on cosmetic surgery, Nureddin Yıldırım, venerated as Nureddin *Hoca* (teacher Nureddin) by his many followers, replied:

> I mean, there are certain ideal standards in the creation of human beings. What is a standard human being? Women are usually 165 cm in height and men about 170 cm. So, if there is one boy who reaches 220 cm at the age of 18, how to account for that? It is an exception to the norm. Then again, if a lady ties herself up and does stretching to grow taller, this is a different matter altogether. The latter is denying God's creation; the former is what we call a malfunction. It is a [medical] problem, because it is an exception from the standard norm. Like being born with six fingers, or having a

crooked finger... These things can be fixed by cosmetic and plastic surgery.
... Being created as an exception to the norm and being fixed by plastic
surgery – there is no problem according to our religion. It is not up to
us to criticize. We also consider it normal to fix a broken bone. But, for
example, if a 45-year-old man or woman makes themselves look the age of
35, this is forbidden by the religion. It may be considered a form of deceit.
... And both the Prophet Muhammad, peace be upon him, and the Holy
Koran prohibit deception.[9]

The quote illustrates how the description of bodily averages and the
establishment of standard measurements, in this case a person's body
height, function as 'a prescription for normality' (Garland-Thomson
2009, 30). Other examples of permissible cosmetic surgery provided later
on in the same interview included the reduction of large noses that made
'a woman look like a man' and the reduction of female breasts so large
that they created backache and could be considered a 'natural disorder.'

In an age of the medicalization and normalization of invasive procedures, whenever possible the treatment of aesthetic 'abnormalities' is
thus regarded as legitimate even by those who were otherwise quick to
condemn the same kind of procedure because of its potentially deceit-
ful impact, or because it was based on a presumptuous intention that
was disrespectful of divine creation. As in other situations of Islamic
decision-making, the final decision is with the believer, who is forced to
scrutinize his or her intention (*niyet*) to undergo surgery. It should be
emphasized that the arguments put forward by religious experts like Şahin
or Yıldırım, which are widely reported and discussed in the Turkish public
sphere, have a legitimizing impact on decisions regarding cosmetic surgery
regardless of whether patients consider themselves pious or not.

Cosmetic surgeons, even more than religious experts, claimed to be
able to objectively establish and measure bodily 'abnormalities' or 'deformations,' often routinely employing tables of standard measurements
in their medical practice. One interlocutor, Prof. Dr. Ismail Kuran, who
was also President of the Turkish Society of Plastic-Reconstructive and
Cosmetic Surgery in Turkey, championed the idea of a 'mathematics of
beauty':

[In cosmetic surgery,] you need mathematics. Even on the face, on most
parts of the body, you can use mathematics. I have been employing these
measurements, not only on the nose, but also on the breast, and now this

[procedure] has become a standard method to decide about the right implant, the right width, the right projection [in breast surgery].... I think mathematics is a very important part of the *scientific* process and for those [who believe that] cosmetic surgery cannot be taken only as an artistic study. It is a combination of science and artistry, so you have to develop some kind of measurements to regulate your practice.[10]

When, for example, I wondered how these measurements responded to patients' different and changing desires, given the recent trend towards smaller breasts, he responded:

Of course, there are fashions, but we should also talk about the *optimum*. I am not talking about trends here. You might want a bigger breast, but there are limits. What happens if your shoe number is 39 and you try to use [a shoe of the size] 35? – it's impossible! What if you use 45? It will be loose. Just like our feet or hands, breasts have a size to start with. This includes the width and height, and if you go beyond your limits, you're in trouble. ... There are more than five hundred different types [of breast implants, in terms of] shape, height, width and projection. So, breasts are an important area for the decision-making process with mathematics, actually.

As will have become clear, Prof. Kuran's understanding of bodily aesthetics relies on the idea of a universal, transcultural 'optimum' that clearly extends beyond cultural or personal taste, not to speak of fashion. Elsewhere in the interview, Prof. Kuran called this quality 'harmony,' with a beautiful person being someone 'who has harmony about her body and face.' This kind of bodily harmony was clearly measurable, and the fact that his medical practice relied on the refashioning of bodies in accordance with a sample of 'standard measurements' indeed qualified it as science, in contrast to an understanding of cosmetic surgery as merely 'artistry.' As Jarrín (2017, 134–35) notes, in Brazil, plastic surgeons conceptualize cosmetic surgery as a strategy for harmonizing patients' somatic features in association with the idea of treating the 'miscegenation' of Brazilian society. On the background of a historical linkage of cosmetic surgery with eugenic thought, Brazilian cosmetic surgeons established a 'right for beauty' that is tied to nationalist narratives of progress (ibid., 54–65).

To sum up, in their medical and theological practices respectively, cosmetic surgeons and religious experts in Turkey likewise assume that 'normal' looks can be objectively established. They regard the treatment of bodies that defy standard norms of appearance as a 'right' untouched by moral objections or religious bans. I will now turn to female patients' cosmetic surgery practices, namely breast and nose surgeries, that are intended to create 'normal-' and 'natural-looking' bodies that no longer defy the norm.

Reshaping 'Turkish' Breasts

Human breasts are a symbol of femininity, and the popular imagination often seems to regard them as its measure. Thus, in her insightful book on *Staring*, Rosemarie Garland-Thomson writes that '[t]oo much breast means too much femininity; too little breast means not enough' (2009, 143). Given that women's breasts come in very diverse shapes and sizes, Garland-Thomson remarks upon the astonishing fact that, in the ubiquitous media images of them, they 'look remarkably uniform' (ibid., 147). This too is the case in Turkey, where women use various techniques, including (push up) brassieres, breast-shaping treatments in beauty salons and cosmetic surgery, to change the size and shape of their breasts, and indeed, as the following account of Özge's breast reduction surgery will show, to 'normalize' them.

Since the early 2000s, there has been a global trend towards smaller breasts, which has also impacted on Turkey, where during the early 2000s, according to the acting general secretary of the Chamber of Turkish plastic reconstructive and aesthetic surgeons, Ali Barutçu, the ideal breast size fell 'from 85 to 80 [cm]', with the exception of performing artists, who apparently continued to prefer larger breasts.[11] The same report goes on to quote him saying that '[b]reast reduction surgery reduces stress in social life while it also improves the quality of women's everyday life and their success in working life.' The following account will help to understand in what ways women's breasts could possibly be linked with social stress, the quality of life and professional success in contemporary urban Turkey.

Özge, a mathematics teacher at a private college and a cheerful woman in her mid-thirties with accurately shaped eyebrows, short black hair and a preference for casual dress, framed her breast reduction surgery within a discourse of patriarchal oppression of the sexualized female body in Turkey. Early on in the interview, Özge distanced herself from 'those women who easily have cosmetic surgery,' stating that for her, 'cosmetic surgery had always been, well, something that popular culture *enforces* upon women.'[12] Instead, she emphasized the health aspect of her surgery, which resulted in the removal of two kilos of fat from her breasts, as her main motivation for undergoing the procedure. However, when I expected Özge to continue talking about backaches, an ailment women seeking breast reduction surgery often reported suffering from, she told me about the restriction of movement she experienced as the result of the 'over-sexualization' of her pre-surgery body. In order to explain what she meant by this, she recounted the restrictive atmosphere of her coming of age as the daughter of rural-urban migrants in a working-class neighbourhood in Istanbul during the conservative post-military putsch era of the 1980s:

> We were raised in the culture of the neighbourhood [*mahalle*]. At those times, girls who had their periods and whose breasts started growing, they couldn't play outside anymore. It was a society that forced you to grow up early. … If this [menstruation and the development of female breasts] happens too early, it is a disadvantage for the girl. I remember feeling ashamed [because of my breasts]. My friends were saying: 'Are they really this big?' Such kind of things really troubled me. I had many problems during adolescence. I felt it [my body/breast] was ugly. … I mean, as a kid, you want to play outside with your friends, but your physique has turned you into a woman from one day to the other. In this [cultural] context, I experienced puberty too early.

During high school, Özge remembered being constantly on a diet, trying to reduce the size of her breasts. Dieting, however, proved useless, she said, because, pointing to her breasts laughingly, 'Everything I ate went there!' While Özge attempted to reduce the sexualized femininity of her body by loosing weight, she felt she was becoming ever more attractive to men:

> Girls are sexual objects in Turkey. For example, if your hips are big, it is not considered erotic. But if you are slim and your breasts are big, you're like 'very sexy.' … Like I said, you can have a big body and just be a fat person, but me – my body was thin, I was so thin. My size in clothes was 36, and my breast measurement was like 100 [cm], so these two things combined made me look too sexy.

This resulted in ever more (self-chosen) confinement, because whenever she ventured out alone Özge felt men staring at her breasts, with some also harassing her verbally. Accordingly, she tried to hide her breasts under 'layers of loose clothing.' It was only after breast reduction surgery that Özge felt she was no longer being stared at and happily proclaimed that now, quoting her cosmetic surgeon, she had 'standard-size breasts.' As soon as the bandages were removed, she went shopping for a new and indeed sexier set of clothes, including tight T-shirts and, for the first time in her life, a bikini. Now that her body was 'normal' and she felt she was in a position to control and regulate her publicly visible attractiveness better, men's stares no longer made her feel vulnerable. While her choice to undergo cosmetic surgery met with a divided response from her feminist friends, Özge felt that it had earned her respect among her female colleagues at the private college where she taught and where many female employees engaged in various forms of aesthetic body modification.

In contrast to Özge, who was single when she undertook breast surgery, many younger interlocutors intended to postpone their breast reduction surgeries until after they got married and had had children, fearing that the surgery might impact on their ability to breastfeed or else harm their attractiveness for their sexual partners, who were commonly assumed to prefer larger female breasts. This was the case with Sevda, the fashion-conscious daughter of a beauty salon owner in the conservative neighbourhood of Fatih, who fantasized about breast reduction surgery. Sevda's large breasts made her feel uncomfortable about her body, especially since she knew from female relatives who suffered from the same kind of 'problem' that these tended to become even larger after giving birth and breastfeeding. While Sevda's maternal grandmother had undergone breast reduction surgery several years earlier, other relatives shunned the procedure out of moral and religious conviction. Among them was her aunt, whose breasts Sevda had recently and accidentally seen naked, an encounter that continued to haunt her. For Sevda, her aunt's breasts made her look like 'the typical old peasant woman (*köylü kadın*),'[13] namely those in her family's hometown in the Black Sea region, who had given birth and breastfed many children. Inheriting this look, Sevda confided, was among her greatest fears.

Talking to me about her breasts shortly before and again shortly after she got married, Sevda was still not prepared to undergo surgery. She knew that her husband actually 'liked' her larger breasts and feared that reducing them might prove risky for their sexual relationship. As a 'good wife,' she hoped to seek his consent in the near future, perhaps after giving birth and breastfeeding, which would provide her with the opportunity to frame the surgery as a form of postnatal 'reconstructive' surgery that also had a health aspect to it, namely the reduction of backache.

In postponing breast reduction surgery, Sevda was juggling contrasting expectations of her as a young urban, modern and sexually attractive woman. These expectations and her related fears were tied to two distinctive connotations of larger female breasts in Turkey, on the one hand the erotic female breast as a strong symbol of sensuality and sexuality, commonly seen as desirable by male sexual partners, and on the other hand the maternal breast, signifying fertility and exuberance but also, in the popular imagination, a characteristic of the devalued peasant woman. As indicated by common caricatures of the *köylü kadın*, as well as media coverage of the topic,[14] if not carried by an urban upper-class woman or a performing artist, larger female breasts risked linking its wearer with a lower social status and those regions most readily associated with peripheral rural life in Istanbul, namely the Black Sea or the Anatolian southeast.

Changing the size of their breasts was never an easy choice for women, one that was commonly hidden from or else had to be negotiated with relatives and/or sexual partners. Within more conservative or, as in Özge's case, feminist circles, decisions about breast reduction surgery were commonly framed within a discourse of medical normalization and health, rather than aesthetics. Moreover, women whose parents, like Özge's and Sevda's, had been part of the large influx of rural-urban migrants to Istanbul in the 1960s and 1970s seemed to be especially haunted by the symbolic connection between larger female breasts and rural cloddishness. However, as exemplified by Sevda's hesitation to undergo surgery and Özge's account of men's predatory stares at her pre-surgery breasts, they were also well aware of the normative link between larger female breasts, sexual attractiveness and gendered roles, carefully weighing their surgery decisions against it. In spite of the high costs, pain and risks involved, the reshaping of breasts seen as 'abnormal' was commonly seen as a powerful way of managing one's adherence to gendered norms. To Özge, her surgical choice to go for more 'standard-size' breasts seemed an almost subversive act against the ever more sexualized, hyper-feminine bodily ideals that for many years had made her the object of dominating male stares and subsequently, restriction of movement. On the other hand, it was also embedded in a professional environment of socially aspiring women, who clearly knew how to take care of themselves and actively participated in the booming beauty service economy.

Reshaping 'Turkish' Noses

As mentioned above, the idea of an aesthetic optimum is deeply racialized in Turkey, with 'large' female breasts and noses being considered especially problematic and widely associated with more peripheral regions in Turkey, and more generally, rural backwardness. Rather than being considered a national characteristic per se, 'big' or 'hooked' noses are linked with the Black Sea region and the Anatolian southeast in particular. For example, in an interview with the *Hürriyet* daily newspaper in 2006, cosmetic surgeon Prof. Dr. Onur Erol, himself a media star in Turkey and internationally renowned for his so-called Turkish Delight-nose surgery technique (Erol 2000), talked about different types of 'deformed' noses in need of correction, differentiating between the 'big and pointed noses' of the Black Sea population and the 'big and fleshy noses' of those originating in the Turkish southeast.[15] As the religious scholar Nureddin Yıldırım, mentioned above, put it, '[w]omen especially are obsessed with their noses ... Actually, in Turkey, in the Black Sea and in eastern regions, women *do* have big noses. So when they migrate to big cities like Istanbul, they think they draw attention to themselves.' While interlocutors rarely linked their decisions about nose surgery with migration directly, they nevertheless often half-jokingly stated their desire to change their 'Turkish' or 'Greek' noses into smaller 'French' ones, reflecting yet another geography of beauty.

Among them was Ruken, a 23-year-old woman who was introduced to me by her uncle, a friend of mine, shortly after she moved in with his family while flat-hunting in Istanbul. About a year prior to our first meeting, she had graduated from university and taken up employment as a lawyer in Izmir, where her family had resettled from the eastern Anatolian region of Tunceli/Dersim during the Kurdish uprising and violent armed conflicts in the region during the 1990s. Shortly before starting to apply for jobs in Istanbul and eventually moving there, Ruken had undergone nose surgery to remove her 'bump,'[16] as she put it. Arriving for our interview in a café in central Istanbul straight from a lecture given by the well-known philosopher and feminist-socialist writer Gülnur Acar-Savran, Ruken joked about the irony of talking to me about her cosmetic surgery right after having listened to a lecture on feminism, something she clearly perceived as a contradiction in terms. She quickly moved on to tell me how important the surgery had been for her, after many years of suffering from a nose that had made her feel 'really ugly,' even 'handicapped.'

She had fantasized about nose surgery ever since her childhood, but was forced to wait until she was finally able to pay for it out of her own savings, this being the first major purchase from her own income. With her new, smaller nose, she felt perfectly equipped to start 'a new chapter in life,' as she told me, and prepared for moving to Istanbul. About ten months after the surgery, with a new position in an Istanbul-based law firm and all signs of surgery gone, Ruken happily recounted how finally she felt 'perfectly normal.' Indeed, she expressed surprise at the fact that her initial euphoria about her long desired new nose had quickly given way to a sense of 'normal everyday life.' While she had not talked to her new colleagues or Istanbul friends about the surgery, she knew of others having had the same type of surgery. She mused that for young upwardly mobile women in Istanbul, a smaller nose or else cosmetic surgery were simply 'part of the deal.'

There is a history of the operated nose in Turkey, with the President of the Chamber of Plastic Reconstructive and Aesthetic surgery in Turkey telling me that 'it used to be a [pre-]fabricated operation before: small noses with upturned tips.' This earlier aesthetics of the 'standard' operated nose, popularized by Turkish celebrities such as pop star and cosmetic surgery afficionada Ajda Pekkan, who had her first nose surgery in the mid-1960s, were now widely rejected as 'overdone,' 'artificial' or even 'tasteless,' especially if performed by patients from lower social strata, who might engage in cosmetic surgery as a form of conspicuous consumption. Instead, many cosmetic surgery patients and surgeons were concerned with what were commonly called 'natural' designs. These were seen as being both in line with the aesthetic standards of the day and hardly recognizable as having been operated upon. Ruken, mentioned above, had also been concerned about acquiring a 'natural-looking' nose and engaged in much research along these lines in preparation for her surgery, especially in the large nose surgery section of the popular online forum Women's Club (*Kadınlar Kulübü*).[17] With the help of this virtual community, she had chosen a surgeon who was renowned for his 'natural' nose surgery designs. When this surgeon suggested that Ruken return with the picture of someone whose nose she liked, her resulting query posted in the forum triggered a long debate on natural-looking designs. While some uploaded pictures of celebrities, whose noses they liked for their naturalness—among them that of the Turkish model and actress Deniz Akkaya, rumoured to have had her own nose modelled after the looks of US American model Liv Tylor by celebrity surgeon Onur Erol—others warned that emulating another person's nose posed a great threat to natural looks.

The common reference to 'naturalness' with regard to bodily aesthetics is closely linked to the ideal of looking 'normal', yet it also relies on a particular aesthetic style that draws heavily on current discourses of the beauty industry. In its claim to produce 'naturalness,' this discourse relies on an understanding of the body as something that has to be made, preferably through the consumption of beauty services and cosmetics, rather than something that has been given. Among interlocutors, naturalness as the outcome of surgery was an important criterion in talking about satisfaction with their surgery, with those remaining dissatisfied claiming that surgery had made them look 'unnatural.' Among them was Sibel, a middle-aged entrepreneur, who, thirteen years after her first nose surgery procedure, lamented that, by changing her 'kind of characteristic nose' into an unnatural-looking smaller one, she had 'turned into a regular cosmetically touched woman.'[18] While for Sibel too 'normalizing' her nose had been a major motivating factor for surgery, paradoxically the standardization of her body as an unnatural-looking one that had been operated on becomes similarly problematic.

Indeed, in the 2010s, the aesthetic modification of noses had become so common among young, upwardly mobile women in Istanbul that the decision of individual women not to undergo surgery was commonly seen as a very 'brave' or 'cool' choice, even as a fashion statement. Talking about her favourite Turkish model, Didem Soydan, a female fashion photographer told me: 'She is blond, she has blue eyes, she's one of the most popular models [in Turkey] – *and* she has a big nose! I think she is *so cool!*'[19]

In an age of consumer capitalism that makes one desire and easily achieve the 'right look' through cosmetic surgery, Didem Soydan's 'big' nose, which seemed to defy the dominant beauty norms, could indeed be interpreted as a 'cool' countercultural aesthetic move. Engaged in by someone who otherwise conformed to dominant beauty ideals, Soydan's 'refusal' of cosmetic surgery of course did little to destabilize the pressure to 'normalize' bodies for Ruken or others. Instead, the decision not to reshape one's 'Turkish' nose (or breast, for that matter) was beyond debate for those less firmly established within the urban geography of fashion and beauty, even if, like Özge or Ruken, they shared feminist positions that were critical of beauty.

Conclusion

This chapter contributes to the debate on standardization in bodily appearance by describing the normalization of cosmetic surgery in Turkey's recent past, especially with regard to women's nose and breast (reduction) surgery. Given the construal of large female breasts and noses as particularly prevalent and problematic in urban Turkey, the treatment of these bodily 'deformations,' in medical language, was commonly narrated as based on an affective desire for, and indeed a right to, a 'normal' rather than (merely) 'beautiful' look.

Whereas early republicans were eager to emphasize that Turks formed a homogenous 'race,' with predominantly light skin and eyes and a straight nose, thereby idealizing the look of the founder of the Turkish Republic, Mustafa Kemal 'Atatürk,' as the perfect representation of this type (Özyürek 2004, 219), in contemporary aesthetic discourses a rather heterogeneous image and ideal of national 'mixed-ness' is emerging. At the same time, hitherto dominant (secular) gendered norms have been challenged by the rise of a conservative urban middle class, as well as ideals and images of hyper-femininity in the global market. Similar to what Edmonds discusses with reference to cosmetic surgery in Brazil, rather than creating room for manoeuvre for women by making it possible for them to conform to one of many different models of gendered beauty, the national ideal of 'mixed-ness' puts additional pressure on women to conform to the demand to 'take care of oneself.' Given the demands of hyper-feminine outer appearances in an age of consumer capitalism and medicalization, taking care of oneself also comes to include invasive forms of beautification, such as cosmetic surgery.

Moreover, similar to Brazil, where northeasterners hope to become upwardly mobile by 'getting rid of the noses that mark them as rural migrants' (Jarrín 2017, 135), there is an imagined national geography of beauty in Turkey, where the large influx of domestic migrants from the Black Sea and south-eastern Anatolia to Istanbul has led to a particular form of social distinction by long-term urban residents. Female breasts and noses, as well as their surgical modification, are imbued with specific meanings in this particular location, with large breasts, for example, connoting both erotic femininity and rural backwardness, depending on who has them and at what point in the lifecourse. Tanıl Bora (2010) analyses the stereotypes of the urban and secular elite, the so-called White Turks, towards those who do not qualify as modern city-dwellers in their eyes as a form of 'racism that has an emphasis on class, relating social differences of people with cultural and even physical characteristics.'

Immigrants to the city or those living in more marginal neighbourhoods are scrutinized visually for not belonging fully and may thus put particular emphasis on reshaping their bodies to conform to certain gendered ideals concerning their appearance. For them, intensive beauty work proves especially tricky, because both their bodies *and* their aesthetic bodily modifications may give away their more peripheral regional backgrounds, especially if the latter produce 'unnatural' results.

To sum up, there are strong normative ideals of gendered images and subjectivity in urban Turkey that are regulated not only by patriarchal control of the female sexual body, but also by affective desires and an ethos of women taking care of themselves. As argued above, the negative hermeneutics of earlier feminist studies of beauty failed to grasp this complexity. Cosmetic surgery patients, many of whom are aware of and even share the feminist critique of beauty, still manage to draw satisfaction from and legitimize their efforts to beautify themselves as a form of 'normalization.' Beauty, writes Alex Edmonds (2007, 371), in his ethnography of cosmetic surgery in Brazil, 'can become a "right" during a neoliberal regime where rights are re-interpreted as access to goods and the antidote to social exclusion is imagined as market participation.' For the young women portrayed in this chapter, the consumption of cosmetic surgery is an often hard-earned, albeit double-edged 'right' that may indeed enable them to move more freely and participate in the urban economy embedded in a particular history of biopolitics within a transnational imaginary.

Notes

1. This chapter is based on a larger study supported by the German Research Foundation (No. LI 2357/1-1) and the Chair for Social Anthropology at the University of Bayreuth, in affiliation with the Department of Sociology of Boğaziçi University.
2. See, for example, Çınar (2005), Gökarıksel (2009, 2012), Gökarıksel and Secor (2009, 2010), Navaro-Yashin (2002, 78–113), Secor (2001), Turam (2013), and White (2002, 29–55, 212–41).
3. See, for example, the Turkish daily *Cumhuriyet Gazetesi* from 17 July 2016, available online at http://www.cumhuriyet.com.tr/video/video_haber/568899/Moda_da_gericiler_cimlerde_oturan_vatandaslara_saldirdi.html (accessed 14 February 2017).

4. The names of research sites and participants without a public role or function have been replaced with pseudonyms throughout this article.

5. Interview with Esma, 3 April 2014.

6. For example, the Religious Commission Committee in Konya prohibited cosmetic surgery in 2000 (*Hürriyet* 2000. Konya müftülügü: estetik günah [Konya Religious Commission Committee: Aesthetic Surgery Is a Sin]. *Hürriyet*, 19 December), the grand mufti of Istanbul, Ahmet Okutan, in 2005 (Ferah, Metin 2005. Ameliyatla güzelligi dinimiz tasvip etmez [Our Religion Does Not Agree to Beauty through surgery]. *Hürriyet*, September 10) and the mufti of Edirne, Ömer Taşcıoglu, in 2009 (*Hürriyet* 2009. Edirne Müftüsü: Estetik yaptırmak günah [The Edirne Religious Commission Committee: To Undergo Aesthetic Surgery Is a Sin]. *Hürriyet*, July 17).

7. Quoted from Özdemir, Şemsinur 2005. Estetik ameliyat ruh sağlığını bozuyor. *Zaman*, 5 June.

8. Şahin, Ahmed 1995. Estetik ameliyat caiz olabilir mi? [Can Aesthetic Surgery Be Permissible?] *Zaman*, 20 July.

9. Interview with Nureddin Yıldırım, 22 October 2013. The following quotes by Yıldırım are also taken from this interview.

10. Interview with Ismail Kuran, 10 July 2014. The following quotes by Kuran are also taken from this interview.

11. Hürriyet 2002. Kadınların tercihi artık küçük göğüs [Women Now Prefer Small Breasts]. *Hürriyet*, 17 March.

12. Interview with Özge, 21 January 2014. The following quotes by Özge are also taken from this interview.

13. Interview with Sevda, 21 July 2014. The following quotes by Sevda are also taken from this interview.

14. For example, in an article about breast reduction surgery published in the *Hürriyet* daily, the focus of reporting on the topic is on southeastern Anatolia, where, the authors claim, the waiting period for breast reduction surgeries is six months in the leading regional university hospital, and surgeons no longer give out appointments (Hürriyet 2010. Bu ameliyat için 6 ay sıra yok [For This Surgery, the Waiting Time Is Six Months]. *Hürriyet*, 28 October).

15. Quoted from Hürriyet 2006. Dünyanın en güzel kadınları Türkler [The Most Beautiful Women in the World Are Turkish]. *Hürriyet*, 6 December.

16. Interview with Ruken, 10 March 2012. The following quotes by Ruken are also taken from this interview.

17. See http://kadinlarkulubu.com/portal/ (accessed 4 March 2016).

18. Interview with Sibel, 15 January 2014.

19. Interview with Demet, 18 December 2013. In spring 2015, the tabloid press reported that Didem Soydan did have nose surgery (see, for example, Posta 2015. Didem Soydan burnunu neden yaptırdı? [Why Did

Didem Soydan Have Her Nose Done?] *Posta Magazine*, 15 May, online: http://www.posta.com.tr/didem-soydan-burnunu-neden-yaptirdi-fotograflihaberi-282173, accessed 28 September 2017).

References

Aydin, Cemil. 2007. *The Politics of Anti-westernism in Asia: Visions of World Order in Pan-Islamic and Pan-Asian Thought*. New York: Columbia University Press.

Bartky, Sandra L. 1990. *Femininity and Domination: Studies in the Phenomenology of Oppression*. New York: Routledge.

Bora, Tanıl. 2010. "Beyaz Türkler tartışması—kırlı beyaz." *Birikim* 260: 25–37 [Turkish].

Bordo, Susan. 1993. *Unbearable Weight: Feminism, Western Culture, and the Body*. Berkeley and Los Angeles: University of California Press.

Çınar, Alev. 2005. *Modernity, Islam and Secularism in Turkey: Bodies, Places and Time*. Minneapolis: The University of Minnesota Press.

Coleman, Rebecca, and Mónica Moreno Figueroa. 2010. "Past and Future Perfect? Beauty, Affect and Hope." *Journal for Cultural Research* 14 (4): 357–73.

Craig, Maxine L. 2006. "Race, Beauty, and the Tangled Knot of Guilty Pleasure." *Feminist Theory* 7 (2): 159–77.

Edmonds, Alex. 2007. "'The Poor Have the Right to Be Beautiful': Cosmetic Surgery in Neoliberal Brazil." *Journal of the Royal Anthropological Institute* 13 (2): 363–81.

Elias, Ana Sofia, Rosalind Gill, and Christina Scharff, eds. 2017. *Aesthetic Labour: Rethinking Beauty Politics in Neoliberalism*. London: Palgrave Macmillan.

Erol, Onur Ö. 2000. "The Turkish Delight: A Pliable Graft for Rhinoplasty." *Plastic & Reconstructive Surgery* 105 (6): 2229–41.

Felski, Rita. 2006. "'Because It Is Beautiful' New Feminist Perspectives on Beauty." *Feminist Theory* 7 (2): 273–82.

Garland-Thomson, Rosemarie. 2009. *Staring: How We Look*. Oxford: Oxford University Press.

Gilman, Sander L. 1999. *Making the Body Beautiful: A Cultural History of Aesthetic Surgery*. Princeton and Oxford: Princeton University Press.

Gökarıksel, Banu. 2009. "Beyond the Officially Sacred: Religion, Secularism and the Body in the Production of Subjectivity." *Social and Cultural Geography* 10 (6): 657–74.

Gökarıksel, Banu. 2012. "The Intimate Politics of Secularism and the Headscarf: The Mall, the Neighborhood, and the Public Square in Istanbul." *Gender, Place & Culture: A Journal of Feminist Geography* 19 (1): 1–20.

Gökarıksel, Banu, and Anna J. Secor. 2009. "New Transnational Geographies of Islamism, Capitalism, and Subjectivity: The Veiling-Fashion Industry in Turkey." *Area* 41 (1): 6–18.

Gökarıksel, Banu, and Anna J. Secor. 2010. "Between Fashion and Tesettür: Marketing and Consuming Veiling-Fashion." *Journal of Middle East Women's Studies* 6 (3): 118–48.

ISAPS. 2017. *The International Study on Aesthetic/Cosmetic Procedures Performed in 2016.* Press Release on 27 June. Available at: http://www.isaps.org/Media/Default/Current%20News/GlobalStatistics2016.pdf (28 August 2017).

Jarrín, A. 2017. *The Biopolitics of Beauty: Cosmetic Citizenship and Affective Capital in Brazil.* Oakland: University of California Press.

Kandiyoti, Deniz. 2015. "The Gender Wars in Turkey: A Litmus Test of Democracy?" In *The State of Democracy in Turkey: Institutions, Society and Foreign Relations*, vol. 4, edited by Katerina Dalacoura and Hakan Seckinelgin, 8–14. LSE Working Papers.

Liebelt, Claudia. 2016. "Grooming Istanbul: Intimate Encounters and Concerns in Turkish Beauty Salons." *Journal of Middle East Women's Studies* 12 (2): 181–202.

Mann, Denise. 2014. "Ethnic Plastic Surgery: What's in a Name?" *Plastic Surgery Practice* 8 (6) (21 August). Accessed 5 October 2016. http://www.plasticsurgerypractice.com/2014/08/editor-ethnic-plastic-surgery-whats-name/.

Navaro-Yashin, Yael. 2002. *Faces of the State: Secularism and Public Life in Turkey.* Princeton: Princeton University Press.

Özyürek, Esra. 2004. "Miniaturizing Atatürk: Privatization of the State Imagery and Ideology in Turkey." *American Ethnologist* 31 (3): 374–91.

Sawicki, Jana. 1991. *Disciplining Foucault: Feminism, Power, and the Body.* New York and London: Routledge.

Secor, Anna J. 2001. "Toward a Feminist Counter-Geopolitics: Gender, Space and Islamist Politics in Istanbul." *Space and Polity* 5 (3): 191–211.

Shissler, Holly. 2004. "Beauty Is Nothing to Be Ashamed of: Beauty Contests as Tools of Women's Liberation in Early Republican Turkey." *Comparative Studies of South Asia, Africa and the Middle East* 24: 107–22.

Slupchynskyj, Oleh. 2005. "Ethnic Rhinoplasty." *Plastic Surgery Practice*, 7 September. Accessed 5 October 2016. http://www.plasticsurgerypractice.com/2005/09/ethnic-rhinoplasty/.

Turam, Berna. 2013. "The Primacy of Space in Politics: Bargaining Rights, Freedom and Power in an İstanbul Neighborhood." *International Journal of Urban and Regional Research* 37 (2): 409–29.

White, Jenny B. 2002. *Islamist Mobilization in Turkey: A Study in Vernacular Politics.* Seattle and London: University of Washington Press.

White, Jenny B. 2013. *Muslim Nationalism and the New Turks.* Princeton and Oxford: Princeton University Press.

Wolf, Naomi. 1991. *The Beauty Myth: How Images of Beauty Are Used Against Women.* New York: William Morrow & Co.

CHAPTER 8

Fashioning the Female Muslim Face: From 'Hiding One's Beauty' to 'Managing One's Beauty'

R. Arzu Ünal

Tesettür is an inclusive term that refers not only to the religiously inspired Muslim dress, but also more broadly to the cultivation of a modest pious self that is not restricted to clothing. Beyond the binary of veiled and unveiled sartorial styles, fashioning a pious, modest self requires a more complex and nuanced way of managing one's appearance. Instead of examining how Turkish-Dutch Muslim women deal with the stigma of being members of a sartorial minority in the Netherlands, my research explores the ambivalent meanings and contested practices of being visibly Muslim by focusing on a more commonly shared practice: the application of makeup among *tesettürlü* women.

Using certain amounts of cosmetics in a proper manner has become a common yet a highly contested practice in fashioning a modest *tesettür* appearance. In particular, wearing make-up is a challenging practice, as it is often promoted to make a person look more attractive. There is a thin, ambiguous line between a healthy natural look and an attractive look.

R. Arzu Ünal (✉)
University of Amsterdam, Amsterdam, The Netherlands

© The Author(s) 2019
C. Liebelt et al. (eds.), *Beauty and the Norm*,
Palgrave Studies in Globalization and Embodiment,
https://doi.org/10.1007/978-3-319-91174-8_8

177

As I will show in this chapter, the tension between proper care of the self and making oneself attractive is a daily dilemma in Turkish-Dutch women's practice of *tesettür*, because looking healthy may also be considered beautiful and attractive.

This chapter is based on ethnographic fieldwork carried out primarily in several Dutch cities between 2007 and 2011 among women from the Turkish immigrant community, along with brief periods of research in Turkey.[1] It draws on a combination of in-depth interviews with fifty-six women, participant observation, and 'wardrobe research' (Woodward 2007), as well as the compilation of a large number of topical life stories focusing on dress and the body. I tried to include pious women from different backgrounds and generations, even if many of my interlocutors were part of the same network of Turkish religious communities (namely *Diyanet*, *Milli Görüş*, the *Nurcu* and the *Süleymanlı* Communities); I also chose to include as many different women as possible in terms of *tesettür* understandings, styles and preferences.

I aim to move beyond the binary between being covered and uncovered, secular and religious, to understand how pious Muslim women strategically fashion their appearance differently in various social contexts. My research thus records changing meanings of beauty and practices of make-up through the accounts of pious Muslim women from different generations and lifestyles, as well as in the course of migration. I argue that fashioning the Muslim female body is not simply a matter of covering (parts of) one's body, in other words, hiding one's beauty, but of managing one's beauty as well.

In the early years of migration, women originally from Turkey were not scrutinized for being recognizably Muslim; Turkish-Dutch women have only been 'discovered' as Muslim migrants in recent decades (Moors 2009a; Sunier 1995). The effects of 9/11 and, more locally, the assassination of the Dutch film director Theo Van Gogh in 2004 heightened the visibility of Muslims in the Netherlands. As across Western Europe more generally, political discourse increasingly targeted Muslims' sexualities, bodily attitudes and clothing as indicative of their unwillingness to join the wider society and of the threat they posed to European identity (Bowen 2011; Bracke 2011; Dwyer 1999; Fadil 2009; Moors 2009b; Scott 2007; van der Veer 2006).

Migration entailed a transformation of sartorial preferences and beauty practices for almost all women, albeit to different extents. Certain sartorial aesthetics and understandings of beauty were seen as indicating women's success or failure to integrate into Dutch society. Women who succeeded in adopting a modern urban dress code attained more privileged professional positions than women who were considered to be 'still' wearing their 'traditional' clothing, whether this was seen as ethnic, rural or religious (Ünal 2013b). Adopting the aesthetics of a modern wardrobe and incorporating the new gestures and postures that these garments required played a significant role in these women's formation as modern subjects.

The typical tendency in academic studies of and discourse about the image of Muslim women commonly revolved around the headscarf, which for decades has been discussed in isolation from wider social, economic and political changes. This strong emphasis on one particular style of headscarf, namely the 'modern Islamic headscarf', reduces the meanings and significations of what it means to look Muslim to ideological explanations. The debate on the 'modern Islamic headscarf' was shaped by binary narratives of submission and resistance, being covered or not, the religious and the secular, the modern and traditional (El-Guindi 1981; Göle 2003; Kavakçı 2010; Macleod 1991), which failed to take into account the complex meanings and ambivalent practices of being visibly Muslim.

The more recent literature has been inspired by consumer studies and urban studies, and latterly by fashion and dress studies, which have enabled new, multiple readings of the headscarf to emerge (Kılıçbay and Binark 2002; Moors and Tarlo 2007, 2013; Navaro-Yashin 2002; Sandıkçı and Ger 2007; Secor and Gökarıksel 2008; Ünal and Moors 2012). Studies of 'Islamic fashion' have directed attention to women's management of visibility, which has also entailed a move away from the focus on headscarves to include the rest of one's appearance (Clarke 2015; Liebelt 2016; Tarlo 2010; Ünal 2013a). Furthermore, new anthropological research has expanded the scope of studies on Muslim female subjects by emphasizing the significance of other activities that women engage in, such as sports and leisure (Deeb and Harb 2013; Rana 2017; Sehlikoğlu 2016; Sehlikoğlu and Karataş 2016), beyond the binary of the un/veiled woman. Contributions from scholars in various fields have articulated multiple new forms of lived Islam, from fashion to sexuality, from architecture to food and music. In doing so, this new literature has begun to convey the more complex, ambiguous character of pious subjectivities and being visibly Muslim (Bilge 2010; Gökarıksel and Secor 2012; Özyeğin 2015; Saktanber 2002; Sandıkçı and Ger 2010; Schielke and Debevec 2012). Similarly, I approached accounts of beauty and make-up as means to move beyond binaries of the existing literature on the female Muslim body and to trace intimate, tactical, nuanced and ambivalent ways of self-fashioning among pious Turkish-Dutch women in the Netherlands.

Knowing the correct amount and style of make-up to apply at the right moment is an important tool of beauty management. A well-groomed face as the marker of proper care of the self and the ways in which such a face is perceived in specific contexts produce different concerns about make-up. Managing one's beauty is about performing 'appropriate femininity' at the right time and place through acquired knowledge and skills (Black 2004, 71–75). The presence of specific individuals (*mahrem* or *namahrem*),[2] spatial boundaries (indoors or outdoors) and different social events (from weddings to funerals) require different ethical and aesthetic judgments in relation to both the quality and quantity of one's make-up. There are certain occasions when the same style and amount of make-up produces the opposite effect, as these occasions require different presentations of femininity and religious modesty. As the following will show, generational differences, lifestyles and religious beliefs all play an important role in shifting interpretations of modesty, practices of beauty and notions of care for the self. Women's narratives about wearing make-up highlight different aspects of this transformation and illustrate the different effects that make-up has on different publics.

The issues surrounding make-up are complex, not only because of different interpretations of women's adornment according to religious understandings of modesty, but also because women refer to different concepts of beauty, intimacy and femininity in fashioning their everyday appearance (Abbas 2015; Liebelt 2016; Moors 2007; Tarlo 2007; Ünal 2013b). Not least, *tesettür* fashion catalogues and magazines closely follow mainstream fashion trends, including with regard to make-up; models often wear a certain amount of make-up, which is deemed necessary for fashion photography. By focusing on distinct styles and amounts of make-up—both commonly worn 'invisible make-up' (minimal make-up) and occasionally worn visible or heavy ('*ağır*') make-up—and their different effects, this chapter shows how women apply different amounts of make-up to accommodate and contest particular understandings of femininity and ideas of beauty in different contexts. It demonstrates how contemporary interpretations of modesty in respect of *tesettür* clothing have evolved towards the 'management of beauty' rather than its concealment.

CARE OF THE SELF AND THE MANAGEMENT OF BEAUTY

Young Turkish-Dutch women frequently draw on notions of care of the self and the management of beauty to talk about the particular aesthetics of a well-groomed appearance. Care of the self is a mode of behaviour instilled in the lives of subjects over time, as Foucault has famously argued. In his words, care of the self consists of 'practices and formulas that people (have) reflected on, developed, perfected and taught' (1984, 45). The notion of care of the self (in Turkish, *kendine bakmak*) is very common in the accounts of the young women I interviewed for this research, and wearing make-up is often referred to as a strong marker of a well-cared-for self. I approach women's efforts and practices aimed at producing a carefully groomed presence as indicators of care of the self. These display a certain mode of knowledge and behaviour in the cultivation of a modern but pious female subject.

Wearing a certain style and amount of make-up has increasingly become an integral aspect of *tesettür*. When discussing what constitutes a modest appearance, the criteria for choosing between wearing and avoiding make-up, as well as when, where and which style of make-up to wear, reveal diverse, if not contrasting practices of *tesettür* and care of the self. Women emphasise the notion of a 'clean,' 'healthy' and 'well-groomed' look as the marker of proper care of the self rather than a 'beautiful' or 'attractive' appearance. They also try to use make-up materials that use the least harmful chemicals and with *helal* (permissible to use according to Islamic knowledge) ingredients. In their narratives, care of the self becomes a new way of talking about particular aesthetic questions related to *tesettür*. Fashioning a modest, healthy, presentable appearance while not appearing attractive in a way that involves negative sexual connotations is a dilemma for many pious young women.

While some pious women see make-up as necessary for their care of the self, others interpret it as an alteration of one's God-given appearance and strictly avoid it accordingly. However, in most cases, the statement 'I don't wear make-up' was followed by comments such as 'Well, perhaps a little bit of mascara, foundation, and lip gloss'; 'Sometimes, when I am bored at home, I wear make-up'; 'I carry make-up in my bag but I do not wear it'; and so on. Even if women do not use make-up on a daily basis, there are special occasions when they do wear it. They feel that sometimes merely dressing up is not enough to achieve a desired appearance. For instance, in the workplace or at school, women feel they need to use a certain amount of make-up to produce a healthy appearance and mien.

Many young teenage women in the Turkish-Dutch *tesettür* scene already own a make-up set which in its most basic form includes a lip gloss, eyeliner and mascara. Through a process of trial and error, young women develop a mode of make-up which they feel is appropriate to *tesettür*. Accounts of learning appropriate make-up reveal very rich and diverse sources: female friends and relatives, in both Turkey and the Netherlands, and also social media networks, especially the make-up tutorials on YouTube and beauty blogs, which introduce different styles and techniques and promote new and trendy make-up materials. Women combine different ideas of beauty and modesty when they choose to wear a particular kind of make-up. Wearing make-up requires devoting extra time and labour to one's appearance. Make-up, interlocutors emphasised, adds an 'extra touch' to one's appearance. There is no single formula for the proper style and right amount of make-up that always goes along with modest *tesettür* clothing. The quantity and quality of make-up applied differs from person to person and occasion to occasion, as well as changing over time.

The reflections of pious elderly women about make-up demonstrate that understandings of femininity and notions of care of the self have changed dramatically in recent decades. In their accounts, a carefully 'neglected self' (*kendini ihmal etmek* in Turkish), as well as a lack of the time and money necessary to producing a well-groomed image are considered markers of modesty. For them, make-up is a novelty that is difficult to regard as a marker of care of the self. This is why elderly interlocutors often criticized the desire of young women, especially their female relatives, to appear well-groomed, seeing these new beautification practices as incompatible with their own notions of modesty and religious convictions. For instance, when I asked Mükerrem, one of the elderly women I interviewed for this research, about make-up, her response focused on her granddaughter. Mükerrem told me that she herself had only used hand cream from time to time when her hands got very dry after long hours working in the fields. She did not even like to put Henna dye on her hands. The only bodily adornment she mentioned was her long, braided hair, which she has never had cut. Thick, long, braided hair was sufficient to mark her as a healthy person, she said. Because of her hair, she was considered beautiful when she was young.

Mükerrem compared herself with her granddaughter in discussing changing understandings of beauty. She was displeased because her granddaughter wears what she considers very heavy make-up:

I have a granddaughter in Germany. It doesn't matter if she's covered or not, she wears heavy make-up. I do not know what she is thinking; she says that she wears make-up to look more beautiful. I call it 'whitewash' (*badana*)...I never plucked a single hair (pointing to her face), I never put anything in my hair. [*Did you cut your hair?*] No, I didn't; I had five very long braids, and my relatives would help me make them.[3]

The methods of revealing and managing one's beauty as markers of one's care of the self have changed visibly, as Mükerrem's comparative account indicates. Her granddaughter considers make-up a necessary means of self-beautification, compatible with her understanding of *tesettür*, even if she is often criticised by her grandmother.

It is not possible to explain this change only on the basis of the individual's level of devotion and piety. Like many provincial women of her generation, Mükerrem had never put on make-up. While this was linked to her pious sense of self over the course of her life, she was not influenced by her religious convictions in any single way. For instance, as she grew older, she became a more devout Muslim. Being in her seventies today, the number of social occasions that require Mükerem to dress up and look beautiful has gradually decreased. Within her close social circle, consisting mostly of Turkish immigrants in the Netherlands, there are specific cultural expectations about the mode of femininity that an elderly, pious woman should embody. Notions of modesty and ideas of beauty are not only formed by the religious convictions of individuals and generational differences, but they are also dependent on social contexts and localities (Black 2004; Liebelt 2016; Peiss 2002). To reiterate, they change over the course of a person's lifetime.

Thus, during the first years following Mükerrem's migration to the Netherlands in the 1980s, her attire changed completely. She replaced her baggy trousers, the attire of Turkish village women, with a more urban style consisting of an overcoat and a small headscarf, and later with a skirt-and-trousers combination. Although she had strictly avoided wearing make-up as a young woman, the reason for this was not just piety, but rather a particular understanding of beauty and femininity among Turkish migrants during the early years of migration. Visible make-up was a sign of inappropriate femininity, an overstatement of one's self-transformation in a context where migrant women from the provinces already perceived the rather common new clothing style as a degenerative effect of the migration experience (Ünal 2013b).

In the younger Turkish-Dutch *tesettür* scene, however, using cosmetics to produce a healthy facial look has become necessary in creating a proper appearance. Nevertheless, some young women share ideas and judgments similar to those expressed by Mükerrem, having given up wearing make-up as a marker of self-care, even though it is expected on the present-day *tesettür* scene. They regard the absence of make-up as a part of their own individual *tesettür*. Some pious young women deem make-up inappropriate because they consider it to be an act of interference with God's creation. In addition to avoiding make-up, leaving one's eyebrows untouched is also perceived as a sign of a higher level of devotion. The practice of leaving one's eyebrows untouched draws its significance from a particular hadith that curses women who change the shape of their eyebrows.[4] However, as one interlocutor stated, it is very difficult to disregard one's bushy eyebrows when every year fashion models appear with differently shaped eyebrows.[5] Leaving one's eyebrows untouched becomes a sign of appreciation of the 'natural beauty' that God has bestowed upon the individual. In recent mainstream fashion, some beauty therapists encourage women to produce a more 'natural' look of beauty by leaving their eyebrows bushy and avoiding artificial effects, while others promote microblading, a form of permanent make-up creating a fuller and supposedly more natural-looking brow.

For another interlocutor, Hülya, a university student who shared a house with three other female students, putting on make-up had been an everyday practice for her, as for many other young students her age, for quite some time. Her make-up practices changed when, more recently, Hülya became a more pious individual as she learned more about Islam. She began to appreciate what she called her 'innocent look' (*masum görünüş* in Turkish) as a result of this transformation. Her account illustrates clearly that ideas of beauty and their relationship to make-up may also change in the process of cultivating a pious self. She saw her natural appearance as innocent because she considered it to be God's meticulous creation. Therefore, she wanted to keep it as it was. Wearing no make-up and leaving one's eyebrows untouched have become strong markers of piety for her. This careful neglect represents a different understanding of care of the self:

> I don't wear make-up anymore, but there were times when I did. When I was in high school, I wore mascara and eye shadow; I was enthusiastic about that sort of thing. Even after I learned that it's a sin, I continued to

wear make-up for a while. Then the same thing happened with plucking my eyebrows. I lost my enthusiasm. I never wore heavy make-up anyway. Everybody was doing it, so I did it too. Because, if you didn't, you weren't normal. Later, I learned that it was very sinful. [*Plucking your eyebrows?*] Ah, yes, it is sinful because eyebrows are very important. God created us meticulously.... every single person, each detail, God created us uniquely. When you give your eyebrows a different shape, you change the look that God has given you. God created everyone with an innocent look.[6]

While the 'innocent look' has become quite prominent on the Turkish-Dutch *tesettür* scene, the argument for a 'God-given' (untouched) appearance may not be sufficient to negotiate the beauty ideals of different environments, such as in one's professional life. Wearing the correct amount of make-up shows that one understands the norms and aesthetics that are suitable in a particular social context. Women modulate their presentation of femininity and modesty by managing their make-up; in doing so, they are able to reveal or conceal certain aspects of the self. There are different degrees and practices of *kendine bakmak*, care of the self, and *ihmal etmek*, neglecting the self, and fashioning a Muslim appearance does not simply mean the subversion of mainstream notions of beauty.

To sum up, generational differences, class aspirations, religious convictions and changing ideals of beauty engender different practices and ambiguous interpretations of wearing make-up on the Turkish-Dutch *tesettür* scene. The following section will explore the common practice of 'invisible make-up' as a crucial part of everyday *tesettür* appearance.

Invisible Make-Up

Minimal, 'invisible' make-up is commonly used by young *tesettürlü* women to produce a healthy, natural look. A cosmetically produced 'natural' look has increasingly become the preferred form of make-up for pious younger women. Indeed, invisible make-up is considered necessary to create a healthy facial appearance, and it is also easily adaptable to *tesettür*, as it attracts less attention. Invisible make-up usually consists of a small amount of foundation used to smooth the skin's texture and colour, some blush on the cheeks, some mascara to pull away the eyelashes from the rim of the eye, kohl eye-pencil and sometimes smooth eye shadow, to create the illusion of larger, more open eyes. Lip-gloss or balm completes one's invisible make-up and produces the image of a well-groomed individual.

Wearing invisible make-up indicates that a young woman knows how to manage her looks skilfully, rather than either revealing or hiding her attractiveness. Managing one's beauty is required not only to satisfy moral concerns but also for professional success. The question 'Have you put on make-up?' was quoted by several interlocutors employed in the service sector in the Netherlands as a kind of compliment for someone who puts on 'invisible' make-up. The statement confirmed that the difference from an untouched look was so minimal as to be hardly recognizable; accordingly, these interlocutors felt it did not spoil the ideal meaning of *tesettür*. Boncuk, a mother of two, described 'invisible make-up' as an ideal style of make-up:

> When you think of the ideal of *tesettür*, make-up should not attract attention. Aaah...young girls with tweezed, thin eyebrows, mascara on their eyelashes and eyes framed with thin lines...I don't find this appropriate. You can use a little make-up, of course; when someone sees it, they should say 'What beautiful eyes and eyebrows you have.' It should look natural.[7]

Minimal eye make-up, specifically eye-pencil and mascara, is more compatible with female Muslim piety due to a hadith in which the Prophet recommends putting on kohl (*sürme* in Turkish) at night for the health of one's eyes.[8] According to interlocutors, the use of kohl 'to clear one's vision' and 'to strengthen one's eyelashes', as the hadith indicates, was common among Muslim men and women at the time of the Prophet. This hadith provides a religious basis and justification for eye make-up, even though make-up products now consist of many different chemicals.

Make-up, some interlocutors felt, may enhance the image of a *tesettürlü* woman both positively and negatively. Women are often confronted with the judgements of others. There is a general assumption that make-up and *tesettür* do not go well together because wearing make-up makes a person sexually attractive. In this context, invisible make-up functions to reduce sexual attractiveness. That is why it is regarded a safe alternative that helps women to appear healthy and modest at the same time. The notion of 'not wearing make-up' while wearing invisible make-up to look more pleasant suits the aesthetics of both Islamic modesty and professional life. Another young woman employed in the service sector in Amsterdam, Serpil, commented on her invisible make-up as a part of her professional look:

Well, they always say that they wear make-up to look well-groomed, but make-up turns you into a sex object, too. You wear make-up to have more attractive eyes, or you wear lipstick to have more pronounced lips. It's a matter of preference. I also use make-up. However, I only wear make-up to look healthy at work. My face is pale; I need to colour it just a little bit. This may not be an excuse, I realize. My everyday make-up is not sexy; my friends often ask me whether I put on make-up or not. It's 'invisible make-up.' It's not noticeable...[9]

As the accounts of young professional women indicate, a tired, pale face should be covered with some make-up in the workplace. Cheeks were coloured with blush, powder or cream to create a healthy, energetic facial appearance. Looking energetic and vibrant is a part of one's professional look, particularly in the service sector, as well as a constituent aspect of mainstream ideals of beauty. Such an appearance gives the impression of being a hard-worker, and therefore, it becomes necessary and desirable, regardless of one's ideas about modesty and *tesettür*. After a long period wearing make-up, women feel quite at ease with their 'natural look' and the make-up they use to create it. They become estranged from their make-up-free look: when they look at themselves in the mirror without make-up, they do not see a healthy, energetic face.

Based on their appreciation of God-given beauty, women develop and adopt different styles of make-up. For instance, they prefer to use eye-pencil instead of eyeliner because the eye-pencil supposedly makes the eyes look less seductive. Şüheda, 35 years old, single and employed as an English teacher, has tried to decrease the amount of make-up she uses, as she aims to practice a more modest, covered form of *tesettür*. Using an eye-pencil instead of an eyeliner on her eyes changes the effect of her make-up, as she describes below:

I like make-up and other cosmetics. I often use eye-pencil. It was very difficult to stop wearing eyeliner. You get used to it. If you don't wear it, you feel different and you look sick. Well, in fact it doesn't matter much. [*Do you feel that way now?*] No... but I still put on eye-pencil, even if it is not to look beautiful. Otherwise, you look as if you've just got out of bed. When I go out, I put on mascara and eye-pencil; they make you look good.[10]

One's God-given appearance, however, may not be entirely suitable in one's professional life. Emine, a 22 year-old university student, decided to begin wearing a headscarf one year prior to our interview. She recalled that it was a very difficult decision for her to adopt the headscarf because her family was completely against it. As a young woman and *tesettür* wearer, Emine felt responsible for how she looked at work. She tried to make her *tesettür* presentable. Make-up was crucial in fashioning this effect:

> You have to pay attention to every detail of your appearance. Your scarf and your make-up are both important... I wear make-up because my face is very pale. I put on blush or powder, especially at work. We go to other companies for meetings; we meet with the police, with families. I need to look good and chic.[11]

In some contexts, it has indeed become impossible to imagine *tesettür* without make-up. The amount of make-up one wears not only changes according to different concepts of *tesettür*, but it also depends on social context. Ebrar is a young woman who sought to change her appearance after beginning her professional life as an account manager in a Dutch firm, where she prepares yearly income and tax reports for companies and entrepreneurs. Ebrar reported wearing make-up to hide her exhaustion. She considered minimal make-up appropriate for both *tesettür* and Dutch professional life:

> I rarely wear make-up. Usually, I only do so for women-only gatherings (such as) henna and wedding parties. I do not like to wear make-up outside. Sometimes I wear eye make-up when I go to work. My eyes look bad because of exhaustion and lack of sleep. Dutch people do not approve of too much make-up in the workplace either.[12]

Women rely on invisible make-up not only to achieve a modest appearance, but also to look professional. In both cases, invisible make-up indicates that a woman is not overly interested in her appearance; too much investment in how one looks consumes both time and energy and may easily be considered morally suspect. As an aspect of self-care, make-up and its changing aesthetics are not formed in isolation. Rather, make-up is embedded in social practice; it embodies social encounters and is situated in wider social relations.

In certain respects, Islamic notions of self-care are similar to the modern notion of care of the self, even if the techniques and practices of self-care in each context are distinct. Care of the self is very important in the formation of modern, professional subjects, but it should be kept within certain limits. In addition to the contradictions and anxieties that heavy make-up creates for *tesettürlü* women, it also produces a less professional or presentable look. The practice of wearing make-up in one's professional life thus shares similarities with the make-up applied by women who are concerned to present a modest appearance, especially with regard to its limits. Invisible make-up may work well in contexts where women interact mainly with non-Turkish Dutch communities, as wearing lots of make-up is often considered 'cheap' and associated with a lower social status in the Netherlands. In the following section, I will illustrate how identical amounts and styles of make-up create different effects in different social contexts.

DIFFERENT EFFECTS OF MAKE-UP

The idealisation of *tesettür* as a marker of one's religious identity plays a significant role in how make-up is practiced and perceived by others. As previously noted, make-up is a medium through which women display their attention to self-care, and different styles of make-up reveal both a particular aesthetics and a particular understanding of *tesettür*. Festive events and social occasions within the migrant community, such as weddings or funerals, play a crucial role in how make-up is practised and interpreted. For a *tesettür* wearer, it is very important to know when to wear which type of make-up. The same amount and style of make-up can produce opposite effects in different social contexts. On certain occasions, it is not make-up itself, but the very display of extra care of the self that is unwelcome and inappropriate.

Funerals are one such occasion at which any style or amount of make-up is open to criticism. Publicly displaying self-care in a context of mourning is considered disrespectful within the Turkish cultural context. In this instance, the purpose of the gathering, rather than its location, plays a significant role, as funerals transform the effects of make-up, as well as the sense of place. While a certain style and amount of make-up may be acceptable when one attends the mosque for religious classes, the same kind of make-up would be considered inappropriate when attending the so-called *Mevlid* ritual after a funeral in the same mosque. Even for women who wear make-up on a daily basis, the undesired effects of wearing make-up on such occasions can be difficult to bear.

Another example of a special occasion on which make-up is considered inappropriate is Ramadan, the Muslim month of fasting. Whereas a pale face at work may be undesirable during the rest of the year, during Ramadan such an appearance takes on very different meaning, when a pale face may become a marker of bodily discipline, piety and the deprived, fasting body. Most women who enjoy wearing make-up on a daily basis avoid it during the month of Ramadan. Glossed or coloured lips in particular are considered reprehensible at this time of the year. Even women who are not fasting tend to wear less or no make-up at all during Ramadan. Make-up, interlocutors often stated, ruins the image of the fasting body. Wearing make-up is also considered disrespectful to those who are fasting in order to discipline their bodily desires and strengthen their spirituality.

The question of whether applying lipstick means one is breaking one's fast is also a matter of debate and divergence of opinion. Although many women and religious authorities agree that wearing make-up is generally reprehensible (*mekruh*), though not forbidden (*haram*), wearing lipstick and make-up is almost inevitably seen as a sign of breaking one's fast during Ramadan. At this time, in the holy month of worship, women also tend to pay closer attention to their religious practice (*ibadet* in Turkish) apart from fasting, for example, attempting to pray five times a day, even if they do not normally do so. They also attend religious meetings and daily recitations of the Quran or so-called *mukabele* gatherings. Thus, the reasons for categorising make-up and other cosmetics such as perfume as reprehensible during this particular time of the year are not only related to questions of attractiveness, but also the use of cosmetics contradicts the ideal of the pure, clean body that is required for worship.

The idealisation of *tesettür* as a marker of religious identity transforms the effects of make-up. A pious person is expected to fashion a modest appearance and cultivate a humble self. In the specific contexts discussed in this section, a heightened degree of spiritual significance transforms ideas of beauty and care, consequently changing the effects of make-up. Wearing make-up without full knowledge of the aesthetic and ethical norms of those present at an event can also easily produce undesired effects. Many *tesettürlü* women regard wearing heavy make-up as tolerable only at women-only gatherings and on festive occasions. In other contexts, the same degree of heavy make-up is criticised as having overly sexual connotations.

Women-only occasions are relatively flexible in terms of dress and make-up because they are considered *mahrem* contexts. However, even in such women-only contexts, wearing a lot of make-up can produce conflicts between women who have different understandings of femininity and *tesettür*. Furthermore, generational differences become a significant factor in shaping narratives about wearing visible, 'heavy' make-up (*ağır makyaj*). Dicle describes her first experience of this kind of make-up and how it created a conflict with her mother:

> I went to the coiffeur with my friends, and they put lots of powder on my face. My face looked very tanned. My eyes had layers of make-up and mascara—it was really cool. My mother saw me at the wedding party; she looked at me and said, 'What kind of make-up are you wearing? Go and wipe your lipstick a little bit, wipe the powder off of your face.' I told her to leave me alone, but I knew that I was wearing heavy make-up.[13]

Dicle does not consider her make-up style suitable for wearing with modest clothing because she thinks it transforms her into a very attractive woman; nevertheless, she continued to wear this type of make-up for women-only gatherings. Her account shows that wearing make-up may also be a joyful and playful kind of self-transformation. Being attractive and revealing oneself as such does not have overtly sexual connotations in women-only gatherings, in contrast to mixed-gender contexts. However, the judgements of older women, particularly mothers, who in the Turkish context are considered responsible for watching over their daughters' 'proper' appearance, are often very different from those of younger women, such as their daughters or granddaughters. According to the common understanding of older women, a presentation of femininity such as that performed by Dicle is inappropriate even within women-only gatherings, not only out of religious concerns, but also because, in their particular understanding of modesty, it does not 'fit' with Dicle's social position as an unmarried woman.

MAKE-UP AND THE INTIMATE SELF

As discussed above, invisible and heavy make-up creates different effects in different contexts. However, in Turkey, heavy make-up is in general heavily loaded with negative sexual connotations. By declaring that she does not wear make-up at all, a woman clearly distances herself from the heightened visibility and negative sexual connotations that some make-up, especially lipstick and colourful eye shadow, create. Women who choose to wear absolutely no make-up tend to abide by specific interpretations of the Islamic textual tradition. The texts used in this context emphasise that the adornment and displaying of a woman's beauty should be intended for intimate spaces in the company of one's *mahrem* exclusively. This means that make-up may play a different role in intimate spaces, especially in the lives of married women, as marriage creates a context in which a sexually attractive self can be performed in a legitimate and desired manner.[14] Even if women oppose the practice of make-up in public, they may find it acceptable or even enjoyable in intimate spaces such as the family home. For some non-make-up wearers, make-up may be a matter of personal entertainment because it produces a different sense of femininity and the intimate self. Others may wear make-up to please or appear attractive for their husbands. However, pleasing one's husband is not always a determining factor, especially if the woman in question finds displaying an attractive self at odds with her construction of a modest and pious self.

Some of my interlocutors only put on make-up for specific, intimate occasions, for example, when they were with very close female friends. Frequently, they showed me smart-phone pictures of themselves wearing make-up taken on such occasions, or when they were alone. For example, one interlocutor, Hanne, was very strict about not wearing make-up outdoors. She told me her concerns about make-up, not so much as a *hoca* or as a *çarşaf*[15] wearer, but as a single woman in her late thirties. She referred to her past as a reference point to highlight her consistency and strength in practising a modest appearance, even though she also considered wearing make-up an option for the future:

> My eyes (*she has green eyes*[16]) are the most beautiful part of my face – of course, when I wear mascara, I look different. Since my eyebrows and eyelashes are light, when I put mascara on they look very different. Others ask me 'Is that you, Hanne?' When I am bored, I put on make-up. I did

so recently, and then I took a picture. I can show it to you…it looks funny because I do not know how to do it properly…Well, in the future, if my husband would like it, and if it would make him happy, I might be able wear it.[17]

Hanne considers wearing make-up 'fun', seeing it as a means of performing different modalities of femininity. Although most women enjoy this unique feeling and its effect on others, Hanne's account illustrates that make-up may be a very personal experience and practice of the intimate self, not one for public display.

Marriage partners may have different ideas concerning make-up and the presentation of sexual and gender roles. Before marriage, a couple must make sure that they share a certain understanding of femininity and ideals of sexual attractiveness. For example, Selcen, a *çarşaf* wearer, thinks that soft, black eye make-up goes well with her black *çarşaf*. Her make-up is very subtle; she only uses an eye-pencil. She chooses her eye-pencil colour to match the colours of her indoor headscarf. Sometimes she wears big, black sunglasses to conceal her minimal eye make-up when she is in public. Selcen told me happily that her husband cherishes her natural beauty. The two of them agree on a certain notion of sexual attractiveness and femininity, an agreement that is very important to her. Early on in their marital relationship, she wanted to make sure that her husband would accept her choice not to wear make-up except for occasional eye make-up, especially after a comment he had made on their wedding day:

> On our wedding day, the party was women-only. On that day, my husband asked me to put on visible eye make-up. I asked whether this would be for the day of the wedding only, and he said that it would. Then I asked him to find a suitable photographer, because if the photographer had been male, I would not have worn make-up. He said that he would arrange an appropriate photography shoot, because he knew a couple who were both photographers. The woman had her own studio. We went there…[18]

Even though Islamic sources permit and even encourage women's adornment as a way of pleasing their husbands, make-up preferences differ significantly among pious married women. Couples may seek tacit agreement on a modest, pious mode of femininity, and make-up becomes an important signifier because it has a direct connection to sexual attractiveness.

Conclusion

Studying Muslim appearances in the context of migration to Western Europe, where Muslims are considered a sartorial minority, demands comprehending the multiple meanings and interpretations of beauty and religious modesty at different historical moments and locations. Fashioning a Muslim appearance does not necessarily imply subverting modern notions of femininity, nor, for that matter, rejecting 'inherited traditional' Islam. As the accounts of Turkish-Dutch women wearing *tesettür* in the Netherlands reveal, there is no single formula for 'appropriate' make-up as part of *tesettür* understanding. Practices and interpretations of wearing make-up change according to different social contexts and relations. Spatial boundaries (intimate-public), the presence of people (*mahrem-namahrem*), generational differences, different lifestyles, interpretations of Islamic sources, religious convictions and different notions of the self all play important roles in shaping how women feel about wearing make-up. Many young women conceive of make-up as an 'extra touch' in fashioning one's appearance and as an indicator of proper care of the self. For them, wearing a certain amount of make-up, namely 'invisible make-up', is necessary to fashioning a healthy look, which simultaneously suits both *tesettür* and one's professional life. To manage their *tesettür* appearance in multiple settings, women must negotiate and articulate different modalities of femininity and beauty. Rather than hiding their beauty, as the first generation of Turkish women migrating to the Netherlands commonly called their attempts at proper self-fashioning, younger immigrant women use different styles and amounts of make-up as a way of managing their beauty.

Acknowledgements I would like to thank Annelies Moors, Julie McBrien, Jeremy Walton, Paula Schrode and Claudia Liebelt for reading an earlier version of this work and providing invaluable comments and suggestions.

NOTES

1. This work formed part of my PhD research at the University of Amsterdam, which started in 2007 as a NORFACE project on the emergence of Islamic Fashion in Europe and was later funded by the Cultural Dynamics Programme of the Netherlands Organization for Scientific Research (NWO).

2. In the Quran, Surah Nur (24), Ayet 31 explains the category of *mahrem* (and its opposite, *namahrem*) in the following way: 'And tell the believing women to reduce [some] of their vision, and guard their private parts and do not expose their adornment except that which [necessarily] appears thereof and to wrap [a portion of] their headcovers over their chest and not expose their adornment except to their husbands, their fathers, their husbands' fathers, their sons, their husbands' sons, their brothers, their brothers' sons, their sisters' sons, their women, that which their right hands poses or those male attendants having no physical desire, or children who are not well aware of the private aspects of women. And let them not stamp their feet to make known what they conceal of their adornment. And return to Allah in repentance, all of you, O believers, that you might succeed.'

3. Interview with Mükerrem, November 2010.

4. This particular hadith reads: 'Allah has cursed those women who practice tattooing and those who get themselves tattooed, and those who remove their facial hair, and those who create a space between their teeth artificially to look beautiful, and such women as change the features created by Allah. Why then should I not curse those whom the Prophet has cursed? And that is in Allah's Book. i.e. His Saying: "And what the Apostle gives you take it and what he forbids you abstain (from it)." This hadith is recorded in the authoritative collections of Sahih Bukhari, Book 72, Number 815, Narrated by the Companion of the Prophet Muhammad, Abdullah.'

5. See Clarke (2015) for a thick ethnographic description of eyebrow beautification practices and their moral implications in the Muslim Pakistani community of Sheffield, UK.

6. Interview with Hülya, June 2008.

7. Interview with Boncuk, March 2009.

8. 'The Prophet Muhammad said: "Among the best types of collyrium is antimony (*ithmid*), for it clears the vision and makes the hair sprout." This hadith is recorded in the authoritative collection of Sunan Abu-Dawud, Book 32, Kitab El-Libas, Number 4050, Narrated by the Companion of the Prophet, Abdullah Ibn Abbas.'

9. Interview with Serpil, March 2010.
10. Interview with Şüheda, July 2010.
11. Interview with Emine, November 2008.
12. Interview with Ebrar, November 2010.
13. Interview with Dicle, July 2010.
14. Abu Lughod's (1990) ethnography of Bedouin women richly portrays emerging forms of differentiation among women based on their involvement in companionate marriages, in which women's attractiveness and individuality seem to be of greater importance.
15. A long, loose, two-pieced outdoor garment considered the most sober form of Muslim dress on the Turkish *tesettür* scene.
16. Green and blue colored eyes are commonly considered attractive in Turkey.
17. Interview with Hanne, May 2010.
18. Interview with Selcen, December 2010.

REFERENCES

Abbas, Saba. 2015. "'My Veil Makes Me Beautiful' Paradoxes of Zeena and Concealment in Amman." *Journal of Middle East Women's Studies* 11 (2): 139–60.

Abu Lughod, Lila. 1990. "The Romance of Resistance: Tracing Transformations of Power Through Bedouin Women." *American Ethnologist* 17 (1): 41–45.

Bilge, Sirma. 2010. "Beyond Subordination vs Resistance: An Intersectional Approach to the Agency of Veiled Muslim." *Journal of Intercultural Studies* 31 (1): 9–28.

Black, Paula. 2004. *The Beauty Industry: Gender, Culture, Pleasure*. New York: Routledge.

Bowen, John R. 2011. "How the French State Justifies Controlling Muslim Bodies: From Harm-Based to Values-Based Reasoning." *Social Research* 78 (2554): 325–48.

Bracke, Sarah. 2011. "Subjects of Debate: Secular and Sexual Exceptionalism, and Muslim Women in the Netherlands." *Feminist Review* 98: 28–46.

Clarke, Hester. 2015. "Shaping Eyebrows and Moral Selves: Considering Islamic Discourse, Gender and Ethnicity Within the Muslim Pakistani Community of Sheffield (UK)." *Sociologus* 66 (1): 1–20.

Deeb, Lara, and Harb, Mona. 2013. *Leisurely Islam: Negotiating Geography and Morality in Shi'ite South Beirut*. Princeton: Princeton University Press.

Dwyer, Claire. 1999. "Veiled Meanings: Young British Muslim Women and the Negotiation of Differences." *Gender, Place & Culture: A Journal of Feminist Geography* 6 (1): 5–26.

El Guindi, Fadwa. 1981. "Veiling Infitah with Muslim Ethic: Egypt's Contemporary Islamic Movement." *Social Problems* 28 (4): 465–85.

Fadil, Nadia. 2009. "Managing Affects and Sensibilities: The Case of Not-Handshaking and Not-Fasting." *Social Anthropology* 17 (4): 439–54.

Foucault, Michel. 1984. *The Care of the Self, History of Sexuality.* Vol. 3. London: Penguin Books.

Gökarıksel, Banu, and Anna Secor. 2012. "Even I Was Tempted: The Moral Ambivalence and Ethical Practice of Veiling-Fashion in Turkey." *Annals of the Association of American Geographers* 102 (4): 847–62.

Göle, Nilüfer. 2003. "The Voluntary Adoption of Islamic Stigma Symbols." *Social Research* 70 (3): 809–28.

Kavakçı, Merve. 2010. *Politics of Turkish Headscarf: A Post-Colonial Reading.* New York: Palgrave Macmillan.

Kılıçbay, Barış, and Mutlu Binark. 2002. "Consumer Culture, Islam and the Politics of Lifestyle: Fashion for Veiling in Contemporary Turkey." *European Journal of Communication* 17 (4): 495–511.

Liebelt, Claudia. 2016. "Grooming Istanbul: Intimate Encounters and Concerns in Turkish Beauty Salons." *Journal of Middle East Women's Studies* 12 (2): 181–202.

MacLeod, Arlene E. 1991. *Accommodating Protest: Working Women, the New Veiling and Change in Cairo.* New York: Columbia University Press.

Moors, Annelies. 2007. "Fashionable Muslims: Notions of Self, Religion and Society in San'a." *Fashion Theory* 11 (2/3): 319–46.

Moors, Annelies. 2009a. "'Islamic Fashion' in Europe: Religious Conviction, Aesthetic Style, and Creative Consumption." *Encounters* 1 (1): 175–201.

Moors, Annelies. 2009b. "The Dutch and the Face-Veil: The Politics of Discomfort." *Social Anthropology* 17 (4): 393–408.

Moors, Annelies, and Emma Tarlo. 2007. "Introduction." In *Muslim Fashions.* Special Double Issue, *Journal of Fashion Theory* 11 (2/3): 133–141.

Moors, Annelies, and Emma Tarlo. 2013. "Introduction." In *Islamic Fashion and Anti-Fashion New Perspectives from Europe and America,* edited by Annelies Moors and Emma Tarlo, 1–30. London: Bloomsbury.

Navaro-Yashin, Yael. 2002. "The Market for Identities: Secularism, Islamism, Commodities." In *Fragments of Culture: The Everyday of Modern Turkey,* edited by Deniz Kandiyoti and Ayse Saktanber, 221–53. New Jersey: Rutgers University Press.

Özyeğin, Gul. 2015. *New Desires, New Selves Sex, Love, and Piety among Turkish Youth.* New York: New York University Press.

Peiss, Kathy. 2002. "Educating the Eye of the Beholder: American Cosmetics Abroad." *Daedalus* 131 (4): 101–9.

Rana, Jasmijn. 2017. "Ladies-only! Empowerment and Comfort in Gender-segregated Kickboxing in the Netherlands." In *Race, Gender and Sport: The Politics of Ethnic 'Other' Girls and Women*, edited by Aarti Ratna and Samaya F. Samie, 148–46. Oxford: Routledge.

Saktanber, Ayşe. 2002. "We Pray Like You Have Fun: New Islamic Youth in Turkey." In *Fragments of Culture*, edited by Ayse Saktanber and Deniz Kandiyoti, 254–76. New Jersey: Rutgers University Press.

Sandıkçı, Özlem, and Güliz Ger. 2007. "Constructing and Representing Islamic Consumer in Turkey, edited by EmmaTarlo and Annelies Moors." *Fashion Theory* 11 (2/3): 189–210.

Sandıkçı, Özlem, and Güliz Ger. 2010. "Veiling in Style: How Does a Stigmatized Practice Become Fashionable?" *Journal of Consumer Research* 37: 15–35.

Schielke, Samuli, and Liza Debevec. 2012. "Introduction." In *Ordinary Lives and Grand Schemes: An Anthropology of Everyday Religion*, edited by Samuli Schielke and Liza Debevec, 1–16. New York: Berghahn Books.

Scott, Joan. 2007. *The Politics of the Veil*. Princeton and Oxford: Princeton University Press.

Secor, Anna, and Banu Gökarıksel. 2008. "New Transnational Geographies of Islamism, Capitalism and Subjectivity: The Veiling-Fashion Industry in Turkey." *Area* 41 (1): 6–18.

Sehlikoğlu, Sertaç. 2016. "Exercising in Comfort: Islamicate Culture of *Mahremiyet* in Everyday Istanbul." *Journal of Middle East Women's Studies* 12 (2): 143–65.

Sehlikoğlu, Sertaç, and Fahri Karakas. 2016. "We Can Have the Cake and Eat It Too: Leisure and Spirituality at 'Veiled' Hotels in Turkey." *Leisure Studies* 35 (2): 157–69.

Sunan Abu-Dawud. Book 32, Kitab El-Libas, Number 4050, Narrated by the Companion of the Prophet, Abdullah Ibn Abbas.

Sunier, Thijl. 1995. "Disconnecting Religion and Ethnicity: Young Turkish Muslims in the Netherlands." In *Post-migration Ethnicity*, edited by Gerd Baumann and Till Sunier, 58–77. Amsterdam: Het Spinhuis.

Surah Nur. 24: 3. Sahih International. Retrieved from http://quran.com/24/31 on 17 April 2012.

Tarlo, Emma. 2007. "Hijab in London: Metamorphosis, Resonance and Effects." *Journal of Material Culture* 12 (2): 131–56.

Tarlo, Emma. 2010. *Visibly Muslim*. London: Berg.

Ünal, R. Arzu. 2013a. "The Genealogy of the Turkish Pardösü (Long Overcoat) in the Netherlands and Beyond." In *Islamic Fashion and Anti-Fashion*, edited by Annelies Moors and Emma Tarlo. *New Perspectives from Europe and North America*, 123–41. London: Bloomsbury.

Ünal, R. Arzu. 2013b. Wardrobes of Turkish-Dutch Women: The Multiple Meanings and Aesthetics of Muslim Dress. PhD diss., University of Amsterdam.

Ünal, R. Arzu, and Annelies Moors. 2012. "Formats, Fabrics, and Fashions: Muslim Headscarves Revisited." *Material Religion: The Journal of Objects, Art and Belief* 8 (3): 308–29.

van der Veer, Peter. 2006. "Pim Fortuyn, Theo Van Gogh, and the Politics of Tolerance in the Netherlands." *Public Culture* 18 (1): 111–24.

Woodward, Sophie. 2007. *Why Women Wear What They Wear*. Oxford: Berg.

PART IV

Skin Colour Politics

CHAPTER 9

Beauty and the Norm Sketches:
A Conversation on a Performative Response

Syowia Kyambi and Anisha H. Soff

In this conversation with Anisha H. Soff, Nairobi-based artist Syowia Kyambi reflects on her performance, 'Working Title: Beauty and the Norm Sketches', which was staged on two consecutive days during the conference that preceded this publication.[1] In this work, Kyambi approaches the topic of beauty norms from the perspective of identity, memory and the self in relation to the wider society. During the performance, Kyambi sat in front of a large dressing table mirror, putting on several layers of make up or marking certain areas of her face with eye liner, surrounded by a watching audience (cf. Figs. 9.1, 9.2, 9.3, and 9.4).

S. Kyambi (✉)
Independent Artist, Nairobi, Kenya

A. H. Soff
Goethe Institute Kenya, Nairobi, Kenya

Fig. 9.1 Syowia Kyambi in front of an audience during her performance 'Working Title: Beauty and the Norm Sketches,' Iwalewahaus, 7 April 2016. Photographed by Anisha H. Soff

Anisha H. Soff: In 2016, you were invited to participate in the conference 'Beauty and the Norm: Debating Standardization in Bodily Appearance' as both a panellist and an artist. Before we discuss your art practice, I would like to start off by talking about your input during the conference. The performances took place on two consecutive days within the conference venue and drew on the conference theme in several ways. What was the background for this specific kind of work, and how was it influenced by the conference?

Syowia Kyambi: I came to the conference with two different agendas. One was to do a performative work that reacted to what was discussed during the conference, which I did on its second day. And the other was an idea I had already formulated before the conference as a response to the topic, loosely based on the academic abstracts from contributors, which were emailed to participants before the conference.

Fig. 9.2 Syowia Kyambi putting on make-up during her performance 'Working Title: Beauty and the Norm Sketches,' Iwalewahaus, 8 April 2016. Photographed by Anisha H. Soff

Doing something performative without an installation component was kind of new for me. I normally don't work that way, and I usually build an installation and use performance as a way to change the installation.

Anisha H. Soff: During the first part of the performance on day one, you were sitting in front of a dressing table, putting on various layers of make-up foundation, alternating lightening and darkening your complexion.

Syowia Kyambi: I guess that when I read the abstracts of what other contributors were going to talk about, one of the things that crept up for me and my own history was skin tone and the variations of how you are treated depending on your skin tone and how you have easier access in Kenya at least to upper-class spaces and gated communities. This is something that I experienced as a kid during family vacations in Diani Beach,[2] where me and my sisters would sneak into hotels and easily gain access to their swimming pools. Yet, when it was time for my parents to come and pick us up, my mother, a white German woman, would

Fig. 9.3 Syowia Kyambi marking her face with eyeliner during her performance 'Working Title: Beauty and the Norm Sketches,' Iwalewahaus, 8 April 2016. Photographed by Anisha H. Soff

have no problem entering the hotel to come and collect us, whereas my Kenyan father would often be interrogated and not permitted entry. This was an awful thing to experience as a child, the acceptance of one parent and the rejection of another due to blatant discrimination and racisms in a post-colonial African country.

The colour of my skin easily changes a few hues lighter and a few darker depending on how much time I spend in the sun. I often feel that I'm singled out or addressed differently depending on my skin tone and dress. So during the performance that you mentioned, I was experimenting with different shades of foundation to see what would happen to my internal feelings, with different tones on my face and how far I could take it; how would I internalise my lighter or darker self, taking into account my childhood experiences of my father being rejected and the resulting psychological trauma, which has been experienced by so many people in Kenya to this day. In retrospect, I find it a

Fig. 9.4 Syowia Kyambi during her performance 'Working Title: Beauty and the Norm Sketches,' Iwalewahaus, 7 April 2016. Photographed by Anisha H. Soff

kind of problematic thing to do because the audience might relate this art practice to African-American history and traditions of blackface.[3] I was reminded of the hurtful history of African Americans by the blackface that I learned during my time at the School of the Art Institute in Chicago (2000–2003), when I became conscious of American-Black culture. To darken my face thus became difficult, because in the back of my mind I knew that the risk of the audience framing the work in this way was very high (cf. Fig. 9.2).

Anisha H. Soff: Watching your performance that day, blackface did cross my mind at some point, and I thought that a white person could not possibly do this kind of performance. Yet, because you, as a non-white person, were in this 'white space' in Bayreuth, it became an even more powerful act. I think what you were exploring then also became clearer in combination with the second day's performance and with the audience focusing on the theme of beauty and norms; the reactions and response that the performance evoked in the viewers were clearly guided by that.

Syowia Kyambi: I also felt like this conference was a safe space to try and explore what I described, but I don't know if I would include it in another public exhibition platform.

Anisha H. Soff: On the second day, the setting was similar, but you were marking certain areas of your face by drawing five black lines onto them (see Fig. 9.3). Sometimes you only did it once, sometimes again and again, with force. These lines reminded me of counting time on the wall of a jail; on the mouth, they looked like a skull, and someone mentioned pirates. So here again one could read a lot of different meanings into that, but in the context of the conference on beauty and norms, the one meaning that imposed itself was that you were actually marking the 'flaws' in your face that you personally don't like. That was the main interpretation pointed out to you by others, right?

Syowia Kyambi: Yes, the markings on the face were a direct response to that day's conference. I think there were a lot of discussions around body modification, and there was a presentation on facelifts and surgical procedures in Iran.[4] What I was exploring was the line between a simple mark on my face, which I could easily deal with because I know it is a temporary situation, like a pimple, and a permanent marking that is constantly commented on and that I struggle to deal with. Those two extremes and the perpetual negotiation of bodily well-being which becomes harder with aging and with noticing marks of age on your body, given that most notions of beauty are connected to youthfulness, are a struggle one has to deal with. One has to navigate what is presented as a normative expectation of beauty and what is the reality of your own beauty (cf. Fig. 9.4).

Anisha H. Soff: Both performances were done in front of a mirror. In the context of the conference and the discussions around beauty, this might seem like an obvious choice. But, since the mirror is repeatedly appearing in your art practice, I think it is quite an important object for you more generally.

Syowia Kyambi: I guess the meaning of the mirror, as part of the performance, was twofold, you know. For me, normally the mirror is about the inclusion of 'the other'. But in this case, it was like the inclusion of 'the other' as being part of myself. There is this documentary film called *1 Giant Leap*,[5] which has a section on identity and discusses the idea of many selves in one body. 'Only you know which self you are referring to when you say "I"' is a statement from that film that I think is a useful reference for this work and my use of the mirror in this specific performance. I was seeing my selves in several different ways in different moments during this performance. In everyday life, we do this consciously and unconsciously, seeing different parts of ourselves and relating them to different ages of ourselves within our psyche. There are many 'others' within my other. I didn't think of this in this way when I was doing the work. That was an afterthought. I think it was the first time that I was using a mirror to initiate a conversation between me and that object which is my body, which is supposedly me, between me and my psyche, which holds different parts of me together (laughs).

Again, I think that's because it was a conference on beauty and bodily standardisation. And I think the performance also had to do with being vulnerable. For example, the line on my forehead is a generational line: my mother had the same line, my father has it, it's like a Kyambi signature, something that is often commented on in my family as a frown, and trying to get rid of this frown is subconsciously an ongoing issue for me. It is a personal issue I have with my face, and in the performance, I tried to mark it and re-mark it until I felt a sense of acceptance of the mark, that I know is never gonna go away; it is probably going to get worse (laughs). The performance was part of a process of learning to accept these marks on my face—in a sense accepting myself as part of my family.

Anisha H. Soff: In what way do you think these issues with your appearance that you tackled in the performance reflect current beauty standards?

Syowia Kyambi: Frowns and wrinkles are a constant target in the beauty and cosmetic industry's marketing campaigns. You see more and more products marketed as age-defying creams. I always expected my relationship with aging being a smooth one, but I do notice my wrinkles more these days and at times, I get frustrated with them and the expectation in the back of my mind that I should look fresh and young, knowing that this sounds like an advert I have heard somewhere before. This makes me even more irritated at myself, having this thought and at the same time questioning whether this is really my thought.

Anisha H. Soff: During the conference, the question came up whether investing in beauty could be seen as a kind of 'aesthetic capital' (Elias et al. 2016). Maxine Craig talked about how a competitive labour market forces women to spend more money on beauty products and services, while the hoped for social climbing fails to materialise in most cases because it is influenced by other structural factors such as racism, sexism and social inequality. Naomi Wolf (1991) called this the 'beauty myth'. What is your take on this?

Syowia Kyambi: I think another factor is that the beauty industry is constantly making you feel insufficient, so you have to buy their products to improve, and at the same time you also buy into their implicit message that you're insufficient the way you are. In my opinion, it's not really about climbing a ladder, but about feeling insufficient, and I think that message is drilled into women all the time in various ways. But it doesn't quite work because most of the products that are produced by the beauty and cosmetics industry are still largely for a white, Western market, so I often feel the product is not for me (laughs). I think that is exactly what Maxine Craig (2006) is talking about when she claims that in the field of beauty studies the interconnections of race, class, gender and beauty have often been neglected. On an everyday basis, it means that either I cannot afford a particular beauty product, or it is not for my skin tone.

Anisha H. Soff: The performances you did during the conference dealt exactly with these intersecting issues.

Syowia Kyambi: Absolutely. I guess I am more interested in norms because—I don't know if one could say that norms shape beauty, but with the reference to the concept of the norm, you can discuss why something is becoming what it is. I guess on the one hand, beauty is very debatable, subjective. I find the whole topic very problematic to discuss from the position of a distant or objective observer, which is a theme that was brought up during the first day of the conference. The fact that beauty is a very personal topic to talk about in my opinion makes it a particularly difficult topic for 'scientific' investigation. What's interesting with this theme is that some contributors declared that they embarked on their research motivated by personal events. As bodily beings, the knowledge we produce cannot be treated as something that fits objective and clear-cut scientific formulas because it is embodied and affective. And I guess, because it runs so deep in our societies in many different ways and is so rooted in various forms of capitalism and forms of acceptance or non-acceptance, I find it quite tricky to reflect about.

Anisha H. Soff: True. While what I consider 'beautiful' does not necessarily have to be considered beautiful by the wider society, how I act in public continues to be influenced by the norms that are in place there. Otherwise I might get sanctioned.

Syowia Kyambi: It is that flux in the relationship between beauty, as a personal assessment, and hegemonic norms that people struggle with.

Anisha H. Soff: This tension is visible in your art practice and that of other female artists we met. Most works draw on personal experience, but they deal with universal issues that a lot of people face but cannot express because of the normative structures that are in place. Can you give an example of how this struggle is part of your everyday practice as an artist?

Syowia Kyambi: I am often confronted with the assumption that all of my work is autobiographical. This is true for some of my earlier works, but not all. I often get the sense that for a female artist working with performance, there is the predetermined expectation that she works from an autobiographical perspective, and I wonder what this does for how a work is represented in the public eye. The assumption that the work is raw and personal makes it harder for a public or to be critical of that work. This can be a disadvantage, because if this is a label typically put on female practitioners' work, it will not be critically discussed and written about beyond a personalized framework. I wonder if I were a male artist, would I have the same issue thrown at me? If I fully accept this role, then my practice gets covered in soft cotton wool kept neatly in storage away from critical discourse. This is something all artists need to be wary of.

Anisha H. Soff: But isn't it at the same time an essentialist expectation of you as a female artist to be emotional and personally driven? Like a prejudice that you are expected to fulfil?

Syowia Kyambi: I suppose so, yeah. I haven't actually found any tools on how to navigate the trajectories built around female artists. I am sure male artists draw on the personal too, but they may not discuss it, or the language that is surrounded by it is different. Is it different for other women artists? And what does referencing a domestic space like the application of make-up in front of a large dressing-table mirror in a public setting do? What language could you employ, and if you employ that language what happens to the message?

Anisha H. Soff: To return to your performance, 'Working Title: Beauty and the Norm Sketches,' at the end of it, you take off all the make-up to become yourself again, or rather, your 'non-performative being' again. For me, there is that moment of acceptance involved in that. As if you looked at yourself in the mirror and discovered everything that does not fit the norm, in order to then be able to let it all go.

Syowia Kyambi: Yeah, and maybe an interesting action would be to do that repeatedly for a number of days, or even over the course of a year or something, and actually write down what you feel. Because at the end of the performance for a moment, I did have that feeling of 'I am fine the way I am,' and momentarily I felt fully content with myself, but I think it only lasted for a few moments (laughs). The other interesting thing is that when I explained it to a few people, they were also shocked that this is what I think about parts of my face.

Anisha H. Soff: Normally you seem quite confident about yourself. So then acknowledging one's feelings about things perceived as flaws is quite a big step.

Syowia Kyambi: Absolutely. I think there are personae I have built, but if you think about it, it's kind of obvious that in the world we live in, people create personae as forms of self-protection. The thing to explore would be, why have I built this self-confident persona, a public persona—which I guess is what we all do to various degrees as human beings when we leave our private, safe spaces and engage with public spaces—and why has this persona been accepted by the public? I think beauty norms are established so early on in life, in interaction with your caregivers, with schoolteachers, friends, in relation to the toys and games you are exposed to and on so many different levels all the time. It is really hard to break free from something that is so substantive, even if it is not necessarily a positive representation of your identity for you. Are you even able to make conscious decisions within these normative structures? Is there a choice involved at all, to wear make-up or to dress your hair, or is it something that you have been conditioned to 'choose' and believe you are choosing freely without even being fully aware of alternatives?

Anisha H. Soff: So what do you think, does the engagement in beauty practices eventually come down to compliance with society and intersecting normative structures?

Syowia Kyambi: I think it's an ongoing struggle, to raise your consciousness, and to keep unearthing who you are and having the space to explore yourself in a true sense, if that's even possible. But oftentimes, we don't allow that space for such a kind of journey, because it may have scary implications, and it's difficult to face situations and emotions that make us uncomfortable. I now feel like I should go and make more of that artwork (laughs) and see what happens, but it feels like a very selfish activity.

Anisha H. Soff: But in the end, what you are drawing from your own psyche works not only as a kind of therapy, but also reflects issues on a more universal level as well; and then it is not only about you anymore.

Syowia Kyambi: Absolutely. This is why I would find it interesting to do this half an hour every day to explore the ripple effects of such a long-term exploration (pauses). 'Know thyself and free the mind'—'beauty' is a lifelong endeavour! (laughs)

Anisha H. Soff: I think we are done here (laughs). It's always a pleasure to connect, and I'm looking forward to many more discussions. Thanks so much for your time.

NOTES

1. 'Beauty and the Norm: Debating Standardization in Bodily Appearances,' Bayreuth University, 6–8 April 2016.
2. Diani Beach is a popular holiday resorts stretching along the south coast of Kenya. While it attracts local as well as international tourists, it is also known as a site of sexual relationships between European women and Kenyan men, the so-called 'beach boys.'
3. Blackface, or 'blacking up', is the practice of a white person wearing make-up in order to look like a Black person or Person of Colour, mostly for entertainment purposes. It has been widely dismissed and criticized as an appropriation of Black culture and a form of misrepresentation, which enforces racist stereotypes.
4. *Kaivanara, Marzieh. 2016.* A Body to Show: An Ethnographic Study of Conspicuous Consumption in Iran. Paper presented during the conference 'Beauty and the Norm: Debating Standardization in Bodily Appearances,' 7 April, Bayreuth University.
5. Directed by Duncan Bridgeman and Jamie Catto, Germany 2002.

REFERENCES

Craig, Maxine L. 2006. "Race, Beauty, and the Tangled Knot of Guilty Pleasure." *Feminist Theory* 7 (2): 159–77.

Elias, Ana Sofia, Rosalind Gill, and Christina Scharff, eds. 2016. *Aesthetic Labour: Rethinking Beauty Politics in Neoliberalism.* London: Palgrave Macmillan.

Wolf, Naomi. 1991. *The Beauty Myth: How Images of Beauty Are Used Against Women.* New York: William Morrow.

CHAPTER 10

Body Beautiful: Comparative Meanings of Beauty in Brazil, South Africa and Jamaica

Doreen Gordon

This chapter focuses on the meanings and gendered norms of beauty in three different locations: Brazil, South Africa, and Jamaica. This comparative approach reveals how these meanings of beauty arise from similar conditions and experiences across the Black Atlantic and are entangled in global and national structures of inequalities and the circulation of ideas about 'race' and difference. In particular, Africa and the African diaspora have tended to be ranked at the bottom of global hierarchies of races, ethnicities, cultures and nations (Basch et al. 1994; Thomas and Clarke 2013). This global racial-cultural hierarchy places Anglo-American culture at the apex and Sub-Saharan African culture at the base. Other cultures (usually with their own complex and dynamic internal hierarchies) jostle to occupy intermediate positions between the two extremes (Brodkin 1999; Frankenberg 1997). Global discourses about race and culture clearly affect the contours of local hierarchies—even while emerging

D. Gordon (✉)
University of the West Indies, Mona, Jamaica

© The Author(s) 2019
C. Liebelt et al. (eds.), *Beauty and the Norm*,
Palgrave Studies in Globalization and Embodiment,
https://doi.org/10.1007/978-3-319-91174-8_10

215

non-white elites in countries such as Brazil and South Africa potentially challenge global inequalities and dominant discourses of race.[1]

Scholars have argued that discourses about race have long been associated with ideas about beauty and physical appearance (Gilman 1998, 2000; Nuttall 2007). The black body has frequently been represented as 'ugly,' closer to nature, oversexed and animalistic—in direct opposition to the supposed aesthetic dominance of the European body (Hobson 2005; Nuttall 2007). Certain physical features associated with 'African' heritage have been negatively valorised—such as having tightly curled hair and a broader nose. This has contributed to an ongoing stigma and a sense of low self-esteem among black populations (Charles 2003; Hall 1995). Some observers have suggested that powerful racial legacies and the internalization of white supremacist classifications have influenced the recent growth of a lucrative hair and skin bleaching industry among black people across the diaspora (Banks 2000; Charles 2003, 2009; Erasmus 1997). However, my ethnographic material demonstrates that peoples' beauty practices and engagement with racial hierarchies and discourses are far more complex and require deeper analysis.

In this chapter, I deploy ethnographic data drawn from a larger, ongoing research project on the circumstances surrounding emerging elites self-identifying as black in Brazil, South Africa, and Jamaica.[2] This project began in 2005 with 16 months of doctoral research in Salvador, Brazil. I subsequently carried out research as a Post-Doctoral Fellow in South Africa (2011–2012), and, to a lesser extent, in Kingston, Jamaica, since 2012. Using an ethnographic approach, I focused on the collection of genealogies and family histories, participant observation in both personal and public spaces, semi-formal and informal conversations, among other techniques. An important finding was that beauty and physical appearance—especially as it relates to dress, skin colour, hair, and physical bodily features—emerged as a meaningful category in peoples' everyday lives, especially for self-identified black women living and working in upscale urban spaces associated with modernity and sophisticated lifestyles.[3] In the upper middle-class social stratum in which I moved, practices and discourses of beauty were particularly significant and underscored deeper, politicized issues about race, visibility, social mobility, and citizenship. Given their potentially strategic position, do upwardly mobile black women challenge racialized norms and hierarchies through their beauty practices? Or do their beauty practices emphasize old as well as newer inequalities? Do black middle-class women seek to conform to western ideals of beauty and global trends towards an increased standard-ization of the body and physical appearance (Garland-Thomson 2009)?

Feminist theorizing on beauty has gained an important place amongst critical scholars, as attested by a wide range of insightful research on the subject. However, beauty's meaning in women's lives continues to be a scholarly problem. On the one hand, feminists have argued that beauty ideals and practices reflect patriarchal domination (Bordo 1993; Wolf 1991). These analyses stress slightly different arguments but seem to coalesce on the point that beauty practices act as a means of social control over the female body. On the other hand, beauty is also seen as a potentially pleasurable instrument of female agency (Cahill 2003; Davis 2013; Gimlin 2002). These writers emphasize women's subjective experiences of beauty and how they might derive personal satisfaction from cosmetic surgery, beautification and self-stylization. This view of beauty as a tool of female agency has proved illuminating for my work, as beauty was an important means through which respondents could have an impact on their everyday experiences. Indeed, recent scholar-ship demonstrates a push towards what Maxine Leeds Craig (2006) calls a more 'complicated' stance on beauty, generating a new wave of work that takes an intersectional approach and explores 'the lure of beauty' (Felski 2006).

From this perspective, beauty is theorized as an experience that does something and in that doing entangles everyday life in unexpected ways. Following on this point, I complicate the approach to beauty by chal-lenging analyses based on an implicit Euro-American reading of the sub-ject. For example, I will show how racial discourses about whitening, racial mixture, and multicultural promotions of black pride in Brazil chal-lenge the dominance of global white beauty standards.

More recently, feminist writing has been focusing on the 'pragmatics' of beauty—that is, 'how is beauty defined, deployed, defended, subordi-nated, marketed or manipulated' (Colebrook 2006, 132). This has been a useful approach in writing this chapter. What people do on a daily basis throws light on how they create, cope with and resist racialized inequal-ities in their own countries—as well as how they establish connections with the world. This research contributes to a growing body of scholar-ship focused on theoretical and empirically grounded comparative work, deepening our understanding of how the meaning of beauty is entangled in wider inequalities such as gender, race and class, which in turn are tied to notions of citizenship and nationhood.

RESEARCH CONTEXT

The legacies of plantation slavery and colonialism in Jamaica and north-eastern Brazil have created similar racial formations (Beckford 1972; Wagley 1957). Despite the significant contributions of African descendants to economic, cultural and social life, they have long been marginalized, to varying degrees, from national processes and equal citizenship. With limited opportunities for upward mobility, strategies of 'whitening' became a means by which African descendants could improve their lives and social position. This could be achieved through marriage to lighter-skinned spouses, thereby producing lighter-skinned offspring, or through adopting the lifestyles and values of the elite and acquiring wealth and education. Either way, such persons could cross racial boundaries to some extent by their association with whiteness. However, in both Brazil and Jamaica, the creation of national ideologies of race mixture, the impact of social movements such as the black conscious movement, the influence of African derived religions, and the implementation of multicultural policies have challenged traditional race relations. Ideas about beauty and racialized perceptions of skin colour and the body inform each other within a dominant discourse on *mestizaje* (racial mixing) within the Latin American and Caribbean context. Seen largely as a positive process, it is nevertheless an unsettled, relational project where 'people are not white or black, but rather, they are whiter than or darker than others' (Moreno Figueroa 2013, 139). Celebrations of *mestizaje* are common to the region; however, this often obscures the hierarchies that are part of the region's historical legacy. In the case of Brazil, for example, the work of Elizabeth Hordge-Freeman (2015) and Alvaro Jarrín (2017) has demonstrated that this discourse of *mestizaje* imposes aesthetic hierarchies where whiteness is valued and blackness is devalued. This beauty norm is not simply a Western hegemonic ideal but part of national ideologies, which means that attempts to revalue black bodies are often met with strong resistance from dominant groups in Brazil.

Unlike Brazil and the Caribbean, South Africa has had minimal experience with slavery except in the Cape. The concept of a coloured or mixed-race identity is quite specific to racial thinking in South Africa. The nature of coloured identity and its heritage of oppression, betrayal and marginalization have been matters of intense political and ideological contestation. Indeed, some have argued that coloured identity in the new South Africa is one of fragmentation, uncertainty, negative racial stereotyping, and confusion, and is experiencing dramatic change since the emergence of the term in the nineteenth century (Adhikari 2005). Competition and conflict between colonial powers in South Africa led to less stability than existed in Brazil where the consistent maintenance of Portuguese rule helped to reduce internal conflict (Marx 1998, 45). Brazil's colonial legacy of greater unity and state centralization brought greater stability to race relations than was the case in South Africa. Unlike South Africa or the segregationist American South, racial categories were not imposed legally. This is not a trivial distinction—when racial discrimination is mandated by law, it operates in a more rigid and inflexible way than in societies in which it is informal and at the discretion of individuals (ibid., 7f.). At the same time, the informality of racial discrimination has made racism difficult to name in Brazil.

Apartheid discourse on race in South Africa legally entrenched unequal access to housing, employment, remuneration, education, health and other social services.[4] However, lived reality sometimes defied apartheid's pure types. People resorted to using the system of racial classification to pass for 'white' or 'coloured' in order to access the rights and opportunities associated with these legal categories (Erasmus 2007). When South Africa emerged from apartheid, the Black Economic Empowerment programme was instituted in 1996 as an affirmative action policy that sought to increase the numbers of non-whites in the public and private sectors. Formerly, white residential areas were opened up and public spaces in general became more racially mixed than before. The race and class basis of social inequality has, therefore, been changing, albeit slowly. A black middle-class has emerged, building on older origins.

Today, Brazil and South Africa are emerging economies yet highly unequal. In Brazil, social and economic indicators continue to demonstrate significant disparities between blacks and whites (Reichmann 1999). In South Africa, blacks have emerged out of extreme forms of racial segregation and discrimination under apartheid, yet there is much debate about their rise. The term 'black diamonds' has been used to describe this politically empowered elite, whose members are said to be characterized by lavish lifestyles and high-end consumerism.[5] Some (such as Mbeki 2009) claim that black political elites are more alienated than ever from the masses of poor, black people. Indeed, black elites are often critiqued in the media for their opulence, vulgarity and lack of style. Physical appearance and self-styling are major concern for the black elite in South Africa. Their situation recalls historical accounts of the birth of mass culture in the United States and Europe in the early twentieth century, when the middle and working classes—especially immigrant communities—had to be taught how to consume. These historical accounts of twentieth century consumption in Europe and the US have explored the history of shopping, advertising and marketing as activities of individuals and as arenas for corporate endeavour (Benjamin 2006; Heinze 1990; Strasser et al. 1998; Zelizer 1997). This is a phenomenon that is ever present in South Africa today. Malls, department stores, the media, lifestyle magazines, financial institutions, the automotive, telecommunications and beauty industries, international companies and brands now target a section of the population who were formerly excluded from certain urban spaces and consumption of particular goods under apartheid. Consumption of a wide array of local and international brands could be one way that black elites link themselves to the nation and to the rest of the world.

To sum up, while in Brazil and Jamaica racial formations were more flexible and allowed for boundary crossing, South African racial categories were more rigid. The dismantling of apartheid has rendered the term 'black middle class' even more meaningful in the policy-driven environment of transformation taking place in South Africa today. As a modern consumer culture expands and targets new groups that were previously marginalized, it creates special conditions for a strong emphasis on appearance among emerging black middle classes. In the following section, I will explore these themes in more detail using ethnographic examples drawn from Brazil and South Africa.

Keeping Up Appearances

On a breezy afternoon in November 2006, I stood in the foyer of the Teatro Castro Alves, a historically important theatre in Salvador, Brazil. The theatre goers chatted while drinking cups of coffee. When members of the Teixeira family walked into the foyer, they represented some of the few darker-skinned faces in the crowd but they did not look out of place. Indeed, they were described by their friends as a particularly stylish, sophisticated and educated family. On this afternoon, the women of the family were dressed elegantly, makeup carefully applied, a hint of perfume, smart handbags, high-heeled shoes and expensive sunglasses perched on top of their well-coiffed hair. In a country obsessed with svelte and sensual bodies, they blended easily into the crowd, exuding confidence, style and glamour. Eventually, Juliana, the matriarch of the family, introduced me to a tall man standing beside her, 'This is Alberto, the plastic surgeon who totally reformed my breasts and stomach after my divorce. His hands are like magic, he is a great artist. I am very happy with my results'. Alberto smiled and lifted his cup of coffee to hers.

While plastic surgery is subsidized by the public health system in Brazil, those who can afford it go to private clinics where the cost could vary from USD$ 6000 upwards (Machado-Borges 2008, 152). In speaking openly about her plastic surgery, Juliana was likely making the point that she was financially able to participate in the consumption of this particular beauty practice in a country where plastic surgeons have been known to state that 'everyone has a right to beauty' (Edmonds 2010, 14). Indeed, one of the more distinctive things about the Teixeiras was the manner in which they presented themselves and managed their bodies—their dress, physical appearance, body language and speech. For example, Juliana stated that she never left her house without her hair being well-groomed (meaning, chemically straightened and dyed black), her skin looking good and her clothes fashionable. I was first introduced to Juliana's three daughters, all in their thirties, at the party of a Brazilian friend who explained to me that, 'They are different from the common person here in Salvador. You can tell because they are *bem educadas*. Look at how beautiful they are!'[6]

According to Juliana, the Teixeira family is descended from an original union between an African slave woman and the son of a wealthy Dutch sugar plantation owner. This man subsequently married a white woman but all of the children from the former union were well taken care of. Juliana's parents lived a comfortable life and were respected in their neighbourhood—her father was university educated, worked for a British shipping company and spoke many languages, while her mother was an educator. They maintained a relatively privileged position for generations. Juliana acknowledged that they have had to downscale in the current economic environment. But none have become poor. Indeed it could be said that they have reformulated their status over time, by selective consumption of particular items of cultural value and by maintaining their social networks.

Juliana stated that in the past, family members preferred to refer to themselves as *mulato(a) claro(a)* (light skinned/mixed race). As a child, she sometimes heard relatives make disparaging remarks about the physical features and moral traits of darker-skinned persons. These racialized discourses surrounding appearance and the valuation of particular, physical traits possibly indicate strategies among non-white elites to distance themselves as much as possible from the negative valuation of blackness and racial discrimination, although they did not always escape it. For example, Juliana related that many years ago, her mother, Rita (now deceased), tried to gain entrance into one of Salvador's most exclusive social clubs. Rita had many long standing, influential friends among the Euro-Brazilian elite who were members of the club. One of them was the *prefeito* (mayor) of Salvador and he wrote a reference letter for Rita. Nevertheless, the club's executive committee rejected Rita's application. Her friends were convinced that their friend's skin colour was the deciding factor. To protest the club's decision, they immediately withdrew their membership.

This story related by Juliana is potentially revealing of everyday social relations in many ways. Firstly, it indicated how personal relationships across lines of colour and class (friendships, kin ties) could sometimes mitigate the negative effects of having darker skin colour, though it did not always protect them from discrimination. Secondly, it could be the case that Rita's friends did not perceive or treat her as black—in other words, she had become structurally and symbolically 'white' by virtue of being seen as a member of their class. Therefore, the story indicates that there were instances in which persons could cross racial boundaries as they become upwardly mobile. Adopting upper middle-class Eurocentric beauty ideals was important for social acceptance, which Juliana achieved through cosmetic surgery, purchasing cosmetic products and prestigious fashion labels, chemically straightening her hair at the salon, and regular visits to the dermatologist to keep her skin smooth.

Some generations later, the growth of an increasingly vocal black movement—as well as the adoption of legislation against racism and policies directed at reducing racial inequality—has led to a more positive valuation of 'blackness' in Brazil (Sansone 2003; Telles 2004). The younger generation of the Teixeira family claim a more politicized, black identity—symbolized by their use of the Brazilian Portuguese term *negro*—while challenging others in their family to take on this identity. For example, they criticized their mother's brother, Bruno, for describing himself as *Brasileiro* (Brazilian), which is a way of stating his claim to a mixed-race identity, in line with dominant national discourses prevalent amongst his generation. Younger people, however, would be more familiar with an international, multicultural discourse of 'race', especially since the United Nation's Declaration of Human Rights in 1948 and the subsequent implementation of multicultural policies into the constitutions of many Latin American nations (Kymlicka 1995).

Unlike her brother, Juliana identified as *negra* and indicated that racial prejudice persists, illustrating her point by referring to the discriminatory way that lighter-skinned shop owners treat her when she enters their expensive stores. Yet she emphasized the family's indigenous heritage when explaining the frequent comments made by others about their 'good looks'. She made reference to the high cheek bones, petite frame and 'finer' hair that many women in the Teixeira family possessed, associated with an indigenous rather than an African background. Here, a statement is being made about culturally preferred physical features, in which the lowest rank is assigned to an appearance associated with an African heritage—such as tightly curled, kinky hair.[7] A darker-skinned person might, therefore, distance themselves from unflattering associations with blackness, claiming an indigenous heritage instead.

In Brazil, it was not uncommon for contradictory discourses about 'race' to exist within the same context—an identification with blackness and a distancing from the more stigmatizing meanings of blackness. What is interesting about the Teixeira family case are the different ways in which its members negotiated unequal society in Salvador, employing discourses or practices centred on the body to erase or stress difference. In this sense, they could move across racial boundaries or categories depending on the context. However, it was a lot more challenging for my respondents in South Africa to transcend racial boundaries, as I will illustrate below.

As the summer was coming to an end in May 2012, I was invited to a pool barbecue in Pretoria. I met Hope—an attractive, middle-aged woman with a lively and warm personality, who offered to be my first interviewee. She invited me to a dinner party at her upscale home in the northern suburbs of Johannesburg. Originally from the city of Durban on the Pacific coast of South Africa, she described her family as having mixed ancestry—East Indian, white and Zulu. They were classified as coloured by the South African government, and this required them to live in a coloured township under apartheid. She described her mother as a housewife, coming from a well-to-do family with substantial land as well as cattle, poultry, livestock and horses. Her father's family was less wealthy. He worked as an administrator in a local company. However, despite their comfortable standard of living, they were marginalized under South Africa's apartheid regime and had to negotiate the limited amenities, services and opportunities available to them as coloured South Africans. Negative stereotypes about coloured people abounded— such as their supposed propensity for alcohol, violence and promiscuity. However, Hope's mother was determined to counter these negative stereotypes by giving her daughter the best life she could possibly offer. She had an excellent command of English and made sure to pass on this skill to Hope, as many persons from the township could not speak or write in English. Hope felt that this skill had been beneficial in her professional and personal life, allowing for some mobility. She applied to work as a receptionist in a travel agency during the 1980s. This propelled her into the social world of white South Africans, since they were principally the ones who travelled. She recalled that at first, her clients were often surprised at seeing who she was after speaking to her on the phone. They had not expected to see a coloured woman in that setting, carrying herself confidently and possessing the required language skills to move in their context.

In this working environment, she was required to attend social gatherings, speak well and dress elegantly. She spent 10 years in this environment which was enough time to get to know some of her clients—indeed, some invited her to their parties and she began to make friendships. While she had access to these social settings, in apartheid South Africa you had to return to the neighbourhood to which you were designated, according to your racial classification. One evening, a senior manager offered to take Hope home in his car. They were stopped by police under the suspicion of being an inter-racial couple. One of the policemen accused Hope of being a 'Transkei beauty queen.'[8] At the time, inter-racial sexual affairs were illegal under the Immorality Act. When it became clear that they were just colleagues the police let them go. Racial boundaries were, therefore, difficult to cross in a legal system of racial segregation.

Eventually, Hope went into television broadcasting as a news reporter. She was chosen for this position because of her ability to speak English and because she presented a pleasing visual appearance, as her managers explained. However, her visual appearance did not suit a changing media industry when apartheid came to an end in 1994. Today, Hope coaches business executives and managers—especially black entrepreneurs who now have access to new economic opportunities. In the competitive business world of Johannesburg where executive boardrooms are still primarily white and male, she assists black South Africans who want to learn how to negotiate these environments successfully and confidently. She focuses on their physical appearance (dress, skin tone, hair, and personal grooming) as well as speech, body language and etiquette. Indeed, Hope's physical appearance is one of the main ways in which she markets herself—she makes sure that her skin, hair and nails are always maintained in good condition and that her clothes are fashionable because she must present to her clients a convincing and successful image of herself. Hope mentioned a case where she had to advise a black executive woman to get her teeth straightened and whitened, as an essential component of her image in the business world. In the case of another business client who attended high profile social events, Hope gave advice on fashion labels and cosmetics. These stories reflect the anxieties of a post-apartheid society where changes in status and the visibility of previously marginalized groups of people in the city lead to a strong emphasis on appearance.

Hope is the manager of her own business. Re-defining herself as a black woman, she has been able to take advantage of government policies that are specially geared towards black women. Hope argues that anyone who was not white under apartheid is black, because all non-whites were formerly subjected to racism and repressive policies. She has built a comfortable life for herself, living in a formerly white neighbourhood, with a vacation home in Port Elizabeth in the Eastern Cape province—a far cry from her life growing up in a depressed coloured township in Durban. Her daughter Maya, on the other hand, has grown up in a more privileged environment, attending private schools and circulating in social contexts where many of her peers are white or light skinned. To counteract Maya's upbringing in a largely white upper middle-class environment, Hope has several works of art as well as musical collections by black South African artists and bookshelves throughout the house stacked with literature on South Africa's diverse history, culture and peoples—especially the struggles of black South Africans for freedom.

In summary, it is clear that Hope had less opportunity in her society to cross racial barriers in comparison to my middle-class respondents in Brazil for whom separate residential areas and enforced segregation was not a part of their daily reality. However, there are some ways in which their experiences are similar. Hope's social mobility, as well as the Teixeiras, is connected to the norms and symbols of what in their respective societies is considered 'white.' After the end of apartheid, Hope could change her racial identity from coloured to black South African. Similarly, my Brazilian respondents were also reflecting on and challenging their own racial identifications in a changing environment that allows for a more positive valuation of 'blackness.' Finally, both cases illustrate that physical appearance can be deployed as a kind of social capital as respondents attempted to negotiate highly unequal societies—even though at times physical appearance could also be the basis of discrimination.

The 'Aesthetics' of Race

While studies of the relationship between race and beauty exist (Banet-Weiser 1999; Banks 2000), feminist writers have tended to emphasize the dominance of Euro-American beauty standards, thereby neglecting alternative cultural logics of beauty. In this section, I will elaborate on the repercussions of dominant western paradigms of beauty, as well as alternative discourses and anti-racist critiques.

Researchers writing primarily on Caribbean and black populations living in the United States and Britain have noted that dominant western paradigms of beauty are reflected in the importance of having 'good hair' (straight or wavy), 'a good nose' (small and narrow), and 'a good complexion' (white or light skinned) among these groups (see Collins 2000; hooks 1993; Weekes 1997). This literature points to an 'aesthetics of race' in black diasporic communities in which some physical features are ranked according to their approximation to whiteness. Physical features associated with blackness, such as curly Afro-textured hair and dark skin colour, tend to be negatively valuated within this schema.[9] These racialized discourses have a special impact on women in relation to dominant notions of femininity that emphasize long, flowing hair. For example, Dorothy, who is lighter-skinned in relation to her peers in Jamaica, lives in an upscale area of Kingston. Her sister, Yolanda, has long, wavy hair while Dorothy's hair has always been curlier, prompting comments from neighbours and friends that she should groom her hair and make sure that it is tidy. Now 45 years old, Dorothy thinks these comments indicate prejudice towards curlier, Afro-textured hair. She related that when she was 15 years old, she told her parents that she wanted to chemically straighten her hair for her high school graduation ball. This was not regarded as an unusual request by her family. Rather, Dorothy's aunt and mother had undergone similar hair straightening rituals as young women. When Dorothy emerged from the neighbourhood salon sporting a shoulder-length, straightened hairstyle, her appearance was praised by several neighbours, friends and family members, signalling her acceptance into established middle-class norms of beauty.

To reiterate, dominant racial hierarchies and beauty norms have real effects on individuals' lives. In Jamaica, this may be reflected in a preference for lighter-skinned or 'brown' romantic partners, deemed to be more attractive—a cultural norm that children learn while growing up, as in the case of Dorothy above (Miller 1969; Mohammed 2000). In Brazil, a hyper-emphasis on *boa aparência* has emerged in competitive labour markets. Traditionally, *boa aparência* meant having lighter skin combined with certain signs of a higher social class position. This concept has specific meanings for female employees in the modern service and financial sectors (Edmonds 2010; Telles 2004). Employers concerned with reflecting an image of modernity, cosmopolitanizm and glamour to their customers hire employees that vary in shade from brown to light skinned and are mostly slim, smooth skinned and young with straight or long hair (Edmonds 2007, 2010). According to Abdullah (1998) and Thompson (2009), it is a common experience for black women with 'natural hair' to be deemed unkempt and unprofessional by employers. For example, in a newspaper article by Janet Silvera (2012) entitled *Policewomen fight to wear Afro-centric Hairdos*, it was reported that policewomen working with the Jamaica Constabulary Force were told that they could only wear fine corn or cane rows. Other hairstyles for Afro-textured hair, such as twists, dreadlocks, and fat plaits were not allowed. By contrast, texturized (chemically straightened) or permed hair was perfectly acceptable. These kinds of lived realities are believed to contribute to the prevalence of beauty practices such as hair straightening and skin bleaching or lightening. Despite the documented physical, medical and psychological effects of skin bleaching practices on the body, it continues to be practiced in many countries across the African diaspora (Charles 2003, 2009; Glenn 2008; Ribane 2006). While it occurred in all three research settings, skin bleaching is dealt with extensively by other authors and will not be discussed in this chapter (see, for example, Hall 1994, 1995; Mire 2001).

The historical roots of these kinds of discourses and practices are to be found in the way that Africa and African bodies have been conceived in Western aesthetic discourses as embodying ugliness and moral decay. According to 'enlightenment' discourse, including in the writings of Kant (2004 [1960]) or, in reference to Brazil, de Gobineau (1855, quoted from Schwarcz 1993, 5), ugliness was particularly visible in the black body. Nowhere is this more emphasized than in the case of the 'Hottentot Venus'—the famed South African Sara (or Saartjie) Baartman, a Khoisan woman who was brought to England and France for public exhibition between 1810 and 1815 (Gilman 1985). The 'Hottentot Venus' came to symbolize both the presumed ugliness and heightened sexuality of the African race Baartman's body was exhibited in nineteenth century freak shows to display her large buttocks and her 'African' physical features, seen to be the opposite of femininity and beauty in Europe (Hobson 2005, 1).[10] More recently, the image of the 'freakish' black female body resurfaced in global debates regarding the gender and sexuality of South African athlete Caster Semenya. After her performance in the 2009 World Championships in Athletics, she had to undergo degrading 'gender testing' and faced brutal scrutiny by fellow athletes, journalists and sport officials. Other well-known figures from across the black diaspora, such as professional tennis player Serena Williams and ballet dancer Misty Copeland, have also faced discrimination from mainly white audiences about their supposedly 'deviant' bodies. This links back to the spectacle of the 'Hottentot Venus,' as these black women's bodies were perceived as deviating from global norms of femininity, gender, and beauty, while occasionally they were also eroticized.

Even as these hegemonic ideas of the 'ugly' black female body are present across Africa and the African diaspora, other discourses of beauty exist that challenge this view. In South Africa, cultural ideals link a larger body shape with affluence, beauty, and prosperity among black and coloured populations (Caradas et al. 2001). Similarly, in the Jamaican context, a cultural preference for voluptuous bodies with a well-rounded bottom ('batty' in Jamaican parlance) is taken rather seriously in Jamaican discourses of beauty and desire. Although a rising fitness and gym culture focusing on slimmer bodies is taking place especially in urban areas, popular culture continues to celebrate the 'fluffy' (curvy) woman, such as in the 2014 carnival calypso song by DJ Killa, 'I Want a Rolly Polly'. The song's lyrics glorify a generous and curvy female shape:

Ah want ah fat gyal, Ah want ah Rolly Polly, Ah want a big gyal, you make me bawl holy moly	I want a fat girl, I want a Rolly Polly, I want a big girl, you make me shout holy moly

Whether in working class dancehall settings or more middle-class carnival celebrations, female bottoms are let loose in uninhibited, glorious celebrations of flesh and sexual energy. While such displays have historically been characterized as riotous and disorderly, such movements of the 'batty' in the contexts of dancehall and carnival invite a public discourse that challenges colonial constructs of decency and white supremacy.[11] The very essence of black women's dancing threatened systems of class, gender, race and nationality. Less feminine and disorderly dances were relegated to the margins—looked down upon by black, mixed race and East Indian elites who imagined a more feminine public persona.

In Brazil and Jamaica, national discourses of race mixture shaped alternative beauty ideals. For example, the *morena* (mixed race brown woman) is the quintessential icon of a long-standing ideology of racial democracy in Brazil, portrayed in eroticized images of carnival, samba and football. The *morena* supposedly embodies the positive characteristics of each race in Brazil. In Jamaica, a national creole identity has been encouraged since independence in 1962, reflected in the national motto, 'Out of Many, One People.' Beauty pageants promoted racial and cultural diversity, thereby linking these contests with dominant constructs of the nation (Barnes 2006, 64–65). Yet beauty contests have received criticism for selecting beauty queens that represent Euro-centric beauty values. However, these beauty ideals are changing, as witnessed in the 2017 Miss Universe Pageant where Miss Jamaica—a dark skinned, 23-year-old woman wearing an Afro—placed in the second runner up position. Her hairstyle stood out from the other contestants' mostly blown-out, straight styles and she was celebrated across social media for wearing her natural hair (cf. Rodulfo 2017).

In South Africa, the promise of a 'Rainbow Nation,' a term coined by Archbishop Desmond Tutu that has come to encapsulate the hopes of a non-racial, post-apartheid South Africa, appear to be going unfulfilled for some, especially in light of recent youth-driven protests and social movements.[12] The lifestyle of a small minority of black elites, portrayed in popular soap operas such as *Generations* and television shows such as *Top Billing*, seem out of reach for the majority of black South Africans.

These programs disseminate images of successful black entrepreneurs to transnational audiences, including in Jamaica, where the show is broadcasted. While *Generations* is an important show in that it conveys a sense of black pride across the diaspora, normative, that is, hegemonic Euro-American ideals of femininity are reflected in the show's most central characters—such as Dineo, a single woman constantly searching for a boyfriend (and ultimately, a husband). She is beautiful, slim, well dressed and glamorous, the editor of a fashion magazine. Her hair is mostly worn straight or wavy—long or short—always in a style associated with sophisticated, modern lifestyles. Accordingly, an alternative soap opera called *Muvhango*, was created by the South African theatre producer Katsenga, focusing on African culture, language and dress and incorporating traditional beauty practices, such as hairstyling practices including short, closely cut hair, braids, tresses and chignons.[13] Recently, Katsenga intervened in a heated social media debate about the hairstyles of an actress, Maggie Benedict, who played the part of Akhona in *Generations*. He stated that comments about her naturally curly hair on social media revealed black peoples' hatred of their own skin, hair and traditional culture. Mr. Katsenga, who was a freedom fighter and a black activist in his youth, argued that the black conscious movement of previous decades did not seem to have had an effect on helping black people to appreciate each other and their bodies. His Facebook post went viral and attracted nation-wide support.

To summarize briefly, this section showed how people both conform and resist normative beauty standards on the background of historical and ongoing devaluations of non-white bodies. In Jamaica and Brazil, the cultural preference and desirability of the mixed-race woman complicates the assumption of a white beauty norm that is dominant globally and invites more exploration. In South Africa, the national ideal of a non-racial society is being challenged by citizens who continue to feel excluded and discriminated against. In both South Africa and Jamaica, the cultural norm of a generously curvy, full figured woman is celebrated among black and mixed-race populations while the ideal of a slim body type holds more sway in Brazil. Picking up on the idea of attitudes to black hair raised in this section, I develop this theme in the following section by underscoring how particular beauty practices centred on hair provide an important window through which to understand black peoples' ongoing struggles to negotiate their identities 'in the power structures of their societies' (Chibnall 1985, 87).

HAIR AND HAIR-STYLING

Researchers have argued that hair is central to black culture and experience across Africa and the African diaspora (Barnett 2016; Batulukisi 2000; Gomes 2006; Mercer 1987; Sieber 2000). In Jamaica and Brazil, colonial discourses about race and beauty often targeted hair styling as a way of disciplining unruly bodies, as reflected in practices such as school rules about hair grooming and preferred hairstyles enforced by employers. Some would argue that these attitudes still exist despite the influence of the black consciousness movement in the 1960s and the resistance of Rastafarians to colonial power structures through the symbolizm of their hair (referred to as 'natty dreads').

Writers such as Erasmus (1997), Fanon (1967), Miller (1969), and Tafari-Ama (2006) are just a few of the scholars who have articulated the perspective that internalized racism has resulted in a sense of shame in African features. Tafari-Ama (2016) has argued that black women are anxiously preoccupied with imitating a Eurocentric identity model, such that they have shifted to imitating Eurocentric hairstyles as a social norm.

Hair is probably one of the most important, visible signs of the social and aesthetic power of a woman in black diasporic communities and is related to meaningful symbols of upward mobility and respectable femininity (Barnett 2016). Although there are a variety of hair practices informed by different influences and historical forces, there is a strong preference among many black women for long or wavy hair, especially in Brazil (Gomes 2006). These beauty practices begin in childhood and include perming, chemically straightening the hair, setting hair on large, plastic rollers or more recently, buying extensions from places like China, Brazil and India and then having a hairstylist sew or glue them unto the natural hair.

In African cultures, hairstyling has a complex and diverse history and hair can reflect 'one's place in the cycle of life, one's status, or one's special condition as a leader (Sieber 2000, 16). Indigenous hair practices have mixed with western beauty ideals as well as discourses and practices from other African countries and the black diaspora. In South Africa, the fall of apartheid meant that women began earning more money and had greater access to beauty products and services (Ojong 2005, v). According to Gugulethu Mhlungu (2014), South Africa's black hair industry has an estimated value of ZAR 6.7 billion a year and was considered to be the largest in Africa by the Professional Hair Care Market 2010 Report. Consumption of a variety of hair products and services has become a major indicator of modernity and performing citizenship in the nation.[14] West African female migrants skilled in hairdressing were quick to seize this opportunity and introduced hair extensions and other westernized and African hairstyles to the South African market (Ojong 2005, v). At the same time, a growing number of local and international brands—such as 'Perfect Choice', 'Revlon', and 'Black Like Me'—entered the market, targeting previously excluded social groups. Increasingly, they have concentrated their efforts on black and coloured townships. For example, Perfect Choice, a brand that focuses on chemically relaxed hair, uses the catchy phrase 'the sisterhood circle.' This is a marketing strategy focused on popularizing straightened hair through kinship and friendship networks.

Women striving for mobility today may experience more social pressure in their work and personal circles to conform to urban standards of normative beauty. Affluent middle-class women may have more information and knowledge about hair care and perhaps more freedom to choose natural hairstyles such as braids, top knots, and dreadlocks. However, their socially powerful position does not protect them from public criticism, as noted in the previous discussion in reference to debates surrounding the hairstyles of TV series characters. In South Africa too, transnational hairstyles such as the African American 'Afro,' or Jamaican dreadlocks, helped to redefine blackness as a positive attribute in the 1960s and 1970s by affording what Mercer (1987, 37) calls a 'liberating rupture' from dominant white styles.

In Brazil and Jamaica, tightly curled hair is associated with an African heritage and frequently defined as ugly and unfeminine. In Brazil, the terms *cabelo ruim* (bad hair) and *cabelo duro* (hard hair) are used in reference to Afro-textured hair. Indeed, it was not long ago when, in July 1996, an album was released in Brazil that included a song *Veja os cabelos dela* ('Look at Her Hair') by Tiririca, a Brazilian singer, comedian and politician. While popularly regarded as playful and humorous, the song included a number of negative stereotypes about black women, highlighting the gendered dimensions of racism. The song refers to a woman who initially captures the singer's attention, but whose hair he finds undesirable, likening it to a scouring pad used to clean pots and pans. His description of her also makes reference to her smell and skin colour, such as:

Essa nega fede, fede de lascar,	This black woman stinks, she
Bicha federenta, fede mais que	stinks horribly, Stinking beast,
gamba	she smells worse than a skunk

The song associates black bodies with ugliness and stench—and in particular, stigmatizes the texture of black women's hair. The lyrics created an outcry amongst black activists and resulted in both Tiririca and his recording label, Sony Music, being sued for racism. However, the song was not seen as offensive by most Brazilians, but rather as a *brincadeira* (joke). Indeed, Brazilian discourses of 'race' have frequently used humour to transmit racist stereotypes (Goldstein 1999; Sheriff 2001). Even when black cultural organizations attempt to resist racist stereotypes and emphasize pride in black features, they encounter resistance not only from dominant groups but also within the intimate sphere of Afro-Brazilian family life. For example, the leader of a black female carnival band in Salvador recounted how one of the members of her organization, a 15-year-old girl by the name of Mariana, was asked to appear on the television show *Domingo Alegria*. Given that her carnival band prides itself on promoting black women's 'natural' physical features, she was surprized when Mariana appeared with her hair wet.[15] She enquired why Mariana had not worn her hair in an Afro as she normally does. Mariana tearfully replied that her grandmother had scolded her for going out of the house with her 'hard' hair, instructing her to properly groom it by wetting it.

Multicultural discourses of race that promote blackness as a source of pride have led to some changes. For example, Brazilian black feminists have organized workshops on hair-braiding and natural hair styling, underscoring efforts to challenge dominant prejudices regarding the hair texture of black women (Caldwell 2007). These efforts have had mixed results, as we can see in the case of Mariana's family above. The popularity of blonde hair extensions among women who are the target of these efforts underscores the need to evaluate more closely conditions of power in the lives of lower- versus middle-class women.

Nevertheless, the increased promotion of beauty practices that express pride in blackness has challenged hegemonic models present in Brazilian society that have tended to highlight lighter skin colour and hair. An expanding black beauty industry (occurring in Brazil and elsewhere) seems to have arisen to address this need (Dos Santos 2000; Gomes 2006). The contemporary concept of *beleza black* (black beauty)—which derives from African-American civil rights struggles during the 1960s—is associated with these black movement discourses. It also reflects links between a national black movement and the global pan-African movement (Sansone 2003). Cultural organizations in the city emphasise blackness as a source of pride and beauty as their members march through the streets in African-style fashion featuring bold prints and colours, their hair in braids and decorated with bright beads. The idea of un-straightened hair has gained currency among some participants in Brazil and elsewhere, especially with the increased availability of hair care products now on the market. Hairstyles such as the afro, braids and dreadlocks signify the embrace of an alternative ideological code of value.

Moral arguments have been put forward that those with straightened hair want to cultivate a 'European' appearance and are, therefore, suffering from low self-esteem and a mutilated black consciousness. Yet respondents asserted their right to style themselves in whatever way they felt like without being judged for it. For example, Nyla grew up in a rural community in Jamaica. Her mother came from a sugar cane district and her father came from a farming family. As she got older, her mother decided to take her to the capital city where she could access more opportunities. They lived in a poor Kingston neighbourhood with an aunt while her mother tried to negotiate her daughter's access to higher quality education. Nyla did well in her high school examinations and entered Law School.

She met her husband shortly after successfully graduating with her degree. His story is similar to Nyla's, in that he achieved considerable professional success against great economic odds. Their marriage cemented their arrival at a privileged social position. For Nyla, this higher class status appeared to involve some anxieties about appearance. She was concerned about maintaining a slim body type and suitable hairstyle as a professional woman and wife of an influential man. She experimented with various hairstyles, including blonde and red highlights, coloured contact lenses, wigs, and fashionable clothes with international labels. Nyla currently uses Brazilian hair extensions for achieving her desired appearance, prompting one of her friends to comment that she was becoming addicted to 'hair crack'—meaning that she was developing a dependency on hair extensions in order to conform to upper middle-class norms of beauty. However, Nyla frequently stresses that she has always been comfortable with her sexuality and likes experimenting with a variety of styles and fashions, including braids and Afro wigs, stating that she has a right to choose how she wants to look.

Research participants such as Nyla, who assert their right to choose amongst a variety of aesthetic options, might be seen to be adopting de-politicized 'post-feminist' stances towards social inequalities in their country. In *The Aftermath of Feminism*, Angela McRobbie (2009) argues that consumer culture in contemporary society offers the illusion of 'freedom of choice' when in reality, new forms of power are enacted that re-establish patriarchal hegemony and the cultural dominance of whiteness. However, other writers are developing more complicated approaches to understanding black women's hair choices (Barnett 2016; Donaldson 2012; Tate 2007), such as noting elements of creative play involved in participants' beauty work. Applying blonde highlights or implanting long hair weaves are also ways of inverting dominant beauty standards. In other words, some participants resisted their positioning by others to a certain racial category or appearance.

Conclusion

In this chapter, I compared beauty practices and discourses in Brazil, South Africa and Jamaica. The chapter revealed how my self-identified black respondents in these settings crossed or blurred racial boundaries through their beauty discourses and practices. Beauty practices could also be used to stress or erase difference depending on the social context. The ethnographic material shows that this seemed easier for Brazilians and Jamaicans than for South Africans where black people experienced enforced segregation. Through my ethnographic examples, I demonstrated how participants both challenged and reproduced racial inequalities in their societies, with potential revolutionary impacts on a larger scale.

The contradictory position of black middle-class women—as representing both a marginalised and an economically better off stratum of the population—poses some complex issues for interpretation. In particular, notions of beauty and femininity in Brazil and Jamaica privilege a brown, mixed raced appearance and are shaped by national creole ideologies. However, shifts in racial thinking have made it less problematic to identify with blackness. In South Africa, indigenous cultural practices have mixed with western hegemonic discourses about beauty as well as discourses and practices from the African diaspora.

Even as some of these practices seem contradictory, Nyamnjoh and Fuh (2014) argue that African identities are more flexible and accommodate varied collective visions of beauty. Meanwhile, some respondents, especially in Brazil and Jamaica, resisted being classified as belonging to any particular racial category when it came to their beauty practices. The spread of consumer culture in South Africa among populations that were previously marginalized invites further research. Writers who analyze the contemporary dynamics of post-feminism such as McRobbie (2009) suggest that consumer culture appeals to ideas about female success and choice while it in fact reinforces traditional power dynamics and ties women into new, neurotic tendencies (such as eating disorders). In the case of research participants, consumption focused on the body (beauty treatments, fashion, surgery) represents a symbolic and material way of positioning themselves within their societies as well as relating to the world—thus becoming 'visible,' that is be recognized as valuable and regarded with favour like any other citizen.

NOTES

1. A recent World Bank report (Ferreira et al. 2013) stated that Latin America and the Caribbean registered a fifty percent jump in the number of people joining the middle classes in the last decade. More specifically, the middle classes in the region grew to an estimated 152 million in 2009, compared to 103 million in 2003. Meanwhile, Javier Blas (*Financial Times*, 18 April 2014) draws from African Development Bank data to show that Africa's middle classes are expanding. Numbering 115 million in 1980, the middle classes are said to have grown to 326 million in the past three and a half decades. However, in comparison to other emerging economies, Africa still has the smallest middle class as a share of the total population. Thus, the African middle classes account for 33% of the population of the region, while in Asia this figure is 56% and in Latin America, 77%.

2. By 'emerging elites,' I refer to the literature on the rise of the middle classes said to be taking place in the developing world, particularly in the emerging economies of Brazil, South Africa, India, and China (see, for example, Davis 2010; Ncube and Lufumpa 2014; Neri 2008; Zhang 2010). When I refer to 'black elites' or 'black middle classes,' more specifically, I include both political and social elites. See Deane (1978), Kuper (1965), Seekings and Nattrass (2005), and Bond (2005) on the origins, trajectories and lifestyles of Black elites in South Africa; Gordon (2015) and Figueiredo (2002, 2003) on Brazil; and Robotham (2000)

on Jamaica. Despite differences in the contours of the black middle classes in each case, my work attempts to carry out a comparative analysis of race and inequality across these different contexts.

3. Studies that focus on masculinity and men's physical appearance and stylization include Bogatsu (2009), Buckridge (2009), Hope (2010), Klopper (2010), Reid (2013), and Wasser (2016).

4. Housing, employment, remuneration, education, health and social services are also highly racialized in Brazil. However, my middle class Brazilian interlocutors often lived in neighbourhoods with white Brazilians and indeed had kin ties with the Euro-Brazilian elite. This degree of racial mixture and integration was not typical of the South African context.

5. South Africa's journalists and marketing specialists have written about the new black middle classes, frequently referred to as 'black diamonds', exploring and debating the signs of its identity and development. Reports from bodies such as the corporate funded Unilever Strategic Marketing at Cape Town University and TNS Surveys have produced reports such as, 'Black Diamond on the Move' (16 June 2007). In this latter document, it was reported that the black middle classes experienced an increase in their average personal monthly incomes from R 1550 in 2005 to R 1650 in 2007.

6. This Brazilian Portuguese term refers to having both formal education and a sense of etiquette and cultural knowledge.

7. For deeper insight into the meaning of racialized features in Brazil, please see Hordge-Freeman (2015) and Alvaro Jarrín (2017).

8. Transkai was a Bantustan or homeland set aside for members of a specific ethnicity in the south eastern region of South Africa, created as part an apartheid policy of 'separate development.' In 1994, it was reintegrated into its larger neighbour, Eastern Cape province.

9. Note that counter-examples exist. For example, Nicolas Wasser (2016) describes how a Brazilian fashion label has incorporated the workers' self-stylization as 'authentically black' into its branding strategies.

10. More recently, Baartman became a national symbol when her remains were repatriated to her country of origin and laid to rest in 2002.

11. The term 'batty' has recently taken on a more negative meaning, especially in homophobic expressions that describe gay men as 'batty boys.'

12. These include the #FeesMustFall social movement across many South African Universities, and the recent protests against school policies towards hair grooming and language at Pretoria Girls High School, with the hashtag #StopRacismAtPretoriaGirlsHigh.

13. According to Sieber and Herreman (2000), some of these hairstyles may be very old in African societies.

14. Scholars writing on citizenship increasingly frame the condition of being a citizen in terms of performance and on-going practices, rather than simply in relation to the attainment of formal status (Isin 2008; Ofer and Groves 2016). Urban citizenship is conceptualized as increasingly dependent on self-organization, creative and cultural practices, consumption, social movements, community building, and social activism rather than being restricted to participation in traditional institutions such as political parties and unions.

15. 'Natural' has a subjective meaning here. Black hair has been manipulated into various styles for centuries, and even so-called 'natural hairstyles' require the application of creams, gels, bees wax, and hair extensions to achieve the desired look.

REFERENCES

Abdullah, Afi Samelia. 1998. "Mammy-ism: A Diagnosis of Psychological Misorientation for Women of African Descent." *Journal of Black Psychology* 24 (2): 196–210.

Adhikari, Mohammed. 2005. *Not White Enough, Not Black Enough: Racial Identity in the South African Coloured Community.* Athens: Ohio University Press.

African Development Fund. 2011. "The Middle of the Pyramid: Dynamics of the Middle Class in Africa, April, 20th." https://www.afdb.org/fileadmin/uploads/afdb/Documents/Publications/The%20Middle%20of%20the%20Pyramid_The%20Middle%20of%20the%20Pyramid.pdf. Accessed 10 April 2017.

Banet-Weiser, Sarah. 1999. *The Most Beautiful Girl in the World: Beauty Pageants and National Identity.* Berkeley: University of California Press.

Banks, Ingrid. 2000. *Hair Matters: Beauty, Power and Black Women's Consciousness.* New York and London: New York University Press.

Barnes, Natasha. 2006. *Cultural Conundrums: Gender, Race, Nation and the Making of Caribbean Cultural Politics.* Ann Arbor: University of Michigan Press.

Barnett, Michael. 2016. "The Politics of Hair: A Focus on Natural vs Relaxed Hair in African Caribbean Women." *Ideaz* 14: 69–100.

Basch, Linda, Nina Glick-Schiller, and Cristina Szanton-Blanc. 1994. *Nations Unbound: Transnational Projects, Postcolonial Predicaments and Deterritorialized Nation-States.* Anghorne, PA: Gordon and Breach.

Batulukisi, Niangi. 2000. "Hair in African Art and Culture." In *Hair in African Art and Culture,* edited by Roy Sieber, Frank Herreman, and Niangi Batulukisi, 25–39. New York: The Museum for African Art; Munich: Prestel.

Beckford, George. 1972. *Persistent Poverty: Underdevelopment in Plantation Economies of the Third World*. London: Oxford University Press.

Benjamin, Walter. 2006. *The Writer of Modern Life: Essays on Charles Baudelaire*. Edited by Michael Jennings. Cambridge and London: The Belknap Press of Harvard University Press.

Blas, Javier. 2014. "The Fragile Middle Class: Rising Inequality in Africa weighs in on New Consumers." *Financial Times*, 18 April.

Bogatsu, Mpolokeng. 2009. "Luxion Kulcha: Fashioning Black Youth Culture in Post-Apartheid South Africa." *Journal of English Studies in Africa* 45 (2): 1–11.

Bond, Patrick. 2005. *Elite Transition; From Apartheid to Neoliberalism in South Africa*. South Africa: University of KwaZulu-Natal Press.

Bordo, Susan. 1993. *Unbearable Weight: Feminism, Western Culture and the Body*. Berkeley: University of California Press.

Brodkin, Karen. 1999. *How Jews Became White Folks and What that Says About Race in America*. Piscataway: Rutgers University Press.

Buckridge, Steeve. 2009. *The Language of Dress: Resistance and Accommodation in Jamaica, 1760–1890*. Mona: University of the West Indies Press.

Cahill, Ann J. 2003. "Feminist Pleasure and Feminist Beautification." *Hypatia* 18: 42–64.

Caldwell, Kia Lilly. 2007. *Negras in Brazil: Re-envisioning Black Women, Citizenship, and the Politics of Identity*. New Brunswick: Rutgers University Press.

Caradas, Ashleigh A., Estelle V. Lambert, and Karen E. Charlton. 2001. "An Ethnic Comparison of Eating Attitudes and Associated Body Image Concerns in Adolescent South African School Girls." *Journal of Human Nutrition and Dietetics* 14: 111–20.

Charles, Christopher. 2003. "Skin Bleaching, Self-Hate, and Black Identity in Jamaica." *Journal of Black Studies* 33: 711–28.

Charles, Christopher. 2009. "Skin Bleachers' Representations of Skin Colour in Jamaica." *Journal of Black Studies* 40: 153–70.

Chibnall, Steve. 1985. "Whistle and Zoot: The Changing Meaning of a Suit of Clothes." *History Workshop Journal* 20: 56–81.

Colebrook, Clair. 2006. "Introduction: Special Issue on Beauty and Feminist Theory." *Feminist Theory* 7: 132–42.

Collins, Patricia Hill. 2000. *Black Feminist Thought: Knowledge, Consciousness, and the Politics of Empowerment*. London and New York: Routledge.

Craig, Maxine Leeds. 2006. "Race, Beauty, and the Tangled Knot of a Guilty Pleasure." *Feminist Theory* 7 (2): 159–77.

Davis, Diane E. 2010. "The Socio-Political Reconfiguration of Middle Classes and Their Impact on Politics and Development in the Global South:

Preliminary Ideas for Future Research." *Political Power and Social Theory* 21: 241–69.

Davis, Kathy. 2013. *Re-shaping the Female Body: The Dilemma of Cosmetic Surgery.* New York: Routledge.

Deane, Dee Shirley. 1978. *Black South Africans, A Who's Who: 57 Profiles of Natal's Leading Blacks.* Cape Town: Oxford University Press.

Donaldson, Chanel. 2012. "Hair Alteration Practices Among Black Women and the Assumption of Self-Hatred." NYU, Steinhardt, Applied Psychology Program: OPUS. http://Steinhardt.nyu.edu/appsych/opus/issues/2012/fall/hairalteration. Accessed 3 May 2015.

Dos Santos, Jocélio Teles. 2000. "O Negro no Espelho: Imagens e Discursos nos Salãos de Beleza Éthnicos." *Estudos Afro-Asiaticos* 38: 49–65.

Edmonds, Alexander. 2007. "The Poor Have the Right to be Beautiful: Cosmetic Surgery in Neoliberal Brazil." *Journal of the Royal Anthropological Institute* 13: 363–81.

Edmonds, Alexander. 2010. *Pretty Modern: Beauty, Sex, and Plastic Surgery in Brazil.* Durham: Duke University Press.

Erasmus, Zimitri. 1997. "Oe! My Hare Gaan Huistoe: Hair Styling as Black Cultural Practice." *Agenda* 32: 11–16.

Erasmus, Zimitri. 2007. "Race." In *New South African Keywords*, edited by Nick Shepherd and Steven L. Robbins, 169–81. Ohio: Ohio University Press.

Fanon, Frantz. 1967. *Black Skin, White Masks.* New York: Grove Press.

Felski, Rita. 2006. "'Because It Is Beautiful': New Feminist Perspectives on Beauty". *Feminist Theory* 7 (2): 273–82.

Ferreira, Francisco H.G., Julian Messina, Jamele Rigolini, Luis Felipe Lopez-Calva, Mana Ana Lugo, and Renos Vakis. 2013. *Economic Mobility and the Rise of the Latin American Middle Classes.* Washington, DC: The World Bank. Online: http://siteresources.worldbank.org/LACEXT/Resources/English_Report_midclass.pdf. Accessed 10 April 2017.

Figueiredo, Angela. 2002. *Novas Elites de Cor: Estudo sobre os Profissionais Liberais Negros de Salvador.* São Paulo: Annablume.

Figueiredo, Angela. 2003. "A Classe Média Negra não vai ao Paraíso: Trajetórias, Perfis e Negritude entre os Empresários Negros." PhD diss., Universidade do Rio de Janeiro, Rio de Janeiro.

Frankenberg, Ruth. 1997. *Displacing Whiteness: Essays in Social Change and Cultural Criticism.* Durham, NC: Duke University Press.

Garland-Thomson, Rosemarie. 2009. *Staring: How We Look.* Oxford: Oxford University Press.

Gilman, Sander L. 1985. *Difference and Pathology: Stereotypes of Sexuality, Race, and Madness.* Ithaca and London: Cornell University Press.

Gilman, Sander L. 1998. *Creating Beauty to Cure the Soul: Race and Psychology in the Shaping of Aesthetic Surgery.* Durham, NC: Duke University Press.

Gilman, Sander L. 2000. *Making the Body Beautiful: A Cultural History of Aesthetic Surgery*. New York: Princeton University Press.

Gimlin, Debra L. 2002. *Body Work: Beauty and Self-Image in American Culture*. Berkeley: University of California Press.

Glenn, Evelyn Nakano. 2008. "Yearning for Lightness: Transnational Circuits in the Marketing and Consumption of Skin Lighteners." *Gender and Society* 22: 281–302.

Goldstein, Donna. 1999. "'Interracial' Sex and Racial Democracy in Brazil: Twin Concepts?" *American Anthropologist*. New Series 101: 563–78.

Gomes, Nilma Lino. 2006. *Sem perder a Raiz: Corpo e Cabelo como Simbolos da Identidade Negra*. Belo Horizonte: Autentica.

Gordon, Doreen. 2015. "Negotiating Inequality: The Contemporary Black Middle Classes in Salvador, Brazil." In *People, Money and Power in the Economic Crisis*, edited by Keith Hart and John Sharp. New York and Oxford: Berghahn Press.

Hall, Ronald E. 1994. "The Bleaching Syndrome: Implications of Light Skin for Hispanic American Assimilation." *Hispanic Journal of Behavioural Sciences* 16: 307–14.

Hall, Ronald E. 1995. "The Bleaching Syndrome: African-American Response to Cultural Domination vis-a-vis Skin Colour." *Journal of Black Studies* 26: 72–184.

Heinze, Andrew R. 1990. *Adapting to Abundance: Jewish Immigrants, Mass Consumption, and the Search for American Identity*. New York: Columbia University Press.

Hobson, Janell. 2005. *Venus in the Dark: Blackness and Beauty in Popular Culture*. New York: Routledge.

hooks, bell. 1993. *Sisters of the Yam: Black Women and Self Recovery*. London: Turnaround.

Hope, Donna. 2010. *Man Vibes: Masculinities in the Jamaican Dancehall*. Kingston: Ian Randle Publishers.

Hordge-Freeman, Elizabeth. 2015. *The Color of Love: Racial Features, Stigma and Socialization in Black Brazilian Families*. Austin: University of Texas Press.

Isin, Engin F. 2008. *Re-casting the Social in Citizenship*. Toronto, Buffalo, and London: University of Toronto Press.

Jarrín, Alvaro. 2017. *The Biopolitics of Beauty: Cosmetic Citizenship and Affective Capital in Brazil*. Oakland: University of California Press.

Kant, Immanuel. 2004 [1960]. *Observations on the Feeling of the Beautiful and the Sublime*. Translated by John T. Goldthwait. Berkeley, Los Angeles and London: University of California Press. Originally published in 1960 by the Regents of the University of California.

Klopper, Sandra. 2010. "'Zulu Dandies:' The History and Significance of Extravagant Hairstyling Among Young Men from Colonial Natal." *Jacana* 1 (Fall): 28–39.

Kuper, Leo. 1965. *An African Bourgeoisie: Race, Class, and Politics in South Africa.* New Haven and London: Yale University Press.

Kymlicka, Will. 1995. *Multicultural Citizenship: A Liberal Theory of Minority Rights.* Oxford: Clarendon Press.

Machado-Borges, Thäis. 2008. "O Antes e Depois: Feminilidade, Classe e Raça na Revista Plástica e Beleza." *Luso Brazilian Review* 45: 146–62.

Marx, Anthony W. 1998. *Making Race and Nation: A Comparison of the United States, South Africa, and Brazil.* Cambridge: Cambridge University Press.

Mbeki, Moeletsi. 2009. *Architects of Poverty: Why African Capitalism Needs Changing.* Johannesburg: Pan Macmillan.

McRobbie, Angela. 2009. *The Aftermath of Feminism: Gender, Culture and Social Change.* Los Angeles and London: Sage.

Mercer, Kobena. 1987. "Black Hair/Style Politics." *New Formations* 3: 33–54.

Mhlungu, Gugulethu. 2014. "Big Hair, Big Business." *City Press*, 23 November. Available at: https://www.news24.com/Archives/City-Press/Big-hair-big-business-20150429 (28 November 2017).

Miller, Errol. 1969. "Body Image, Physical Beauty, and Colour Among Jamaican Adolescents." *Social and Economic Studies* 15 (1): 72–89.

Mire, Amina. 2001. "Skin Bleaching: Poison, Beauty, Power and Politics of the Colour Line." *Resources for Feminist Research* 28: 13–38.

Mohammed, Patricia. 2000. "But Most of All mi Love Me Browning: The Emergence in the Eighteenth and Nineteenth Century Jamaica of the Mulatto Woman as the Desired." *Feminist Review* 65: 22–48.

Moreno Figueroa, Mónica G. 2013. "Displaced Looks: The Lived Experience of Beauty and Racism." *Feminist Theory* 14 (2): 137–51.

Ncube, Mthuli, and Charles Leyeka Lufumpa. 2014. *The Emerging Middle Class in Africa.* London and New York: Routledge.

Neri, Marcelo Côrtes. 2008. *The New Middle Class.* Rio de Janeiro: Fundação Getulio Vargas/ Centro de Politicas Sociais. Available at: http://www.cps.fgv.br/ibrecps/M3/M3_MidClassBrazil_FGV_eng.pdf (23 November 2017).

Nuttall, Sarah. 2007. "Introduction: Re-thinking Beauty". In *Beautiful/Ugly: African and Diaspora Aesthetics*, edited by Sarah Nuttall, 6–29. Durham: Duke University Press.

Nyamnjoh, Francis, and Divine Fuh. 2014. Africans Consuming Hair, Africans Consumed by Hair. *Africa Insight* 44: 52–68.

Ofer, Inbal, and Tamar Groves. 2016. *Performing Citizenship: Social Movements Across the Globe.* New York: Routledge.

Ojong, Vivian Bessem. 2005. "Entrepreneurship and Identity Among a Group of Ghanian Women in Durban, South Africa." PhD diss., University of Zululand, Durban, South Africa.

Reichmann, Rebecca. 1999. *Race in Contemporary Brazil: From Indifference to Inequality.* University Park: The Pennsylvania State University Press.

Reid, Graeme. 2013. *How to Be a Real Gay: Gay Identities in Small Town South Africa*. Scottsville, South Africa: University of KwaZulu-Natal Press.

Ribane, Nakedi. 2006. *Beauty...A Black Perspective*. Scottsville, South Africa: University of KwaZulu-Natal Press.

Robotham, Don. 2000. "Blackening the Jamaican Nation: The Travails of a Black Bourgeoisie in a Globalized World." *Identities: Global Studies in Culture and Power* 7 (1): 1–37.

Rodulfo, Kristina. 2017. "Miss Jamaica Wore an Afro at Miss Universe 2017, and We Are so Here for It." PopSugar, 27 November. Available at: https://www.popsugar.com/beauty/Miss-Jamaica-Davina-Bennett-Afro-Miss-Universe-2017-44301922. Accessed 28 November 2017.

Sansone, Livio. 2003. *Blackness Without Ethnicity: Constructing Race in Brazil*. New York: Palgrave Macmillan.

Schwarcz, Lilia Moritz. 1993. *The Spectacle of the Races: Scientists, Institutions, and the Race Question in Brazil 1870–1930*. New York: Hill and Wong.

Seekings, Jeremy, and Nicoli Nattrass. 2005. *Class, Race, and Inequality in South Africa*. New Haven and London: Yale University Press.

Sheriff, Robin E. 2001. *Dreaming Equality: Colour, Race and Racism in Urban Brazil*. New Brunswick: Rutgers University Press.

Sieber, Roy. 2000. "History." In *Hair in African Art and Culture*, edited by Roy Sieber, Frank Herreman, and Niangi Batulukisi, 18–24. New York: The Museum of African Art.

Sieber, Roy, and Frank Herreman. 2000. *Hair in African Art and Culture*. New York: The Museum of African Art.

Silvera, Janet. 2012. *Policewomen Fight to Wear Afro-centric Hairdos*. Jamaica Gleaner, 28 February.

Strasser, Susan, Charles McGovern, and Matthias Judt. 1998. *Getting and Spending*. Cambridge: Cambridge University Press.

Tafari-Ama, Imani M. 2006. *Blood, Bullets and Bodies: Sexual Politics Below Jamaica's Colour Line*. Kingston: Multimedia Communications.

Tafari-Ama, Imani M. 2016. "Historical Sociology of Beauty Practices: Internalized Racism, Skin Bleaching and Hair Straightening." *Ideaz* 14: 1–19.

Tate, Shirley. 2007. "Black Beauty: Shade, Hair and Anti-Racist Aesthetics." *Ethnic and Racial Studies* 30: 300–19.

Telles, Edward E. 2004. *Race in Another America: The Significance of Skin Colour in Brazil*. Princeton and Oxford: Princeton University Press.

Thomas, Deborah A., and M. Kamari Clarke. 2013. "Globalization and Race: Structures of Inequality, New Sovereignties, and Citizenship in a Neoliberal Era." *Annual Review of Anthropology* 42: 305–25.

Thompson, Cheryl. 2009. "Black Women, Beauty, and Hair as a Matter of Being." *Women's Studies* 38: 851–56.

Unilever Institute of Strategic Marketing. 2007. Black Diamond on the Move: Spending Patterns, Communication, Media Usage, Black Diamond Segment. Online: http://www.uctunileverinstitute.co.za/research/black-diamond-on-the-move/. Accessed 12 April 2017.

Wagley, Charles. 1957. "Plantation America: A Culture Sphere." In *Caribbean Studies: A Symposium*, edited by Vera Rubin, 3–13. Seattle: University of Washington Press.

Wasser, Nicolas. 2016. "Regulating Sexy Subjects: The Case of Brazilian Fashion Retail and its Affective Workforce." In *Intimate Economies: Bodies, Emotions, and Sexualities on the Global Market*, edited by Susanne Hoffmann and Adi Moreno, 57–78. USA: Palgrave Macmillan.

Weekes, Debbie. 1997. Shades of Blackness: Young Black Female Constructions of Beauty. In *Black British Feminism: A Reader*, edited by Heidi Safa Mirza, 113–26. London and New York: Routledge.

Wolf, Naomi. 1991. *The Beauty Myth: How Images of Beauty are Used Against Women*. New York: Harper Collins.

Zelizer, Viviana A. 1997. *The Social Meaning of Money: Pin Money, Pay Checks, Poor Relief, and Other Currencies*. Princeton: Princeton University Press.

Zhang, Li. 2010. *In Search of Paradise: Middle Class Living in a Chinese Metropolis*. New York: Cornell University Press.

CHAPTER 11

'In This Country, Beauty Is Defined by Fairness of Skin.' Skin Colour Politics and Social Stratification in India

Nina Kullrich

The sky which gives light is blue and my mother was not dark but she was a virtuous lady [...] I thought this is an injustice with my body – my dark features were my due but had come to me by some misunderstanding [...] In my childhood I was familiar with the description of the Prince of the stories. But my husband's face didn't fit in the frame created in my mind. His complexion was same as mine. (Tagore 2009 [1916], 8–9)

The novel *Inside Outside* (*Ghare Baire*, 2009 [1916]) by the Nobel Prize-winning Bengali writer Rabindranath Tagore (1861–1941) tells the story of a woman, Bimala, who is torn between participating enthusiastically in the Indian independence movement[1] and rejecting growing nationalism. At the very beginning, Bimala starts telling her life story, first describing her mother's complexion, then depicting her own, darker skin tone, and finally characterizing her husband's. As early as the first page, she declares: 'In this country, beauty is defined by fairness of skin'.

N. Kullrich (✉)
Bayreuth University, Bayreuth, Germany

© The Author(s) 2019
C. Liebelt et al. (eds.), *Beauty and the Norm*,
Palgrave Studies in Globalization and Embodiment,
https://doi.org/10.1007/978-3-319-91174-8_11

245

Even today, a century after this novel was first published, Bimala's observation seems to be more than accurate if one contemplates the images of normative beauty that dominate the public media. The popular Indian actress Nandita Das, who is an ambassador of the awareness campaign 'Dark is Beautiful', even identifies an upward trend for 'fair'[2] skin to become a norm of beauty. On her weblog, she states: 'I am shocked to see the rise in the number of fairness creams and dark actresses looking paler and paler with every film, magazines, hoardings and films and advertisements showing only fair women.'[3]

In this chapter, I elaborate on the politics of skin colour in contemporary Delhi. Desires for fair skin in India are interrelated with local and global discourses on beauty and with religious and caste identities, as well as with colonial and global capitalist (colour) hierarchies. Whereas ideals of beauty have always differed between Indian regions and shifted over time, recent research on the New Indian Woman,[4] Indian beauty queens and Bollywood cinema have demonstrated that the white standard of beauty has indeed become a globally powerful imperative, not despite, but precisely because it incorporates constructs of 'diversity' that are mostly defined by closeness to 'European whiteness' (e.g. Osuri 2008; Parameswaran 2005). Accordingly, scholarship on skin lightening has situated the practice of bleaching primarily within the context of (post-) colonial racism (Hunter 2005; Castro Varela and Dhawan 2005) and a global 'white supremacy' (Mire 2000; Blay 2011). These notions have been further complicated by recent literature on colourism. Rather than interpreting bleaching as 'a manifestation of "false consciousness"' (Glenn 2009, 187), it is here understood as a representation of 'an anxious love for the "other"' (Nadeem 2014, 224f.). Following Nadeem, this chapter argues that bleaching in Delhi is neither (exclusively) a result of internalized racism, nor (primarily) about destabilizing racial categories, but rather a form of demarcation from social others. Thus, by thoroughly examining shades of meaning of skin colour and different social functions of skin bleaching in Delhi, this chapter shows how skin colour is (re)produced as a political signifier and embodied materiality of social, primarily class and gender, relations. I argue that if skin bleaching was solely understood as a kind of legacy of colonialism and/or an imitation of western ideals of beauty, there would be a risk of ignoring both pre-colonial and non-western perspectives on beauty and arguing from a Eurocentric perspective.

Therefore, in order to extend current approaches to skin bleaching, I wish to take the debate on bleaching beyond the focus on colonialism and examine the role skin colour plays in complex systems of social stratification that not only predate but also came to intersect with those of the British Raj. By exploring references to colour in ancient sources, I demonstrate that colour discourses in India have been both transnational and pre-colonial. Whereas the term 'race' is often discussed in works on colourism (cf. Harris 2009), as well as in those that aim to understand the Indian caste system (cf. Robb 1995), I argue that searching for any 'indigenous' Indian concept of race would imply it existed independently of western race theories in the first place. Angela P. Harris (2009) identifies three approaches taken by contemporary scholarly discussions on racism, namely, the 'prejudice' approach (racism as interpersonal), the 'white supremacy' approach (racism as institutional) and finally, the attempt to analyse the constitution of racism through 'economies of difference' or, more specific, 'economies of colours' (ibid., 1). The latter is based on the assumption that colourism and racism are not coinciding, but, though they are intimately linked, can move independently from each other. Colourism can thus operate 'sometimes to confound and sometimes to restructure racial hierarchy' (ibid.). My work builds upon precisely this concept of 'economies of colours', which has to be embedded in other categories of social stratifications that are relevant for the Indian context, in particular caste. Analysing a 'desire for whiteness' in India, Bhattacharya also distinguishes between 'colourism' and 'racism', defining the former as a crucial element of racism while it also constitutes a specific phenomenon in itself, as it occurs both inter- and intra-racially (2012, 123f.). Even though colonial racism must be understood as continuation of the 'European project of modernity' (Gilroy 1995), I also agree with Kapil Raj (2007), who emphasised that race theories were not only western theories but also a result of the colonial entanglement itself.[5]

In, therefore, seeking to go beyond conventional postcolonial approaches, I propose to understand whiteness as a travelling and relational concept. Furthermore, in the Indian context, I suggest analytically distinguishing between the concepts 'Indian fair' and 'European white'. From here follows a central aim of my project: to contribute to the decentralizing and decolonizing (Tate 2010) of whiteness within beauty studies. Hence, in my work, I analyse colourism in India neither as an exclusively colonial legacy nor as a particular phenomenon of *the* Indian culture (cf. John 1998; Reddy 2005; Chakrabarty 2000, 2002), but rather focus on the intersecting politics of skin colour and its particular localisations in Delhi by aiming to understand the various shades of meaning of skin colour and the different social functions of skin bleaching in pre-colonial, British and contemporary (North) India.

This chapter draws primarily on qualitative interviews conducted during research in Delhi in 2014. Whether and how fair skin is desired or rejected relates to different social contexts and positions. As I will argue, both performances of as well as attitudes towards skin bleaching provide avenues for navigating the self through a system of social stratification and thus striving for social acceptance. This finding relates to Hunter's argument (2002) about fair skin as 'social capital.' Even though I argue for an understanding of skin colour as a social construct, it should be realised that what I call 'fair fiction' has an actual counterpart in interviewees' experienced reality: during the interviews, fair skin was predominantly associated with gaining an advantage in both the marriage and job markets. Interviewee Vani, a feminist activist, explained: 'There are different fair spectres within each caste and community [...] there is a valuable and fluent understanding of what fair is'. Notwithstanding, interviewees commonly associated lighter shades with the Indian north, upper castes and classes, certain religious affiliations (namely Sikh and Muslim), as well as with modernity and cosmopolitanism; whereas darker shades were attributed to southern India, lower castes, working migrants or rural Indians.

Finally, in this chapter, I enlarge upon two aspects of the discourse on Indian fairness. First, I demonstrate how desiring fairness means changing skin *shades*, not colour per se. Second, I show how fair skin functions as an identifying narrative in the context of fairness as a beauty ideal that is associated with an (upper) middle-class, urban, cosmopolitan lifestyle, whereas aspirations for fairness are associated with a lower class status and a rural, 'backward' mind-set. Building on these assumptions, I argue that skin bleaching in 'post-liberalisation' and 'post-globalisation' (Phadke 2017) Delhi is a beauty practice whereby individuals aim to overcome structural inequalities against the background of capitalist competition and consumption. However, this can also lead to new boundaries and exclusions, especially within the context of class and gender relations.

This chapter is made up of two parts. The first part outlines my theoretical approach to beauty and my methodological access to the field and historically embeds fairness as an Indian ideal of beauty. The second part introduces the findings of my empirical analysis, enlarging upon the meanings of fairness and the practices and social functions of skin bleaching in contemporary Delhi.

BEAUTY WORK, STATUS AND THE BEAUTY MATRIX

Skin bleaching as social practice is predominantly performed within the context of beauty and body work[6]—hence, my analysis starts from the perspective of beauty. For my interviewees, to bleach their skin meant to also bleach facial and body hair—typically in a beauty parlour—or to apply facial creams or body lotions at home. The general notion that 'the beauty is the fair and the fair is the beauty,' as expressed by one interviewee,[7] prevailed in most of the interviews I conducted in Delhi 2014. Before looking more closely at how interrelations between fairness and beauty were narratively negotiated, I briefly summarize my theoretical conceptions of and approaches to beauty.

First, I follow Nina Degele (2004), who clearly distinguishes her conception of beauty from (a) aesthetic judgments, (b) attractiveness as applied by sociologies of the body, and (c) socio-biological concepts of beauty (2004, 11). Accordingly, she defines beauty as 'a perception produced by mass media, which is relevant in everyday life as a hegemonic norm commonly contrasted with, in mediated public discourse, non-beauty, that is, ugliness' (ibid., my translation).

Secondly, my study follows Maxine Leeds Craig's suggestions for further 'complicating' the analysis of beauty politics. This means I consider it important to pay attention to the social positions of the subjects who are speaking about their beauty perceptions and practices, instead of referring to a 'racially unmarked, implicitly heterosexual woman, of unspecified class' (Craig 2006, 162), which Craig claims has been dominant in much of the research on beauty. Hence, I aim at sorting and unravelling the complex, competing and complicated 'glocal' beauty standards I encountered in Delhi, thereby deconstructing the myth that there is any universal western or white norm of beauty. Here, I follow Shirley Anne Tate's request for beauty studies to be decolonized, especially the 'myth which still circulates in feminist writing on beauty. That is, that all "Black women want to be white"' (Tate 2010, 195). Moreover, I challenge the prevailing practice of focusing solely on subjects socialized as 'female' when researching beauty by including the voices of male socialized subjects in my data and discussion, instead of postulating a 'singular beauty standard enforced by a unified male gaze' (Craig 2006, 159). Lastly, I pay attention to the ambivalent relationship between understanding beauty practices as part of self-empowerment and agency on the one hand and as disciplinary regimes on the other, because, as Villa argues, 'every self-empowering body practice [...is] always also a submission under social norms [...] we can do all kinds of things with our bodies but not everywhere is everything possible for everybody' (2008, 250–52).

Recent scholarship on the politics of beauty suggests that, within the context of 'neoliberal and postfeminist governmentality and capitalism's move to colonise all of life' (Elias et al. 2017, 33), social demands on (female) beauty and bodies have significantly increased, which I argue necessitates an analysis of the interrelations of the politics of skin colour and neoliberal capitalism. Thus, following Elias et al. (2017), I understand contemporary consumers of skin bleaching practices and products to be 'aesthetic entrepreneur[s]' and 'neoliberal subject[s]', whose beauty is 'yet another project to be planned, managed, and regulated in a way that is calculative and seemingly self-directed' (ibid., 39).[8] According to post-feminist narratives, to confront and overcome gender discrimination, each and every individual woman is urged to gain more 'confidence', particularly in respect to her bodily self-image, in order to became (a) 'better economic subject[s]' (Banet-Weiser 2017; McRobbie 2009).[9] Against this background, I ask, what potential for resistance lies in either performing or rejecting bleaching? How are questions of agency negotiated within the context of these omnipresent neoliberal discourses, celebrating body confidence, women's empowerment or beauty diversity? For example, cosmetics companies now promote beauty as a 'source of confidence, not anxiety' (Dove), celebrate 'diversity' and 'beauty for all' (L'Oréal) or promise to 'empower a woman to change her destiny' (Fair & Lovely).[10]

Thirdly, I understand skin lightning as a beauty practice performed for social acceptance and advancement and, therefore, as a practice of beautification as defined by Nina Degele, namely as 'a medium of communication that serves the representation of one's own external image in order to gain attention and ensure one's own identity' (2004, 7, my translation). From such a perspective, I understand interviewees' narrations of skin lightening as processes of identification and practices of social positioning. Within beauty studies, bodily expressions have often been understood as performative. In my view, skin bleaching too is a performative beauty practice because it simultaneously presents and produces social arrangements, relations and hierarchies.[11] Consequently, not only is the practice of bleaching performative, but, as I will go on to show, so is also the act of speaking about it.

Whereas all these definitions of beauty ideals and practices seem to refer to bodily beauty, beauty can also be used and understood as a non-material matter, for instance, within the context of religious philosophies and practices. In this respect, beauty may relate to 'transcendental' values or intellectual quests for 'truth'.[12] Thus, different concepts of beauty circulated during my interviews. In most conversations, beauty was readily understood as a kind of social status that can be achieved by grooming the body; but in many interviews, beauty was also understood as a status of mind that cannot be acquired by body work (alone). Particularly at the beginning of interviews, many research participants (in particular beauticians) were eager to emphasize how for them beauty was about the 'inner heart', 'inner thoughts', 'feelings', 'personality', 'behaviour' or 'beliefs', while later they acknowledged the role of outer appearance. Other interviewees, however, admitted that 'external beauty' was very important indeed, particularly because 'society' demands it. Here, they are referring to what I suggest calling 'the beauty matrix' to grasp those (partly paradoxical) effects of the beauty discourses that individuals (re)produce and to which they react in their everyday lives even when they are perfectly aware of the constructedness of beauty standards. When participants emphasize that inner beauty entails 'good thinking' or a 'simple life', while on the other hand associating fair skin with being 'nice' and 'good', the intersections and overlapping of these supposedly distinct 'inner' and 'outer' qualities of beauty become clearly visible.

METHODOLOGY AND RESEARCH PROCESS

Until now, there has been relatively little research on the subject of colourism in India, which is why I approach the topic from as many different perspectives, or genealogies, as possible. This chapter is part of my research for a PhD project that examines different kinds of narratives of fairness. It draws primarily on thirty qualitative, individual and group interviews I conducted in Delhi in 2014. The interviewees were 55 Indian women and men aged between 16 and 50 from different social, religious, caste and class backgrounds, who were living both at the centre of India's capital and on its outskirts and in informal settlements.[13]

I found my research participants in various beauty parlours throughout the city,[14] intending to talk to people who sell and perform practices of skin bleaching (that is, beauticians and salon managers), as well as those demanding hair or skin treatments (their clients). In addition,

I approached potential interviewees outside these parlours, where a discussion of beauty was less likely to be predefined by the spatial context, starting with the campus of the University of Delhi, with which my project is affiliated. Later I contacted three local NGOs, concerned with economically and socially disadvantaged communities in Lajpat Nagar II, residents of Kathputli Colony[15] and people involved in feminist politics in Defence Colony, respectively, to diversify my data with regard to social background.

Furthermore, I work with literary texts, historical narratives, religious scripts, myths and legends. I also include in the analysis (TV) commercials, the self-portrayals and campaigns of cosmetic companies producing skin bleaching products and the manifestos and actions of groups fighting the fair skin ideal. Lastly, I investigated the space- and labour-related conditions of skin bleaching performances.

I began the analysis with the narrations of the interviewees and followed their references to history, mythology or cultural and social phenomena, then looked for determinants and explanations in the wider context of the political, social and economic order, paying particular attention to the aspect of power (Foucault 1988, 114; Smith 1987). For my heterogeneous empirical material, the applied methods of analysis differ accordingly: Thus, I used a mixture of methods derived from Grounded Theory (e.g. Strauss and Corbin 1990) (Narrative), Discourse Analyses and Literary Analyses.

Skin Colour and 'Shadeism' in India Within and Beyond Colonialism

Under colonialism, skin colour became a category that made visibly clear the distinction between rulers and oppressors that was legitimated through European race theory. It also demonstrates the ruling elites' power to decide when Indians were to be marked as *āryan* ancestors (thus providing the colonizers with an intellectual past) and blacks (thereby legitimating colonial exploitation) at the same time. However, the label 'black' as ascribed to subjugated Indians was not applied homogenously, any more than the term 'white' was for British *sahibs*, even when they attempted to present themselves as a consistent elite (cf. Fischer-Tiné 2009). Furthermore, these ascriptions never remained unchallenged. Political movements lead to changes in colonial literary descriptions—to an increased use of the n-word, for instance (cf. Chaudhuri 1994). They also caused changes in colonial visual representations, such as a ban on the production of 'Indian yellow' for the colonial colour palette (cf. Bailkin 2014). Moreover, they led to anti-colonial re-adoptions of black within anti-colonial and anti-caste movements, as is apparent in the case of the Dalit Panthers, an organization seeking to combat caste discrimination, which was inspired by the Black Panther Movement in the US. There was also evidence suggesting that fairness was not always and everywhere regarded as desirable, especially within the context of (post)colonialism: 'white kinship' was sometimes disguised in order to conform to caste rules of purity (cf. Abraham 2006).

When cultural theorist Arjun Appadurai (1993) told the story about his 'becoming a person of colour' in the 1990s, he indicated the different shades of colour and shades of meaning this process entailed:

> I am now well advanced on the road to becoming a person of colour. It's not exactly that I thought I was white before, but as an Anglophone academic born in India and teaching in the Ivy League, I was certainly hanging out in the field of dreams, and had no cause to think myself black. As a child brought up with a profound sense of colour in a Brahmin household in Bombay, I was always aware of the bad marriage prospects of my darker female relatives, of the glorious 'milky' skin of my father's dead father, of the horrible 'blue' blackness that my mother swore I acquired when I played in the mid-day sun in Bombay. So even though I was as hip as the next person to the fact that black was beautiful, I preferred to stay brown myself. (Appadurai 1993, 801)

Appadurai's brief narrative shows how for him the (re)appropriation of colours has been an ongoing process shaped by global colour hierarchies in which black is assigned the lowest and white the highest social position, as well as by a colour hierarchy adhered to by his Brahmin family ranging from 'the horrible "blue" blackness' to 'the glorious "milky"' colour. He began to self-identify as 'brown', not only realizing his 'non-whiteness', but also rejecting the description 'black'. Does his Brahmin family's colour consciousness merely reflect a colonial and post-colonial bias? What role did colour play in pre-British India?

Taking a closer look at how social orders were established in pre-colonial Indian societies, one finds that skin colour did not seem to be a necessary or consistent criterion for group constructions. Systems of social stratification were mainly based on territory, technical skills, language and religious purity (Thapar 1971). Moreover, the boundaries erected upon these categories were open to transformation whenever the territorial boundaries were extended or constellations of power changed. This becomes vivid in the concept of the 'degenerate Kṣatriya'[16] within the general process of 'Āryanizing',[17] an attempt made by Āryan-speaking immigrants to include and rank the non-Āryan-speaking but yet powerful 'indigenous' or other migrated rulers within their social order, the *varna* system. Selected non-Āryan speakers were accepted as 'Kṣatriyas' by origin, but described as 'degenerate' due to their non-performance of the sacred rites (Thapar 1971, 419). As 'Mlecchas,'[18] they were excluded from marriage relations with Āryan-speakers and more generally described as polluting, though not always as 'dark skinned.'[19] Furthermore, the term 'Mleccha' was also applied to migrants from Europe (Greece) or Central Asia (Iranian Huns). Not least, fair skin was already a marker of female beauty particular in early pre-colonial India, as well as during the Mogul Empire. Ancient Hindu scripts have descriptions of the 'fair' and 'golden' half of the goddess Parvati or Gaurangi (cf. Doniger 2009)[20] and legends praise the 'fair skin' of the dancer Anarkali (sixteenth century). In her study of media representations of fairness in Indonesia and within the Indonesian Diaspora in the US, L. Ayu Saraswati (2010) shows how the ideal of fair skin cannot be thought of as a 'colonial import' alone, and she makes an extremely valuable reference to its formation being historically transnational. Alluding to the Indian and Indonesian versions of the sacred Hindu text, the *Ramayana*, where 'beautiful women are described as having white shining faces, like the full moon' (19), Saraswati suggests that the 'preference for light-skinned women in Indonesia predates European colonialism,' and that 'the light-skinned beauty standard in pre-colonial Indonesia should not be read as merely a "local" or "indigenous" construction' (ibid.). I suggest the same is true of the Indian context.

With regard to caste, it can be noted that colour was not a clear factor in caste distinctions but played a role in depicting the lower castes, such as the Dalits[21] and lower social classes.[22] At least for one of the higher caste groups, the Chitpavan Brahmans, fair skin became a relevant marker of distinction (Johnson 1970). Moreover, colour played a specific role in anti-colonial struggles, when independence and anti-caste movements sought proximity to civil rights and anti-racist movements outside India and identified as black to do so (e.g. the Dalit Panthers) or challenged the colonial imaginary of skin colour, as in the arts and literature, for instance. However, the phenomenon of 'passing', as it is known within racialized social orders, 'is an unacceptable option in the caste system' (Gupta 2000, 93).

Thus, it can be stated that, while the desire for fair skin is closely interrelated with (post-)colonial white privilege and global white supremacy, fair skin as a beauty norm clearly predates European notions of skin colour and race. Nazia Hussein (2010), for example, explicitly bases her study of skin lightening in South Asia upon the concept of 'intra-group racism,' refusing to follow Hunter's (2002) use of the term 'colourism' for fear it could 'reduce the seriousness of the power play involved in racist behaviour within an ethnic group' (408). I prefer to speak about 'colourism' or 'shadeism' to emphasize that colour as a hierarchical category in India does not work along the lines of racial differences alone, but rather is deeply intertwined with the histories and continuities of caste, class and gender differentiations. Thus, I argue, approaching colourism from a perspective that goes beyond its interpretation as internalized (post-)colonial racism permits a deeper understanding of how the ideal of the fair skin is locally embedded.

This understanding is attentive to how transnational beauty norms intersect with and transform other categories of social differentiation in contemporary Delhi. In one interview, for instance, I was told that 'they [people from northeast India] may be fair but [...] those women are not necessarily desirable [...] because they are different, so in that sense race comes in the picture' (interview with Virmati, 22 February 2014). From this, it follows that 'race' can override the colour category within a particular Indian geography. This relates to Harris's observation that 'colourism and racism are not coinciding, [...] they can move independently, but are still intimately linked' (2009, 1). How colourism and classism enforce each other, with 'dark' becoming a signifier for the migrating working classes, for instance, became apparent during a conversation with Zahra, who talked about her childhood in Kashmir:

> You have labourers of [from] Bengal and Bihar [in] some parts of India...they are there in Kashmir, so obviously they are all synonymously known as Biharis, even if they are [from] any part of India. [...] they [other children] would tell me they [Biharis] have left you here, that's why you have a darker complexion than we have. (interview with Zahra, 9 February 2014)

As these two examples indicate, not only is a historical reading of the meanings and functions of skin colour modifications essential, but also is a consideration of the concrete material contexts (cf. Erevelles 2011, 26) that impact on living conditions in contemporary Delhi. Therefore, I now turn to the analysis of my empirical data to show how fairness is defined and when it is desired by my interviewees.

SHADES OF FAIR, SHAPES OF BEAUTY AND SHIFTS OF STATUS

When interview participants talked about beauty (ideals), it became evident that fair skin was generally referred to as a hegemonic beauty norm. It became equally clear that not one concept of fairness exists, but many. Therefore, I will not speak of fairness as a singular beauty norm, or even as a fixed shade or colour, but rather of the different shades of fairness that people learn to perceive and ascribe to. As outlined above, this means understanding fairness as relative and relational regarding different social positions and contexts. Many of the people I spoke to favoured a skin tone they identified as 'natural fair', 'Indian fair', 'middle complexioned' or 'wheatish colour', and some of them explicitly dismissed a skin colour they described as 'too fair' or 'European white'.

One of the most insightful encounters at the beginning of my fieldwork was a conversation with Chayanika,[23] a 22-year-old beautician, who was working in a small women-only beauty parlour in Kamla Nagar I. When asked her to show me what exactly she meant by using the term 'fair' with the help of 23 photographs I had brought along, she first picked out three pictures, but later corrected herself that she had actually selected 'European whites'. If I had asked for 'normal fair' she would have chosen differently, as that was what 'Indians' preferred, namely a 'mixed complexion'. Interviewees also quite often differentiated between beautiful and fair. While flipping through the photographs, interviewee Sita, for instance, categorized them into three different groups, saying 'this is beautiful, but this is fair [...] these are *gora* [light-skinned] [...], but this is beauty with fair'. A group of schoolgirls[24] explained during an interview that 'too much fairness is also not good looking, and this one [the picture showed a woman with very light complexion and blonde hair], she is looking like a witch; there was a movie where a ghost looked like that' (Veena, group interview, 21 March 2014).

The comparison or equation of a white-skinned woman with a 'witch' or a 'ghost' most clearly contradicts the widespread assumption of white (skin) being the ultimate ideal of beauty. When the girls were asked to show me the most beautiful women in the pictures I showed them, they unanimously selected two as 'the most beautiful ones,' which they distinguished from two others, selected as the fairest. But taking the perspective of what they perceived as the 'majority of the Indian population's view', the girls assumed that the woman they had depicted as the fairest but not the most beautiful 'in India, [...] will be the number one'.

The photo-elicitation also showed that the terms 'fair' and 'white' seem not always to fall within the same (skin) tone category. During the interviews, people used a wide range of (additional) adjectives to describe or specify skin tones they themselves have identified as 'fair'. These detailed specifications included further gradations and shades of colour, as in 'yellow', 'pink', 'red' or 'white'; as well as in *savla, gora* or *gora chitta* (Hindi, respectively, for 'brown', 'fair' and 'very fair' complexion[25]). Moreover, they contain allusions to region or origin (as in 'Persian', 'Indian', 'British' or 'āryan'), binary concepts of the 'other' (as in 'foreign') and the 'self' (as in 'normal' or 'natural'), food metaphorical comparisons (as in 'milky' or 'wheatish'), connections to hair colours ('blonde-white') and general designations of brightness ('light', 'glow'). These varied categories, not to mention the wide range of different social positions that were associated with being fair, such as regional belonging or religious, class or caste status, indicate how colour perceptions and descriptions vary with the study participants. Preeti, a 24-year-old beautician[26] who runs her own small unisex beauty parlour together with her husband in Kamla Nagar II, perceived a wide range of colour shades when looking at the photographs, differentiating between 'pinkish' and 'yellow' shades, describing 'fair' as 'wheatish' and preferring 'white-pinkish', but also using 'white' and 'fair' interchangeably (interview with Preeti, 21 February 2014).

Whereas relations between signifier and signified are socially learned and continuously performed, the ambiguity here points to the variety of meanings and definitions available in Indian colour discourse(s). However, it is impossible to clearly assign the terms interviewees use to the concepts they refer to. Therefore, it is crucial to note again that the distinction between Indian 'fair' and European 'white' I have proposed is an analytical one. In (language) practice, these distinctions are never strict, clear or unambiguous to begin with, and they vary widely from one interviewee to another. When interviewees use the term 'white', they might not refer to the concept of European whiteness; when using the term 'fair', they might just as well do so. This further means that different participants can talk about different concepts using the same terms and vice versa.

According to Roland Barthes (1986 [1964]), the linguistic sign (the signifier) adapts itself to different concepts (the signified). In the primary semiological system (signum 1), the sign (e.g. *gora*) refers to a certain gradation of colour (e.g. 'pink white'), and in the secondary semiological system (signum 2), the sign (e.g. 'gora') refers to a social concept of categorization (e.g. 'foreign'). Whereas in signum 1, a wide range of colour shades exists, signum 2 alternates between two 'spatial' poles, such as 'Indian' and 'foreign/European'. Applied to my research, this means that, in order to understand skin colour preferences, one has to examine the different contextual uses of labels such as 'white' and 'fair' even to be able to identify a tendency. When looking again at the respective situations in which specified descriptions were used, it can be noted that 'milky', 'mixed', 'Indian', 'glowing', 'Persian', *savla*, 'normal', 'natural' and 'wheatish' were used when explicitly referring to an Indian fairness, whereas 'British', 'āryan', 'blonde-white', and 'foreign' were used to designate European whiteness, even though interviewees could simultaneously classify all these tones consistently as 'fair', *gora* or 'white'.

The Practice of Skin Bleaching: Changes of Shades, Not Colours

Having elaborated on the range of skin tones interviewees referred to, in this section I address the practice of skin bleaching, focusing on the effects to which beauty salon consumers aspire. I argue that skin bleaching can be understood as a means to change *shades*, not colours. Even though I do not equate skin bleaching with skin tanning, I take interviewees' comparisons of these two practices as my starting point. In most conversations, skin tanning was referred to as a beauty routine practiced *outside* India, predominantly in order to explain skin bleaching as beauty practice performed *within* it. A tanned skin was neither brought up as an Indian ideal of beauty, nor was the practice of tanning among the services offered in the parlours I visited. As a beauty trend, it came up just once in an interview I conducted in one of the most expensive, popular and fashionable beauty parlours I visited during my stay in Delhi:

You know, if people want dusky skin also...some people are very fair, but they want some tanning all over the body...so they go for the tanning or to the beach also...so they apply a lot of amount of oil all over their body, and they will tan their body. (interview with Shalini, beauty parlour Model Town, 14 February 2014)

On another occasion, a friend of mine disclosed that some of her upper-class acquaintances in Poona would desire a tan to show they had spent their holidays on Goa's beaches. When tanning was otherwise mentioned, it usually had the function of 'normalizing' and 'ranking' bleaching as just another beauty practice among others. During the interviews, the practice of bleaching was often defined as 'de-tanning' and bleaching and skin lightening creams were compared to tanning and to tanning lotions.

Aditi, for instance, the owner of a beauty parlour in Khan Market, understood both bleaching and tanning as different ways to attain the same goal: feeling beautiful. Student Jyoti also reflected on how the desire to be or to be seen as beautiful leads to different kinds of beauty work in different parts of the world. Whereas in India a 'fair' skin is desired, in New York, to which her sister had moved, people would aspire to become 'tanned' and to possess an 'Indian skin':

They go for skin tanning on the beaches [laughs] they do like the Indian skin [...] they do the tan skin but here [in Delhi] yes of course the ultimateness is the beauty that lies in the fairness. (interview with Jyoti, 7 February 2014)

In accordance with narratives presenting bleaching as part of a regular beauty *routine*, in the beauty parlours bleaching often comes in a package with the usual 'facial'. Whether the bleach is part of it varies depending on the customers' 'needs', defined as 'personal taste', 'social demands' or 'cosmetic requirements.' Beauty manager Aditi gave two main reasons for recommending bleaching to their female clients: one's profession or a special occasion in one's life such as getting married. Whereas for the profession she only stated that 'they [women] need to do it,' with regard to marriages, she explained that 'she [the bride] likes to look extremely stunning.' In the first case, Aditi explicitly spoke about 'presenting yourself in public', whereas in the latter case, the public was not mentioned. During wedding festivities, however, the bride is also presented, even if only in a supposedly 'private' sphere, to her husband, relatives, in-laws and friends. Yet, whereas the expression 'they need to' implies an external obligation, the phrase 'she likes to' suggests acting solely upon individual choice or taste. However, later Aditi also defined the need from her own beauty expert's perspective and linked fairness to the aspect of skin health[27]:

> we usually don't recommend bleach [...] but sometimes it is good when you have black blemishes and black patches [...] it helps make your skin look very clean and healthy. (interview with Aditi, beauty parlour Khan Market, 14 April 2014)

Thus, just like the alleged contrast between 'inner' and 'outer' beauty I mentioned above, whatever is marked as either 'individual taste' or 'social demand' is already heavily intertwined. For most interviewees, 'social demands' primarily appeal to both the marriage and the job markets. Generally, fair skin was understood as enabling opportunities for what the political activist Virmati described as 'urban-based careers':

> India has been, like, undergoing very rapid economic changes over the last thirty years...offshoot of that has been that women are much more visible in employment and much more active in the economy...obviously, the economy is also pushing women to join the work force, and pushing women to join skin labour...and obviously, this exploitation is happening in a different level altogether...women's wages are not equal still, women's benefits in employment are not there anymore, contract labour is becoming the norm of the day, which is even more hurtful for women, but in case of the advertisement, fairness is also becoming attached to this idea of upward mobility. (interview with Virmati, 22 February 2014)

Depending on the social backgrounds of the interviewees, the 'social demands' and thus the 'skin labour', as Virmati put it, differed further. For a group of female interviewees living in Kathputli Colony, for instance, it meant the possibility to get a job or to move freely beyond the geographical confines of the neighbourhood, commonly regarded as a male privilege. As one participant put it, 'the girl can become a boy' (Usha, group interview, 22 April 2014). For one female student I met on Delhi University campus, it meant attaining a status of equality in the mate-seeking process, for example, achieving a position from which a woman could also demand fairness in a prospective groom (interview with Jyoti, 7 February 2014).

Shalini, the manager of a small beauty parlour in Lajpat Nagar I, described bleaching as follows: 'It is a chemical that removes tanning; people use it to look more beautiful and fair' (interview with Shalini, 14 February 2014). Poonam, a beautician who runs her own salon in Faridabad, also defined bleaching as 'de-tanning' and explained that the (facial or body) hair becomes the same colour as the skin (interview with Poonam, 3 April 2014). Aditi, a beautician from a beauty parlour in Khan Market, likewise emphasized that through bleaching 'facial hair becomes brown' (interview with Aditi, 14 April 2014). She further stated that the bleach is 'good for dark blemishes and patches'. Sarover, an employee in a beauty parlour in Model Town, specified that by bleaching, 'de-tanning' is 'possible', but 'you have your own skin colour, nobody can change that' (interview with Sarover, 29 March 2014). Kavita, a beautician in a beauty parlour in Lajpat Nagar II, described the effect of skin bleaching as 'not a very big change: the tanning is gone and the hair looks golden' (interview with Kavita, 14 February 2014). In these descriptions, it becomes apparent that changing one's complexion is not the (only) objective of bleaching, it is also about making the dark facial or body hair less visible ('brown'), invisible ('same colour as the skin') or lighter ('golden'), as well as making the complexion and the overall appearance of the skin bright(er) or (more) 'glowing'.

This emphasis on gold, glow and shine can be further linked to what Laila Abu-Er-Rub (2017) identified as a central element of female beauty in neoliberal India, especially within the Indian fashion industry. Gold, she argues, marks the very essence of Indian aesthetics. Historically, gold has played a significant role in Hinduism, in Indian rites of passage or festivities, being associated with status and prestige, but also serving as material security for the lower classes. Today, gold is used by industry, the media and government ('Nation Branding') to mediate visually between what is considered Indian tradition or authenticity on the one hand, and the increasing commercialization of a 'modern national identity' on the other, to encourage urban (upper) middle-class consumption, and to secure India's growing economic power (cf. Abu-Er-Rub 2017).

In contrast to the standard of bleaching, both the facial and the body hair, the head hair is virtually never bleached or dyed blonde. Here, dark colours are preferred over lighter tones. As one interviewee put it, 'colour, yeah, they do get colour for the streaks and all, but not as much they prefer their blackness. They use *mehendi*[28] henna, but not as much, they don't go for the blonde colour' (interview with Jyoti, 7 February 2014).

It is apparent that the politics of skin and hair are deeply intertwined, for, in a place where dark skin is unwanted, facial or body hair is equally unwelcome. Consequently, the skin bleaching procedure as performed in the beauty parlours I visited always included the removal or dyeing of facial or body hair. Just like the skin, head, facial, body and pubic hair is culturally read. Those who do not conform to dominant beauty norms are 'seen as anomalous beings by another, often dominant, segment of the social order' (Obeyesekere 1998, xiii). Thus, bleaching often seems to be understood as a practice of 'normalization' rather than of 'beautification' (cf. Davis 1995; Gimlin 2002). Here, I understand 'normalization' not as opposed to 'beautification', but rather as a particular form that beautification can adopt: whereas the latter describes compliance with, dissent from or the transformation of dominant beauty norms; normalization describes an adaptive modification that is not experienced as being beauty work at all.

Moreover, other beauticians explained that bleaching was desired by those whose skin had been 'polluted' by the Indian weather and who wanted to 'clean up' their 'dull', 'dusky', 'dark', 'black' and 'uneven' skin tone (interview with Kamla, 14 February 2014). Accordingly, some people didn't use the words 'fair' or 'white' at all but talked about getting a 'shine' or 'glowing skin' (interview with Dwani, 29 March 2014).

Lastly, the definition of bleaching as de-tanning in the statements quoted above resembles the beauty industries' advertisement narrative. Whereas sun-tan lotions and sun-tanning studios in Europe usually promote a summer complexion (e.g. the German product 'Nivea Visage Sommer Teint Lotion,' a 'facial summer complexion lotion'), fairness cream commercials in India promote winter fairness (e.g. 'fair and lovely winter fairness cream'). The reference to seasonal change may be another indicator of how bleaching practices are not aimed at changing consumers' skin colour, but rather at not letting one's skin tone be changed by the season or the weather. Thus, de-tanning is a cosmetic practice with the aim of preserving the supposedly 'original' or 'natural' tone. The range of bleaching products available in the shops and beauty parlours also points to desired shades beyond white, such as 'gold', 'saffron' or 'chocolate' bleach.

Not least, bleaching is often defined as a means to repair skin 'damage' and to restore the skin's 'original condition'. However, this is not the case for bridal treatments, which clearly stand out of the daily beauty routines. Generally, marriage and the family were always referred to by interviewees when talking about learning, experiencing and the passing on of colourism, whether by a mother constantly worried about marrying off her supposedly dark-skinned daughter or a husband not letting his wife play golf in the sun for fear she might tan. Thus, the activist mentioned above claimed that 'any discussion on skin whitening will be within the framework of marriage' (interview with Virmati, 22 February 2014). Participants explained that women have to be fairer than usual on their wedding days, but most importantly, the bride has to be fairer than the groom. The notion that a woman's skin tone is evaluated and rated in comparison to her husband's, especially during weddings, exemplifies once more that fair skin is a highly gendered norm[29]:

> The whole Indian ideology, that a woman should be fairer than a man, you know, like a man can be dark you would never see...it is very rare to see a couple where the man is really really fair and the woman is dark... it's really...I'm talking about a very average Indian couple – it's usually the other way round...where do you get all these fair women from? It's really...what happens to all the dark women? (interview with Radhika, 1 February 2014)

Respondents of all genders stressed that women were more severely affected by rigid beauty norms and skin colour discrimination. Whereas in regard to men, other status factors such as income, employment or education could easily outweigh a lack of fairness in regard to women beauty pressures came on top of other social demands. Lighter skin was of particular importance to men who experienced discrimination due to their low caste and class background, regional origin and, in one case, homosexual desire.

The specific standing of (pre-)bridal treatments becomes evident from the menus in the beauty parlours. Every beauty parlour I visited offered a wide range of beauty treatments, but all included a particular bridal beauty package, including waxing, body polishing, threading eyebrows, manicure, pedicure, facial, make-up, hair colour/cut/style/spa etc. A beautician from Lajpat Nagar I explained that, for a wedding, they would offer special treatments only 'if they [clients] have a hair or a skin problem'. Otherwise, they would do just the 'normal' beauty package:

> If they have no problem, we don't do anything, just the normal [...]. Like 'normal' in the sense [of what] we do, [of what] we call 'pre-bridal'. In the pre-bridal, we do hair-cutting, all-the-body-bleach, facial, manicure, pedicure, and that's it. Everything [from] head to toes... (interview with Shalini, 14 February 2014)

The expression 'normal' is opposed here to having a particular (beauty) 'problem'. If there is no such thing as a 'problem,' then the 'normal' procedure will be followed. Whereas a 'normal' bodily state has the consequence of 'not doing anything', a 'problem' leads to a special wedding treatment. 'Not doing anything,' however, turns out to entail many different beauty practices, such as 'hair-cutting', 'all-body bleach' or a 'facial', in fact, 'everything from head to toes'. Describing the 'normal procedure' simultaneously as 'not [doing] anything' and '[doing] everything' indicates that a lot of beauty work is required even to attain or sustain 'normality'. Hence, naturally grown facial or body hair is not considered 'normal' and has to be bleached, threaded or waxed, either removed or made less visible.

To conclude this section, it can be stated that in India bleaching the skin is not only and necessarily a 'racialized' practice (Tate 2016), but also and perhaps primarily a routine beauty practice. The stated aim of beauty salon customers is not (always) to obtain or even approximate to a white skin colour, which is commonly perceived as 'foreign', but rather to re-claim a supposedly 'original' and 'natural' skin tone, irrespective of whether such a tone ever existed or is only an imagined ideal. This ideal is often mediated by parents. Interviewee Arjun, for instance, explained how 'she [his mum] is also saying this, that I was good looking in my childhood and that I lost my fairness by playing in the sun' (interview with Arjun, 18 April 2014). These colour constructions are further reproduced by the cosmetic industry's advertisements for bleaching products when they proclaim that they 'bring back the healthy, fair skin you always had'.[30]

THE DESIRE FOR FAIRNESS AS A DESIRE OF THE 'OTHER'

Most of my interlocutors emphasized that 'skin colour' did not play any role in their own personal lives or their own communities, but either they were still very much aware of the problem of colourism itself, or at least knew about the effects it had on other people. Thus, they preferred to talk about their own observations of the experiences of other people rather than about their own personal views or feelings. Though people certainly did notice colour discrimination in their everyday lives, they ascribed it to 'society' or a specific part of it that usually did not include themselves. These 'boundaries' between the self and (the) other(s) were mostly drawn along spatial (cosmopolitan cities/centre vs. the rural area/periphery) and class lines ('uneducated', 'backward' or 'traditional' vs. 'educated', 'modern' or 'rational'). In other words, strategies of self-identification and differentiation regarding class and space were partly negotiated on the basis of skin colour.

In my conversation with Radhika,[31] she mentioned a debate in the media about the popular Indian actress Deepika Padukone, who was called 'from the village' due to her 'dark skin' by a journalist, who, according to Radhika, was 'not fair' herself:

> [...] when [...] Deepika Padukone, the actress, came into the movies, she [the journalist] called Deepika Padukone 'from the village': 'This girl looks like she is from a village, how can she be an actress?' [...]. [There was] a lot of media who went cry about it that you call a dark skinned girl – just because she is dark skinned – 'from the village', and you, an educated woman of today, who is dark skinned and successful and living in a metro city travelling the world, if you cannot accept her, how can you know the masses accept dark-skinned beauties? I think it's gonna take a lot of time for this conditioning in Indians to change... (interview with Radhika, 1 February 2014)

It is interesting how, first, Deepika was called 'from the village' because she was identified as 'dark skinned' by a journalist; secondly, how 'from the village' has a completely negative connotation; thirdly, how the media condemns the journalist's discriminatory statement with the argument that she was dark skinned herself; and fourthly, that the outrage seems to have been exacerbated by the fact that the journalist was 'very, very educated', a 'women of today', 'successful', 'living in a metro city' and 'traveling the world'. Thus, it follows not only that fairness is associated with a kind urbanism or cosmopolitanism, but also that colour discrimination is seen as inconsistent with the image of an educated urban woman. Aspiring fairness is, therefore, associated with rural life, immobility and a lack of education. Interviewee Jayani explained accordingly: 'You wouldn't find this [preference for fair skin] in Delhi...you will find this only if you go to some very, very remote places' (interview with Jayani, 5 February 2014). It is important to note that preferences for fairness were disclaimed not only by interviewees living in the centre of the city, but also by those living on its outskirts or informal settlements. As one interviewee from the outskirts of the city put it, '[there is] no exclusion, envy, jealousy amongst us, no differentiation on the basis of beauty, no preference for skin colour; others might prefer fairness' (interview with Shruti, 19 April 2014). Thus, one may conclude that colourism is in both spaces defined as a 'problem of the other', that is, a problem of both others and other places.

Being modern and preferring fairness was often seen as being mutually exclusive, a fact that can also be attributed to a need to emphasize exceptions. Interviewee Radhika, for instance, stated that her cousin still suffered from earlier discriminatory childhood experiences, despite being a 'modern' adult now, implying that a truly modern woman would remain unaffected by colourism:

> She was not getting married until she was thirty, and there were guys coming over seeing her day [in] and day out [...]. We would hear our parents speak to each other: 'okay, she is dark, she's not getting married, she's not beautiful.' [...] She went through a lot of rejections for that and to an extent, I think, whenever you speak with her now I see some...[her] holding back some of that. [...] She's very modern, she was working in Singapore [...] But you can always see her hold back something from her childhood memories... (interview with Radhika, 1 February 2014)

Here, modernity is associated with working abroad. The same idea, that it is unlikely that 'modern' people desire fairness, is referred to by Radhika when talking about her own marriage. She called her husband 'open-minded' because 'he's a golfer', 'very well-travelled', and because he dated both 'Indian girls' and 'white women'. However, despite being 'open-minded', his actions seemed inconsistent to her when he claimed to enjoy his wife's honeymoon suntan but would not let her play golf in the sun, fearing that she would tan. Yet, Radhika did not perceive this as an attack on her autonomy and introduced it as 'a really, really funny recent thing', explaining that her husband is just as conditioned as herself and everybody else.

In contrast to the view cited above, in which a preference for fairness was linked to less educated people from rural areas, other interviewees explained that the fairness discourse affects people independently of their level of education or place of origin or living. Virmati stated, for instance:

...and I mean, this has nothing to do with education or anything – even as you go up the social ladder and as you are a good scientific[ally] educated or rationally thinking educated [person], I think it doesn't change. Even if you are more urban [and] you are more exposed to these things, [it] doesn't change. I have an aunt who just returned from the US, she lives in the US, and she just had a baby and the baby is fortunately – according to her – 'fair' and she says things like: 'Oh, you know, if [it] had been born darker, I don't know what I would have done' and I'm like, 'You would have loved the baby less?' [laughs] ... and this is someone who has worked. She is someone who is very well educated, she is in the US, and she is not like a 'housewife'. She is out and she is about, so even someone like her can hold these ideas. So it's not like fairness loses its appeal or fairness loses some kind of prestige, even if you get more aware of Indian realities and so on... (interview with Virmati, 22 February 2014)

In this statement, being 'scientific[ally] educated,' 'rationally thinking,' 'urban' and 'living in the US' are all listed under the same category and are all opposed to the life of "a housewife," who, according to Virmati's argument, would be more likely to think or act on the basis of colour discrimination. Yet, Virmati also highlights that colourism develops independently of people's level of education or social status. In referring to 'Indian realities', it seems as if Virmati is locating colourism within Indian society. Thus, she implies that even living abroad (in the US) cannot change her aunt's conditioning. The possibility that her aunt's prejudice was not reduced but maybe even reinforced because she was exposed to a predominantly light-skinned majority population or because she wants her child to 'pass' within this society does not cross her mind.

Fair skin thus also functions as an identifying narrative, especially when fairness as an ideal of beauty is associated with an (upper) middle-class, urban, cosmopolitan lifestyle. In contrast, aspirations towards fairness function as narratives of social distinction, especially when equated with backwardness, underdevelopment, or rural life. Thus, fair aspirations are ascribed to an imagined Other, what I interpret as yet another strategy for further demarcation from the 'lower classes', particularly lower-class women. This aspect becomes particularly evident in a comment made by the popular Indian actress Roopa Ganguly, who declared in a documentary on the preference for fair skin that 'the product Fair&Lovely is only bought by domestic help[ers], those kinds of products [...] I would never want to do something so stupid'.[32] Thus, on the one hand, colourism is linked to some kind of ignorance, leading interviewee Anand to conclude that '[skin colour] discrimination disappears when the level of education increases' (interview with Anand and Prakash, 18 April 2014). Accordingly, campaigns against colourism are usually directed towards changing individual attitudes. The Indian awareness campaign, 'Dark is Beautiful', for instance, claims: 'We aim to educate and empower consumers to make wise choices'.[33] These interventions, however, do not generate critical discussion of the concepts and contents of education or on the social and economic conditions that impact on people's lives, nor do they address global political systems, (trans)national markets, local governments or the various social groups that profit from the maintenance of social inequalities and further spread the powerful narrative of the 'neoliberal subject' who is held accountable for his or her own exclusion from social participation and/or economic resources.

CONCLUSION AND OUTLOOK

The research presented in this chapter reveals a beauty matrix in which fair skin is defined as the central beauty norm. Even though many interviewees stated that they personally do not perceive fairness as the most important criterion for beauty per se, they nevertheless referred to 'society' or 'Indians' who indeed prefer fair skin. In this sense, it is important to note that the descriptions and definitions of what fair means vary widely: they include colour spectra ranging from 'yellow' to 'pink', from 'wheatish' to 'milky', from 'mixed complexion' to 'very white'. Moreover, fair skin tones were commonly associated with North Indian regions, as well as with Pakistani or Iranian origin, with Islam and the Mogul Empire. They were further linked to the upper castes and upper-class status, as well as to women and the feminine body. Definitions of fair skin given to me by my interlocutors ranged roughly between what I suggest calling 'Indian fairness' and 'European whiteness', with the latter being associated with foreigners, namely the British, Europeans, or Aryans more generally. However, as many interviewees pointed out, these various shades of colour cannot be classified within any binary order ranking from black to white. Whereas categories like 'dark' and 'black' were indeed related to lower social positions, 'mixed' complexions ranked further up in the hierarchy of beauty than tones identified as 'white', which were perceived as rather weird or even spooky. Hence, whereas most interviewees preferred Indian fairness, European whiteness was almost unequivocally rejected.

In this, shadeism in India is different from the kind of colourism prevalent in African or American contexts, which has been studied so prominently in the literature. A preference for fair skin in India, particularly in Delhi, I argue, is not primarily about a sense of belonging to a specific 'ethnic' community. Moreover, lightening the skin is not solely about either 'imitating' or 'faking' 'colonial whiteness' (Fisher-Tiné 2009), 'postcolonial whiteness' (López 2005), 'cosmopolitan whiteness' (Saraswati 2010) or 'transnational whiteness' (Osuri 2008) by means of 'mimicry' (Bhabha 1994) or 'lactification' (Fanon 1967).[34] Rather, it can be seen as a beauty practice with a long and locally rooted history. As mentioned above, this is supported by the existence of the fair-skinned pre-colonial beauty icons mentioned by interviewees, such as the legendary dancer Anarkali. Interviewees also often quoted ancient home remedies predating industrial bleaching products.

This chapter has also shown that bleaching as a social practice is aimed at changing shades, not colours. This means that bleaching is rather perceived as a form of 'de-tanning', that is, of restoring one's 'original' or '(winter) seasonal' skin tone. Moreover, bleaching procedures performed in beauty parlours emphasized the dyeing of facial or body hair to make the skin appear more 'shiny' and 'glowing,' rather than the transformation of skin colour per se.

Not least, this chapter has focused on the social functions of bleaching procedures. Even though I argue for an understanding of skin colour as a social construct, it should be acknowledged that aspiring to fairness includes desires for upward mobility and the accumulation of social capital that, to a certain degree and for some research participants, indeed turned out to materialize. The fair fiction thus has its actual counterpart in interviewees' experienced reality. Particularly within the context of marriage, recognition of fair skin can indeed compensate for low-caste status, poor financial standing or a lack of education. Interviewees observed that fair skin can have a material counter-value on the marriage market, and vice versa: if families cannot 'offer' fair-skinned daughter, they can compensate by giving their financial resources to the prospective family-in-law.

Therefore, the practice of bleaching, and beauty work in general, can be understood as alternating between compliance with an oppressive beauty regime on the one hand and an agentive strategy on the other. As mentioned above, in interviews, fair skin was predominantly associated with advantages in the competitive marriage and job markets.

Given that the social significance of marriage for women is primarily linked to social and economic inequalities within a patriarchal caste and class system (Saheli 2007; Chakravarti 2004; Dube 2008), marriage and labour can be regarded as closely related fields of status negotiation for women. Both are fields in which women commonly envisage improvements to their economic and social situation.

On the one hand, interviewees talked about their desire to adhere to the stereotypical gender roles assigned to them by society, for example, by becoming a particular type of 'bride' or an 'urban career woman'. On the other hand, they talked about breaking away from these roles. For example, some interviewees linked fairness to male privilege and strove for fair skin in order to circumvent patriarchal restrictions of movement ('a girl can become a boy'). Other participants talked about rules of conduct enforced upon them by over-protective parents or spouses, who did not allow them to play or exercise outside, fearing they might tan.[35]

One approach to examining skin bleaching as potentially transforming (post-colonial) colour hierarchies is offered by S. A. Tate. She asks whether, in the Black Atlantic context, skin bleaching could also be understood as a 'decolonizing practice':

> If we think of skin bleaching as decolonizing practice we decentre whiteness and tropes of authentic Blackness in terms of skin. Instead, as decolonizing practice bleaching reinstates Black skin multiplicity as normative and as achievable cosmetically. (Tate 2016, 31)

As shown above, bleaching in Delhi is not (primarily) about destabilizing racial categories. Yet, Tate's approach raises some key questions regarding the transformation of social exclusionary systems and agency. It could be asked whether and how (far) 'buying' instead of 'being born with' colour capital changed and continues to change social stratifications in contemporary Indian societies. Under what circumstances can either bleaching or rejecting bleaching in contemporary Delhi be understood or experienced as an individual strategy of empowerment? Moreover, can such an understanding be simultaneously read as a strategy subversive of dominant beauty standards or as a perpetuation not only of beauty, but of neoliberal regimes more generally?

With the liberalization of the Indian economy since 1989, new political and economic interests in women and female bodies have emerged. On the one hand, middle- and upper middle-class Indian woman (were) turned into 'cosmopolitan consumers' supposedly striving for 'world citizenship' rather than national belonging (Deshpande 1993). On the other hand, the (trans-) national market 'discovered' India's rural areas as sales markets, following the slogan to recognize the 'poor not as victims, but consumers':

> In part, lack of choice is what being poor is all about. In India, a young woman working as a sweeper outdoors in the hot sun recently expressed pride in being able to use a fashion product — Fair and Lovely cream, which is part sunscreen, part moisturizer, and part skin-lightener — because, she says, her hard labour will take less of a toll on her skin than it did on her parents. She has a choice and feels empowered because of an affordable consumer product formulated for her needs. (Hammond and Prahalad 2004, n.p.)

In the case presented here, 'buying fairness', and thus lightening the skin, permits 'obscuring' the material and social contexts in which the 'young woman working as a sweeper' is discriminated against as a lower class and lower caste woman. Ironically, as demonstrated above, her choice of a particular bleaching cream marked as 'lower class' might actually further her social exclusion by the dominant segments of the society, rather than elevate her social status.

Social change, Young writes, 'will not come by emancipating signs from totalities but by displacing the relations of productions' (2009, 7; cited by Erevelles 2011, 63). Thus, I argue that most of the shifts of both shade and the 'social self' (Villa 2008) envisaged by my interviewees are ultimately linked to *individual* strategies to transcend structural social and economic boundaries.[36] While colour awareness campaigns may effect change on the individual level, they will hardly do so on a more structural level. These recent campaigns seem to offer little help in that they likewise draw on neoliberal subjectivity: just as cosmetic companies promote the fair skin ideal and define empowerment as a consumption choice, the colour awareness campaign mentioned above, 'Dark is Beautiful', in rejecting and fighting fairness of skin as a norm, focuses on individual changes of attitude, 'aim[ing] to educate and empower consumers to make wise choices.' In order to fully understand what facilitates the changing but continuing power of shadeism in urban neoliberal (North) India today, I argue, the interrelations between the politics of skin colour and neoliberal capitalism need to be further examined.

Notes

1. 'Swadeshi' ('self-sufficiency') describes an economic strategy within the Indian independence movement that involved both the boycott of British products and the revival of domestic products and production processes.

2. Throughout this chapter, I find myself in conflict with the marked contradiction between arguing for an understanding of 'skin colour' as a social construction on the one hand and the necessity of working with precisely these categories to have a shared linguistic or conceptual basis for debates on colourism, at least to some extent, on the other. I would have liked to mark colour categories such as 'fair' or 'white' as socially constructed classifications of differentiation, not least to stress how these shades of colour are significantly co- and re-structured in and by my work. However, in the interests of better readability, I refrain from setting these terms in quotation marks in the following.

3. http://nanditadas.com/nanditawrites30_inc.htm (accessed 31 October 2017).

4. The concept of 'The New Indian Woman' encompasses both supposedly 'western' as well as 'Indian' features. On the one hand, it demands women to be 'modern', educated and working, while on the other, they should also be 'traditional' and 'Indian', with strong family values. This ideal image corresponds to the urban Hindu middle class prototype, the so-called 'Globo-Indian.' The anti-colonial image of the New Indian Woman was constructed as a counterpart of 'western' women, emphasizing women's purity, spirituality, as well as their role as mothers. Since the 1980s, the desire for distinction from 'common' women has gained importance and Titzmann (2014) now sees this figure in contrast to what political feminism in India stands for, weakening and silencing women and women's movements in times of social and economic change.

5. For debates on race and racism in contemporary India, see McDuie-Ra (2015).

6. Following Kang (2010, 20), I define beauty labour as 'commercialized exchanges in which service workers attend to the physical comfort and appearance of the customers, through direct contact with the body (such as touching, massaging, and manicuring) and by attending to the feelings involved with these practices' (for a similar approach, see also the concept of 'holistic labour,' Jie Yang 2017, 117–32). Beauty work, on the other hand, is understood as beautification practices performed at and by the self, or collectively; treatments are either offered unpaid or given in exchange. Within this categorization, skin-lightening can be seen as an individual daily (care) routine work performed at home. Among interviewees, its treatment was also offered as a gesture of friendship, or given

in exchange for a haircut, *mehendi*, make-up or the like, especially when a visit to the beauty parlour was unaffordable.

7. Interview with 22-year-old student Jyoti, 7 February 2014. She refers to her religion as Sikh, to her caste as Bakshi, and describes her family background as middle class.

8. Whereas the concept of the 'aesthetic entrepreneur' places the emphasis on an economic subject that 'works upon itself in order to better itself' (du Gay 1996, 124, cited by Elias et al. 2017, 39), it is not always, and not by a long chalk, the 'self' that takes care of itself. Thus, Miliann Kang's (2010) study has impressively shown that much beauty work is rather passed on to less privileged and predominantly female 'Others' (in her case, Asian migrants in the US).

9. In contrast to these postfeminist and neoliberal narratives, see what Kavita Krishan (2013), an activist with the 'All India Progressive Women's Association' (AIPWA), demands from women's movements. See also Nancy Fraser (e.g. 2013) on the liaisons between neoliberal capitalism and women's movements and Federici's (2004) history of the body in transition to capitalism.

10. http://www.loreal.com/group/diversity, https://www.hul.co.in/brands/our-brands/fair-and-lovely.html, https://www.dove.com/us/en/stories/about-dove.html#!, https://www.fairandlovely.in (last accessed 5 November 2017).

11. Cf. Degele (2004) and Koppetsch (2000), who both make use of Harold Garfinkel (1976), Erving Goffman (1973), and Pierre Bourdieu (1976).

12. On perceptions and practices of beauty in India, see Dehejia and Paranjape (2003). The variety of concepts underlying the term 'beauty' is further apparent in the wide range of meanings in Hindi. The Hindi-English Online-Dictionary *Shabdkosh*, for instance, lists 25 phrases for the English word 'beauty'—one of them, *rup*, has again 45 different meanings, entailing e.g. 'look', 'figure', 'position', 'design', 'nature' or 'picture'.

13. Respondents were asked to provide the following personal information: name, age, place of birth, current place of residence, sexual orientation, marital status, children, gender, caste, religion, languages spoken, occupation and parents' occupations. Accordingly, the majority of interviewees were Hindus, born in Delhi, female, heterosexual, below the age of 30, unmarried and childless. All interviewees spoke Hindi, though most had at least some command of English. In terms of belonging to caste and class, respondents were rather diverse, though most interviews were conducted with self-identified members of the middle class. In the text, background information is provided only when this seems fit for a better understanding. In congruence with my respondents' notion of beauty being relevant for women, rather than men, in the present chapter, I

focus on women's perspectives and practices. However, many interviewees reported that men were becoming increasingly beauty-conscious, an observation that is also reflected in the growing number of unisex or men's beauty parlours and fairness products targeting men.

14. For the beauty parlours, I made an attempt to cover diverse districts of Delhi, such as Kamla Nagar, Kalkaji, Alaknanda, Lajpat Nagar, Model Town, Green Park, Khan Market and Kathputli Colony (Shadipur), an informal settlement located between Tuqhlagabad and Ohkla Industrial Area; and lastly, a home-integrated beauty salon in Faridabad, bordering New Delhi but belonging to the state of Haryana.

15. The informal settlement, Kathputli Colony in Shadipur Depot, West Delhi, is named after string puppet theatres native to Rajasthan and was until recently home to almost 3000 itinerant street performance families. At the moment, the Colony is undergoing a redevelopment plan by the Delhi Development Authority (DDA) of the Government of Delhi, amid to a wide range of protests and resistance by its inhabitants.

16. The term 'Kṣatriya' describes one of the four varna categories (Brāhman, Kṣatriya, Vaiśya and Śūdra). The indeed inevitable amalgamations of existing local cultures leads to the problem that, with the passage of time, not all social groups could be given a precise varṇa status. Thus, mixed castes (sankīrṇa jāti) were admitted, given the rank of Śūdras, and many of them were described as 'Mlecchas' (Thapar 1971, 413). A new problem arose with the arrival of the Greeks, Śakas and Kuṣāṇas: they were all powerful rulers who started to patronize and use Sanskrit, and married into local ruling families. Āryan speakers responded to this development by inventing and approving a new rank: the 'degenerate Kṣatriya' (vrātyakṣatriya).

17. The process of 'Āryanizing' included granting Kṣatriya status, 'overlooking' Mleccha antecedents, especially in areas where Mleccha rulers were powerful.

18. 'Mleccha' was the Āryan-speakers' term for the indigenous population (for its etymology, see Thapar 1971, 409–10). Since occupations were hierarchically ordered from 'clean' to 'polluting,' as expressed in the four varna categories of Brāhman, Kṣatriya, Vaiśya and Śūdra, 'Mlecchas' were assigned the lowliest occupations and, therefore, also a low ritual status (ibid.).

19. However, the Sanskrit term 'varna' translates as 'colour' and the four varnas are each assigned a colour: Brahmans white, Kshatriyas red, Vaishyas yellow, and Shudras black. The association of Brahmans with the colour 'white' in particular requires a closer examination of the interrelations between colour and caste.

20. Padma Purana, one of the eighteen major Puranas, a vast genre of ancient Hindu texts.

21. The term Dalit is a self-designation of indigenous populations in India who have been excluded from the varna system as so-called 'untouchables'.

22. Also, research participants in Delhi commonly associated colour with high caste status, as exemplified by Zahra: 'They say Brahmans are fairer you know. If you know about Hindu mythology, Brahmans are the uppermost part of the body, so Brahmans are expected to have a certain tone, a certain "skin colour" or certain mannerisms which will define their identity (...)' (interview with Zahra, 9 February 2014).

23. Chayanika was born in Delhi, identifies as a Hindu, refers to her caste as 'Rajput' and indicates that her father 'works in a shop' and her mother as a 'housewife'.

24. The group consisted of five female students between 15 and 20 from economically and socially disadvantaged communities in south Delhi, who attended a course on basic technology (in this case, computers). With the exception of one Christian girl, all were Hindu. They spoke Hindi and had no command of English. They were all unmarried and childless.

25. Whether the interviews were conducted in Hindi or English, both the English terms 'fair' and 'white' were used, as well as the Hindi word *gora*, whereas *safed*, the Hindi for 'white', was never used in the context of skin, body or beauty, as it usually refers to objects rather than people. The Hindi term *savla* was also used regularly, but the English translation 'brown' quite rarely: interviewees translated *savla* rather as 'of mixed complexion'. The etymological origin of the Hindi term *gora* is the Sanskrit *gaura*. In Turner's *Comparative Dictionary of Indo-Āryan Languages*, the given source is the Rgveda, in which its meanings cover the spectrum 'white, yellowish, pale red'. In a Hindi-German Dictionary (Gatzlaff-Hälsig 2002) *gora* is translated as 'light (skinned)', 'beautiful', 'light skinned person', a 'European' or 'American'. As shown above, this word was not (only) used to describe people from Europe or America. Moreover, the designation 'American' primarily reveals assumptions made by the book's editor, who obviously imagines America as 'white' in the first place.

26. Preeti described her religion as Hindu and her caste as Kanojia. She was born in Manipur; her parents worked as a 'police officer' and a 'housewife'. Preeti told me that her family suffered from existential financial problems in her childhood; therefore, she started working as beautician at a young age to support them.

27. Almost all the beauticians I talked to referred to the potential health risks of bleaching, but in most cases only after being questioned about them. The disclosure of the potential health risks differed in extent, but never included severe or long-term effects caused by ingredients like hydroquinone, topical corticosteroids or mercury. For example, beauticians

reported sometimes having to treat rashes and burns on bleached skin. On the health risks of skin bleaching, see WHO (2011), Sahu et al. (2014), and Mire (2000).

28. Artistic henna designs created on the body.

29. See also Glenn (2009, 166) on the gendered correlation between skin colour and attractiveness.

30. Advertising slogan in a commercial for 'Nivea Whitening Cell Repair Body Lotion', https://www.youtube.com/watch?time_continue=8&v= Bc8y8JPcdXs (last accessed 4 August 2017).

31. Radhika is a 29-year-old, married fashion designer. She gave her caste as Gupta and her religion as Hindu, but preferred to describe her religious belief as 'spiritual'. Her parents work as a 'chartered accountant' and a 'housewife'.

32. Ganguly stresses that one should take care of one's skin, look after one's skin, use products to make the skin 'better,' not 'fair'—it remains unclear, though, whether she is talking about the health risks of bleaching or whether she doubts the product's ability to lighten skin tone. She also compares complexion to body height and demands that a 'short guy' who does not meet the beauty norm of 'tall' should 'not feel ashamed or bad or sad about it' but should 'accept that, yes, I am short, I have to make most of it with my performance;' thus, she too lays emphasis on changing individual attitudes (*'Fair?'—A Documentary about Skin Colour in India*. Directed by Vishnupriya Dia Das, filmed by Thomas Mallon). https:// www.youtube.com/watch?v=TT7x1BIEhY0 (last accessed 19 July 2017).

33. 'Dark is Beautiful', an awareness campaign against colourism launched by the Indian NGO 'Women of Worth', see http://darkisbeautiful.in/, or http://womenofworth.in/ (last accessed 5 November 2017).

34. '[T]o dream of a form of salvation that consists of magically turning white' (Fanon 1967, 44).

35. When S. Niranjana (2001) rethinks gender theory through the lenses of spatiality and the body in rural Karnataka, she introduces the concept of *olage-horage*, which refers to the continually shifting 'inside-outside' matrix, the 'axes along which their [women's] world is ordered.' In my interviews, constructions of fairness were also strongly related to concepts of 'inside' and 'outside'. It was either about 'getting in' (an employment relationship, marriage, social group, cultural event), or 'getting out' (move beyond the community' boundaries, escaping social stigmas). This movement, however, never comes to an end: it keeps people working constantly on their bodies.

36. This relates to Hunter's examination (2011, 158) of the beauty and public health discourses on bleaching in Africa and African diasporas.

REFERENCES

Abraham, Janaki. 2006. "The Stain of White: Liaisons, Memories, and White Men as Relatives." *Men and Masculinities* 9: 131–51. https://doi.org/10.11 77/1097184x06287764.

Abu-Er-Rub, Laila. 2017. *"Goldene Zeiten: Mode und Körper im neoliberalen Indien"* ["Golden Times: Fashion and Body in Neoliberal India"]. Unpublished PhD thesis, University of Heidelberg.

Appadurai, Arjun. 1993. "The Heart of Whiteness." *Callaloo* 16 (4): 796.

Bailkin, Jordanna. 2014. "Indian Yellow: Making and Breaking the Imperial Palette". In *Empires of Vision: A Reader*, edited by Sumathi Ramaswamy and Martin Jay, 91–110. Durham: Duke University Press.

Banet-Weiser, Sarah. 2017. "'I'm Beautiful the Way I Am': Empowerment, Beauty, and Aesthetic Labour." In *Aesthetic Labour: Rethinking Beauty Politics in Neoliberalism*, edited by Ana Sofia Elias, Rosalind Gill, and Christina Scharff, 265–82. London: Palgrave Macmillan.

Barthes, Roland. 1986 [1964]. *Elements of Semiology*. New York: Hill & Wang.

Bhabha, Homi K. 1994. *The Location of Culture*. London: Routledge.

Bhattacharya, Shilpi. 2012. "The Desire for Whiteness: Can Law and Economics explain it?" *Colombia Journal of Race and Law* 2 (1): 117–147.

Blay, Yaba Amqborale. 2011. "Skin Bleaching and Global White Supremacy: By Way of Introduction." *The Journal of Pan African Studies* 4 (4): 4–46.

Bourdieu, Pierre. 1976 [1972]. *Entwurf einer Theorie der Praxis*. Frankfurt/Main: Suhrkamp.

Castro Varela, M., and N. Dhawan. 2005. "Of Mimicry and (Wo)Man: Desiring Whiteness in Postcolonialism." In *Mythen, Masken und Subjekte. Kritische Weißseinsforschung in Deutschland*, edited by M. Eggers et al., 318–336. Münster: Unrast.

Chakrabarty, Dipesh. 2000. *Provincializing Europe: Postcolonial Thought and Historical Difference*. Princeton, NJ: Princeton University Press.

Chakrabarty, Dipesh. 2002. *Habitations of Modernity: Essays in the Wake of Subaltern Studies*. Chicago, IL: University of Chicago Press.

Chakravarti, Uma. 2004. *Gendering Caste Through a Feminist Lens*. Calcutta: Stree.

Chaudhuri, Nupur. 1994. "Memsahibs and Their Servants in Nineteenth-Century India." *Women's History Review* 3 (4): 549–62. https://doi.org/10.1080/09612029400200071.

Craig, Maxine Leeds. 2006. "Race, Beauty, and the Tangled Knot of a Guilty Pleasure." *Feminist Theory* 7 (2): 159–77.

Davis, Kathy. 1995. *Reshaping the Female Body: The Dilemma of Cosmetic Surgery*. New York: Routledge.

Degele, Nina. 2004. *Sich schön machen. Zur Soziologie von Geschlecht und Schönheitshandeln*. Wiesbaden: Springer.

Dehejia, Harsha V., and Makarand Paranjape, eds. 2003. *Saundarya: The Perception and Practice of Beauty in India*. New Delhi: Samvad India Foundation.

Deshpande, Dipesh. 1993. "Imagined Economies: Styles of Nation-Building in Twentieth Century India." *Journal of Arts and Ideas* 25–26: 5–35.

Doniger, Wendy. 2009. *The Hindus: An Alternative History*. New Delhi: Penguin/Viking Press.

Dube, Leela. 2008. "Caste and Women." In *Women's Studies in India: A Reader*, edited by Mary E. John, 466–74. New Delhi: Penguin Books.

du Gay, Paul. 1996. *Consumption and Identity at Work*. London: Sage.

Elias, Ana Sofia, Rosalind Gill, and Christina Scharff, eds. 2017. *Aesthetic Labour: Rethinking Beauty Politics in Neoliberalism*. London: Palgrave Macmillan.

Erevelles, Nirmala. 2011. *Disability and Difference in Global Contexts: Enabling a Transformative Body Politic*. New York: Palgrave Macmillan.

Fanon, Franz. 1967 [1952]. *Black Skin, White Masks*. New York: Grove Press.

Federici, Silvia. 2004. *Caliban and the Witch: Women, the Body and Primitive Accumulation*. New York: Autonomedia.

Fischer-Tiné, Harald. 2009. *'Low and Licentious Europeans': Race, Class and White Subalternity in Colonial India*. New Delhi: Orient Blackswan.

Foucault, Michel. 1988 [1969]. *Archäologie des Wissens*. Frankfurt/Main: Suhrkamp.

Fraser, Nancy. 2013. *Fortunes of Feminism: From State-Managed Capitalism to Neoliberal Crisis*. London: Verso.

Garfinkel, Harold. 1976. *Studies in Ethnomethodology*. Englewood Cliffs, NJ: Prentice-Hall.

Gatzlaff-Hälsig, M., ed. 2002. *Handwörterbuch Hindi-Deutsch*. Hamburg: Buske.

Gilroy, Paul. 1995. *The Black Atlantic: Modernity and Double Consciousness*. London: Verso.

Gimlin, Debra L. 2002. *Body Work: Beauty and Self-Image in American Culture*. Berkeley: University of California Press.

Glenn, Nakano Evelyn. 2009. "Consuming Lightness: Segmented Markets and Global Capital in the Skin-Whitening Trade." In *Shades of Difference: Why Skin Colour Matters*, edited by Evelyn Nakano Glenn, 166–87. Palo Alto: Stanford University Press.

Goffman, Erving. 1973 [1959]. *Wir alle spielen Theater*. München: Piper.

Gupta, Dipankar. 2000. *Interrogating Caste: Understanding Hierarchy and Difference in Indian Society*. New Delhi: Penguin Books.

Hammond, Allen L., and C. K. Prahalad. 2004. "Selling to the Poor." *Foreign Policy*, 20 November 2017. Available at https://foreignpolicy.com/2009/10/27/selling-to-Inthe-poor/.

Harris, Angela P. 2009. "Introduction." In *Shades of Difference: Why Skin Colour Matters*, edited by Evelyn Nakano Glenn, 1–5. Palo Alto: Stanford University Press.

Hunter, Margaret L. 2002. "'If You're Light You're Alright': Light Skin Colour as Social Capital for Women of Colour." *Gender & Society* 16 (2): 175–93.

Hunter, Margaret L. 2005. *Race, Gender, and the Politics of Skin Tone.* Abingdon: Routledge.

Hunter, Margaret L. 2011. "Buying Racial Capital: Skin Bleaching and Cosmetic Surgery in a Globalized World." *The Journal of Pan African Studies* 4 (4): 142–64.

Hussein, Nazia. 2010. "Colour of Life Achievements: Historical and Media Influence of Identity Formation Based on Skin Colour in South Asia." *Journal of Intercultural Studies* 31 (4): 403–24.

John, Mary E. 1998. "Feminism in India and the West: Recasting a Relationship." *Cultural Dynamics* 10 (2): 197–209.

Johnson, Gordon. 1970. "Chitpavan Brahmins and Politics in Western India in the Late Nineteenth and Early Twentieth Centuries." In *Elites in South Asia,* edited by Edmund Leach and S. N. Mukherjee, 95–118. Cambridge: Cambridge University Press.

Kang, Miliann. 2010. *The Managed Hand: Race, Gender, and the Body in Beauty Service Work.* Berkeley: University of California Press.

Koppetsch, Cornelia, ed. 2000. "Introduction." In *Körper und Status. Zur Soziologie der Attraktivität,* 7–16. Konstanz: Universitätsverlag Konstanz.

Krishan, Kavita. 2013. "Sexuelle Gewalt und Widerstand." In *Speak up! Sozialer Aufbruch und Widerstand in Indien,* edited by Elina Fleig, Madhuresh Kumar, and Jürgen Weber, 154–65. Hamburg: Assoziation A.

López, Alfred J. 2005. *Postcolonial Whiteness—A Critical Reader on Race and Empire.* Albany: State University of New York.

McDuie-Ra, Duncan. 2015. *Debating Race in Contemporary India.* Basingstoke: Palgrave Macmillan.

McRobbie, Angela. 2009. *The Aftermath of Feminism: Gender, Culture and Social Change.* London: Sage.

Mire, Amine. 2000. "Skin-Bleaching: Poison, Beauty, Power and the Politics of the Colour Line." *Resources for Feminist Research* 28 (3 and 4): 13–38.

Nadeem, Shehzad. 2014. "Fair and Anxious: On Mimicry and Skin-Lightening in India." *Social Identities: Journal for the Study of Race, Nation and Culture* 20: 2–3. London: Routledge.

Niranjana, Seemanthini. 2001. *Gender and Space: Femininity, Sexualization and the Female Body.* Thousand Oaks: Sage.

Obeyesekere, Gananath. 1998. "Foreword." In *Hair: Its Power and Meaning in Asian Cultures,* edited by Alf Hiltebeitel and Barbara D. Miller, xi–xiv. Albany: State University of New York Press.

Osuri, Goldie. 2008. "Beauty and the Bollywood Star: Stories of Skin Colour and Transnational Circulation of Whiteness." In *Cultural Theory in Everyday Practice,* edited by Nicole Anderson and Katrina Schlunke, 96–205. Oxford: Oxford University Press.

Parameswaran, Radhika. 2005. "Global Beauty Queens in Post-liberalization India." *Peace Review: A Journal of Social Justice* 17 (4): 419–26. https://doi.org/10.1080/10402650500374702.

Phadke, Shilpa. 2017. "How to Do Feminist Mothering in Urban India? Some Reflections on the Politics of Beauty and Body Shapes." In *Aesthetic Labour: Rethinking Beauty Politics in Neoliberalism*, edited by Ana Sofia Elias, Rosalind Gill, and Christina Scharff, 247–62. London: Palgrave Macmillan.

Raj, Kapil. 2007. *Relocating Modern Science: Circulation and the Construction of Knowledge in South Asia and Europe 1500–1800*. New York: Palgrave Macmillan.

Reddy, Deepa S. 2005. "The Ethnicity of Caste." *Anthropological Quarterly* 78 (3): 543–84.

Robb, Peter. 1995. *The Concept of Race in South Asia*. New Delhi: Oxford University Press.

Saheli Women's Resource Center. 2007. *Talking Marriage, Caste and Community: Voices from Within*. New Delhi: Saheli Women's Resource Center.

Sahu, Ramakant, Poornima Saxena, and Sapna Johnson. 2014. *Heavy Metals in Cosmetics*. Centre for Science and Environment. New Delhi. Accessed 4 November 2017. Available at http://www.cseindia.org/userfiles/Heavy_Metals_in_Cosmetics_Report.pdf.

Saraswati, L. Ayu. 2010. "Cosmopolitan Whiteness: The Effects and Affects of Skin-Whitening Advertisements in a Transnational Women's Magazine in Indonesia." *Meridians* 10 (2): 15–41.

Smith, Dorothy. 1987. "Women's Perspective as Radical Critique of Sociology." In *Feminism and Methodology*, edited by Sandra Harding, 84–96. Bloomington: Indiana University Press.

Strauss, Anselm L., and Juliet M. Corbin. 1990. *Basics of Qualitative Research*. Newbury Park: Sage.

Tagore, Rabindranath. 2009 [1916]. *Inside and Outside*. New Delhi [Ghare Baire]: Fusion Books.

Tate, Shirley Anne. 2010. "'Not All Women Want to Be White: Decolonizing Beauty Studies." In *Decolonizing European Sociology*, edited by Encarnacion Gutierrez Rodriguez, Manuela Batca, and Sergio Costa, 195–212. Ashgate: Farnham and Burlington.

Tate, Shirley Anne. 2016. *Skin Bleaching in Black Atlantic Zones: Shade Shifters*. Basingstoke: Palgrave Macmillan. https://doi.org/10.1057/9781137498465.0004.

Thapar, Romila. 1971. "The Image of the Barbarian in Early India." *Comparative Studies in Society and History* 13 (4): 408–36.

Titzmann, Fritzi-Marie. 2014. *Der indische Online-Heiratsmarkt. Medienpraktiken und Frauenbilder im Wandel*. Berlin: Frank & Timme.

Villa, Paula-Irene, ed. 2008. "Habe den Mut, dich deines Körpers zu bedienen! Thesen zur Körperarbeit in der Gegenwart zwischen Selbstermächtigung und Selbstunterwerfung." In *Schön normal. Manipulationen am Körper als Technologien des Selbst*, 245–72. Bielefeld: Transcript Verlag.

WHO. 2011. *Mercury in Skin Lightening Products*. Geneva, Switzerland. Accessed 5 November 2017. Available at http://www.who.int/ipcs/assessment/public_health/mercury_flyer.pdf.

Yang, Jie. 2017. "Holistic Labour: Gender, Body and the Beauty and Wellness Industry in China." In *Aesthetic Labour. Rethinking Beauty Politics in Neoliberalism*, edited by Ana Sofia Elias, Rosalind Gill, and Christina Scharff, 117–32. London: Palgrave Macmillan.

Young, Robert. 2009. *Signs of Race in Poststructuralism: Toward a Transformative Theory of Race*. Lanham, MD: University Press of America.

CHAPTER 12

Skin Colour Politics
and the White Beauty Standard

Shirley A. Tate and Katharina Fink

In this contribution, Shirley A. Tate and Katharina Fink converse on skin colour politics and the White beauty standard. Critical to the discussion is art and its potential to mobilize revolt. This conversation evolved as a series of vignettes exchanged in the digital sphere.

Katharina Fink: Dear Shirley, in the course of the conference, "Beauty and the Norm: debating standardization in bodily appearance" (Bayreuth University, 6–8 April 2016), we discussed a number of features of the *dispositif* of 'the beautiful' in both its restricting aspects and its subversive ones, its cracks, so to speak, which can be used to create space for alternative ways of living 'beautiful' lives. Nonetheless, White supremacy reigns within standards of beauty till today. This idea of 'the beautiful' is not a superficial affair, but runs deep. Recent transnational protest movements such as #blacklivesmatter and, in the South African context, where you are a Visiting Professor, #fees must fall/#fallism

S. A. Tate
Beckett University, Leeds, UK

K. Fink (✉)
Bayreuth University, Bayreuth, Germany

© The Author(s) 2019
C. Liebelt et al. (eds.), *Beauty and the Norm*,
Palgrave Studies in Globalization and Embodiment,
https://doi.org/10.1007/978-3-319-91174-8_12

pointed to the racism inherent in the state's dealing with racialized bodies. The recent election campaigns in the US have, once again, as if one needed a reminder, shown that the body marked 'female' is at the centre of standardized discussions. And all these sites also show the creativity of protest, which leads to the core theme of my work—the potential of artistic resistance and aesthetic expressions of dissent and utopia. I'd love to begin this conversation by discussing the possibilities of alternative visions of 'the beautiful,' dimensions of the 'future' within ideas of beauty and their relation to power.

In particular, from the perspective of your work, could you please elaborate on the entanglement of the idea of the nation state with its inherent dimension of 'modernity' and time more generally, and the standardized body of the ideal citizen? For you, do these notions interact, and if so, how?

Shirley A. Tate: These are really nice entanglements that you are developing already. I think that maybe what I would like to do is to begin with a possible re-phrasing of the question, if I can? This is also about my own theoretical shortcomings, as I do not work on time, so it is not about anything wrong with the questions themselves. Perhaps, what I would like to ask is, would it be possible *not* to have body norms which represent the power of the ideal citizen? Let us begin with the USA, where it seems to me that, in the run-up to Trump's election as President, there was an incredible rawness to anti-Black woman racism—'misogyny noir'—that we had not seen so publicly aired for some time. The particular incident I am talking about occurred on Facebook. Clay, West Virginia, resident Pamela Ramsey Taylor posted, 'It will be refreshing to have a classy, beautiful, dignified First Lady in the White House. I am tired of seeing a [sic] Ape in heels.' The mayor of Clay, Beverly Whaling, responded to this post with, 'Just made my day, Pam'.[1] Such overt racism meant that she had to resign, but nonetheless she felt that she could applaud these words. Let's leave aside for the moment Taylor's lack of knowledge of English (a ape rather than an) and look at the words themselves and the oppositions that they create in our thoughts.

'Classy', 'beautiful' and 'dignified' refer to the white hyper-feminized body of incoming First Lady Melania Trump, which would refresh white supremacist heteropatriarchal sight, psyche, power, privilege and feminized beauty ideals. However, incumbent First Lady Michelle Obama is an 'ape in heels.' An 'ape in heels'—let us pause on this and submit it to some interrogation. This white supremacist, anti-Black woman phrase has a history. It is textured by a history which leaves a bitter taste in the mouth. A history of colonialism, enslavement, terror, trauma and violence in which the Black woman's body was reproduced as mere flesh during the Middle Passage and in plantation economies (Spillers 2003) in British, French, Portuguese, Spanish, and Dutch colonies in the Western Hemisphere. As flesh, Black women's bodies were torn apart, sexually and physically violated, and made to suffer psychically through a white supremacist-constructed and socially instituted inferiorization so that whiteness could be superior.

One of the technologies for producing the flesh of the Black woman was that of their dehumanization and defeminization alongside hyper-sexualization. It is in this past that only white women were beautiful, while Black mixed-race women who could be their (un)acknowledged sisters, cousins and nieces might be capable of having an exotic beauty because of being mixed; but unmixed Black women were relegated to ugliness. Within this hierarchy, Black women were spoken about as apes and orangutans, for example, by Jamaican planter Edward Long (1774). White men in the then British West Indies were warned about the hypersexuality of Black women, including those who were mixed race, called "Sable Venus" and "Saffron Venus," respectively, by Jamaican planter Bryan Edwards (2010 [1794]). The pervasiveness of this colour hierarchy and its necessity for supporting the nation which sees itself as white can be seen in the painting of Modesto Brocos (1895), *A Redenção de Cam* ('The Redemption of Ham'), which is regarded as an image that represents racial politics in Brazil's racial democracy based on whitening the nation. In this painting, the Black grandmother lifts her hand in praise to God for removing the stain of Blackness from her family through her mixed-race daughter, who has a white child with a white man. This painting implies that in three generations, it is possible to be the desired "white" within Brazil through progressive reproductive whitening. Whiteness as power, privilege and aesthetics remains key to Brazil's racial democracy, as much as it is to 'post-race' states such as the UK and USA.

Black, darker-skinned women such as Michelle Obama have never stopped being 'apes in heels' to white supremacists because of the colonial enslavement history and discourses briefly sketched above. Successful darker-skinned women seem to be a visceral reminder for these two women in West Virginia and that of their white supremacist community that white beauty is not all that matters. As such, the possibility of Black beauty, dignity and grace has to be denied by such shared racist vitriol in order to reorient their white world to ensure white supremacy in all things, including aesthetics. Beauty is not just a matter for the individual, nor something that comes from within, nor is it 'race'-neutral. Beauty, like race, is socially constructed, and as colonialism has shown, once norms have been constructed, they are difficult to dis-assemble within social structures, national psyches and global aesthetic regimes.

For example, would Beyoncé have been taken up globally as beautiful if she was darker skinned, like Kelly Rowland? Would Rachel Christie ever have been Miss England if she was not lighter-skinned, mixed race? Would Dame Jessica Ennis-Hill and Thandi Newton ever have been the international faces of Olay if they were not lighter-skinned, mixed race? It seems to me that we still drag colonial conceptions of skin colour and beauty into the twenty-first century through the work of multinationals aiming to 'open up' new markets, whether that be in the hip-hop music industry, the cosmetics industry or the beauty pageant industry. This is significant, because 'mixed looks' could now well be the new global norm, rather than whiteness.

Of course, I should also say here, as I have said in my work generally (e.g. Tate 2009, 2015), that whiteness now is only one of a variety of beauty norms globally and locally. The measurement of beauty no longer begins solely from whiteness in our contemporary world, even though it is still pervasive. For example, if we think of Lupita N'yongo as Lancôme ambassadress, when a few short years ago she spoke of growing up feeling ugly because she was darker skinned, and only being saved from the shame she felt by seeing the South Sudanese-British model Alek Wek. On the Lancôme US site, the global cosmetic giant describes her as having 'instinctive and sophisticated talent and one of a kind beauty both delicate and exuding strength.' Of course, we can also spend time with this description, 'one of a kind beauty both delicate and exuding strength,' because we can say that this is both a form of infantilization and masculinization, while both these tropes are constructed to equate with Black darker-skinned women's bodies.

'One of a kind' also can mean 'unique' without the possibility of repetition by other darker-skinned Black women. Of course, if we are cynical, we can say that, in choosing N'yongo as ambassadress, they are attempting to corner the cosmetics market of a whole continent and its diaspora.

Katharina Fink: Yes. But the question is also if being cynical leads anywhere at all. Since you mention the market—you currently are a visiting professor in a country, South Africa, in which the politics of race very overtly define identity and structure all fields of social and political debate, from schooling to the tourism business. I also think of forms of commemoration, such as in the Apartheid Museum in Johannesburg, where I worked for my Master's thesis in Museum Studies and where a superficially declared 'non-racialism' governs the museum's narrative. And yet, the whole endeavour was set up by people who made their fortune with skin lightening creams. I mean, to your mind, and based on your work and experience, in a site like this, a museum, can one really avoid or side-step the confrontation with 'race' and its continuing structural dimension?

Shirley A. Tate: I myself visited the museum last year and came out less than half way through really upset because of the images and narratives. I knew about it being built from the profits made from skin-bleaching creams. I was also told that that was the trade-off for the nation to enable the building by these same people of the Gold Reef City Complex of which the museum is a part, the Gold Reef City casino, theme park and hotel. I am not so sure that the museum side-steps confronting race at all. What it might do is erase apartheid history by sanitizing it in a way which the prisons at Constitution Hill cannot and do not. It could be as well that a museum, as a 'heritage practice,' makes pain and continuing racism disappear as something of/from the past, which we need not remember because, to build a future, these past injuries and deaths are best forgotten. The active word here is 'past' because, as we know from contemporary South Africa, these hurts and deaths are not past but keep being re-stimulated with each new racist injury. For example, the students at Pretoria High School, a former whites-only institution, were recently being told that they could not wear their hair in an Afro to school, which led to student protests. Heritage practice might attempt to erase continuing racism within societies structured by racial dominance, but daily life and its continuing injustice refuses this erasure.

I guess I should say something about skin lightening creams and their use. I have written on this topic (e.g. Tate 2015), and what I said has caused much debate when I have presented my work in public. This is because I did not start from the position of skin bleaching, lightening and toning as being a colonial practice based on a white supremacist model of beauty, which as Black beauty we continue to adhere to. I think that it is important to remember that women all over the world bleach. For example, Japanese women are the biggest market for skin bleaching, lightening and toning products. Bleaching cuts across class, sexuality, ability, race and gender and is a multi-million-dollar business worldwide which involves global, national and local entrepreneurs. What interests me particularly about skin bleaching, lightening and toning is that, outside of physical harms to the body, it is very publicly problematized only when it is practised by poorer, darker-skinned women. Here, women are seen to be suffering from the psychological harm of white supremacist lighter-skin preference. I won't be a naysayer of this type here, but rather remind us that we can also start from reading Black skin-tone practices as critiques of existing political economy, as well as intimate economies and their skin colour preferences within the Black Atlantic diaspora's post-racial contexts. It is time to step away from a point of view which says 'it's white supremacy that did it' and think about the variety of motivations underlying skin bleaching, lightening and toning.

Some brief questions here might help this orientation. If white supremacy's lighter-skinned preference is so pervasive, why don't all Black people bleach, irrespective of skin tone and global location? In fact, why do white women use products which illuminate (bleach) or correct dark spots without even a second thought? Why is it that people whose skin shows signs of bleaching, lightening or toning are not employed within corporate Jamaica? Why is skin bleaching, lightening and toning only seen as self-hatred when it is related to Black women's bodies? Why do cosmetic surgery clinics world-wide offer skin bleaching, lightening and toning with glutathione without this being a problematized practice?

Katharina Fink: Important questions which complicate the field of skin colour politics in relation to the White beauty standard. At the beginning of your response, you mentioned that there had been a debate regarding your work and writings in that direction. What exactly were the discomforts with your more detailed and complex description of the realities of bleaching?

Shirley A. Tate: There was a critique of my work because I do not say that women should not bleach, lighten or tone their skins, because this practice is an expression of self-hatred of being Black and of low self-esteem due to practitioners having bought into white supremacy. That is the position taken by some scholars and activists. I prefer to complicate this view because these are patently not the only reasons, and we need a much fuller account, which also includes political economy and colourism and shade-ism within Black communities.

Katharina Fink: During the conference, we talked about the limitations and even the 'necropolitics' (Mbembe 2003) of beauty standards, particularly in regard to bodies marked as female. I want to move our conversation into the direction of talking about the potential of performances of beauty which do not meet hegemonic standards, namely those performances that use queer and joyful strategies to challenge them. I think of body modifications, make-up, fashion etc. as forms of protest, of shifting understandings of 'the norm'. So I would like to pick up one question from the workshop again: 'What does the increasing consumption of aesthetic body modifications mean for the particularities of our bodies, our everyday lives, as well as for the ways we determine what is good, beautiful, healthy and "normal"?'

Shirley A. Tate: Many academic commentators said that our bodies have become projects through which we show who we are or want to become. The body then is malleable rather than taken as a given, in the state of becoming rather than of being. Aesthetic body modifications are a broad group of practices which, I guess, can be seen as focused on normalization towards some bodily ideal determined by the surgeon, patient/client, the body itself or the available technology. There has been an increasing normalization of procedures such as face lifts, neck lifts, blepharoplasty (eyelid surgery), breast augmentation or reduction, cosmetic dentistry, rhinoplasty (nose jobs), bottom implants, 'Botox' injections, lip fillers, skin lightening, labiaplasty, liposuction, chin augmentation and bariatric surgery, for example. These are all aimed at enhancing the body. Enhancement is the byword of the aesthetic surgery industry, one that has been taken up as well by its clients. To enhance something which one already has perhaps denies the possibility of being called vain and downplays the time, money, risk and pain involved in the changes made. Vanity is not good, healthy, beautiful or normal, but beauty is something to be aspired to. Indeed, we are all asked to engage in beauty work to develop more desirable bodies in terms of a hegemonic norm. Men likewise have access to the above procedures, as well as, for example, gynecomastia (fat removed from their breasts) and hair implants. Of course, the body which is most under pressure to be beautiful is the woman's body, especially the ageing one. Moreover, and as we know, the disabled body stands outside of beauty because of its socially constructed inability to embody 'the good, beautiful, healthy and normal'. These words are not neutral, as we have seen when we have spoken of age and disability just now. They are words which are also racialized, gendered, sexualized and classed, as well as relevant for age and disability. An example might suffice here. In the UK, we romanticize breast-feeding mothers as 'beautiful', 'good', 'normal' and 'healthy,' but what about chest-feeding fathers? Are they equally romanticized, or do they make us draw back in horror because of our cis-gender orientations and heteropatriarchal normativities?

We need to admit, though, that what is beautiful must have undergone transformation over the centuries. Not least, there is not the one global ideal and there never has there been one, as even Immanuel Kant, who wrote extensively on the experience of beauty and aesthetic judgement (1790), himself admitted. What is interesting, though, is how 'good', 'normal' and 'healthy' go together with beauty. It is good, normal and healthy to be beautiful. What happens to those with bodies that are not deemed beautiful, such as those with a disability, for example? If beauty matters to you and you think that it relates to the surface, then you must work on your body through aesthetic (surgery) interventions, whether invasive or non-invasive, to become beautiful. This demands money, time and effort, and can also be the source of physical and psychic pain and risk, because we insist that our bodies are malleable enough to achieve what we need to feel good about ourselves. As body-conscious people, are we ever truly content with how we look, or are we doomed to keep trying for perfection until our bodies simply cannot take it anymore? Can the striving to be beautiful become unhealthy, bad and abnormal?

What is interesting about aesthetic modification is the fact that if it is 'natural looking' then it is acceptable, but if it does radically change, not 'enhance,' then it is vilified. We can see this with lip fillers, which get a negative press when they produce 'trout pouts' or face work which radically changes one's look, as is the case for actor Mickey Rourke or hip-hop artist Li'l Kim. These celebrities have made radical changes to how they look facially, and both have been critiqued for this. Li'l Kim, for instance, has been referred to as attempting to deracinate herself, to become more European-looking or to appear like a Latina because of her face work and her skin lightening. The question is, of course, can aesthetic surgery really deracinate your appearance to the extent that it enables you to change 'race'? Or might it just enable you to pass as someone else within contexts in which you are not known? This makes us wonder about the possibility for 'racial play' and what it might produce in the case of Li'l Kim in our 'post-race' moment. If we think that what she is doing is becoming a whitened version of herself, then we can say, perhaps, that she is engaging in a racial play which pushes at the limits of whiteness. However, this 'play' is always subject to failure because that very 'race performativity' (Tate 2005) enabled by aesthetic surgery reproduces her as not white, but as a Black woman with a difference. As I have said previously, rather than thinking of her body modification as having to do with whiteness, I would look instead at the different looks that Black women embody across the Black Atlantic diaspora. That is, I would see her body work as being about producing a Black woman, rather than someone who wants to be white. We know that being white is an impossibility because of the way 'race' works in terms of the one-drop rule. Thus, women can be pale and with so-called 'European features,' but still identify and be identified as Black quite unproblematically. For me, she makes it plain that beauty is a commodity that can be bought, as is also the case for 'healthy', 'good' and 'normal'.

Katharina Fink: Beauty is a *dispositif* with many aspects. On the one hand, it limits, restricts, demands and even kills. It's a tool in the hands of the powerful and the rich; it's an issue of class. On the other hand, it may also be considered a tool of power in the hands of those considered powerless. Beauty is also about empowerment, and can be seen as a form of taking control over one's self-presentation and performance in a matrix of power. This is where many of the truly interesting moments are situated: in a grey zone. In an interview with a German newspaper, Turkish writer Aslı Erdoğan spoke about her imprisonment for 132 days in a women's prison in Istanbul. She spoke about the injustice and the insecurity of her situation—and about beauty. What made the women around her endure the insecurity of life in prison was to watch a seedling raised on an egg shell with few drops of water. To see life unfold in the absence of support for all living was described as empowering and in the language of beauty. So, is there something in the mobilization of the 'beautiful' that may trigger and even inspire radical social change, justice and equality?

Shirley A. Tate: The mobilization of the beautiful for radical social change, justice and equality is an intriguing idea. Intriguing, because I think that the beautiful itself needs to be deconstructed, decolonized and critiqued. It is only *within* such decolonial deconstructive critique that we can begin to see bodily beauty's potential for radical social change, justice and equality. What is commonly seen as bodily beauty, in whichever context we inhabit, can indeed lead to social mobility and thus to social change through this mobility. So, beauty is not just a matter for the individual or the interpersonal, but is a matter for political economy and materiality. Of course, what this question also orients us to is the injustice and inequality related to 'the norm', in whatever way it might be configured. The question of what can radically changing the ideal of bodily 'beauty' do, and, indeed, the question of how, if at all, that norm can be changed? This latter is a massive if not impossible task because it potentially involves inculcating across society different beauty tastes, which are focused on countering the norm. Something like this demands time, effort and money, for example, from beauty entrepreneurs themselves, as we can see in the Dove ad campaigns in the UK, which are aimed at encouraging women to see the diversity of their bodies, thus breaking normative appearance ideals. However, to inculcate tastes which counter the norm must also be taken up by social movements in order to enable more widespread political and individual engagement, as we can see from the Black Power Movement's slogan 'Black is beautiful,' which still has a resonance today.

Katharina Fink: Do you see shifts regarding standardized beauty in recent media discourse? For example, I'm thinking of Caster Semenya, South African runner and sports star, on the cover of the South African *ELLE* magazine in December 2016—which was celebrated by some as a 'leap forward' for feminism.[2] Personally, I don't share this view, as it seems to affirm the market-wise operations of global media houses more than anything else, though I truly believe in the possibilities of pop culture, its power to confuse productively by involuntarily changing iconographies, by side-stepping, bootlegging etc. But what do you think the production of an image such as this one does to spark a critical debate on 'race', 'sex' and power? Does it change anything at all regarding beauty and its normalization, commonly understood as an intersectional affair in which race, class and gender come together?

Shirley A. Tate: I don't think that it does anything for the wider debates that need to be had about the marginalization of transgender bodies, non-gender binary-identified bodies more generally and lesbian bodies, not to mention Black women's bodies in society. These bodies are all marginalized, so perhaps we could see *ELLE* South Africa as doing something to make these bodies more visible, which might be described as a 'leap' for feminism. Which feminism do they mean, though? How does Semenya contribute to this leap through her objectification? Again, do we see a Black woman's body being used to service a white feminism read as providing liberation, much as we have done since Sojourner Truth critiqued this constructed sisterhood by highlighting the differences between women based on race and its intersections?[3]

I am not an *ELLE* South Africa reader, so I cannot say how the image would have been taken up in terms of 'race', sex and power by South African readers. However, I think, rather than rushing to celebrate this as a leap forward for feminism, what we should remember is the daily lives lived by lesbians, non-gender binary-identified people and transgender women and men in South Africa and elsewhere in the world. Their lives are not ones of physical or psychic safety, nor are they ones of social acceptance. Homophobia, transphobia and heteropatriarchal normativity are everywhere and continue to create unliveable lives. What interests me, though, is that Semenya's image on the cover of *ELLE* South Africa is only spoken about in terms of feminism. If we look back at *ELLE* South Africa covers, we can see that they are dominated by white or lighter-skinned women. Is there not a need for Semenya's cover to also be commented on as a device for combatting the anti-darker-skinned racism that we know to exist in South Africa and elsewhere? Why is there such a skirting of this particular issue through a focus on a non-racialized, non-sexualized, non-classed, able-bodied, cis-gendered feminism? Which feminism is kept in play here and which erased—a variety of African feminisms, or its Euro-US American sisters? What does the feminism being spoken about mean for the continuing subjugation of women and the kind of feminist politics that must be engaged in in South Africa and elsewhere in our contemporary moment, when prevailing discourses on women as neo-liberal subjects would make us believe that women in the Global North West can be whatever they want, can have choices, can have control over their lives and, in fact, no longer need the liberation promised by second-wave feminism? The question it is necessary to ask here, of course, is whether the sort of feminist battle that needs to now be engaged can be fought from the cover of a women's magazine only.

Katharina Fink: I am currently working in a project concerned with visions of the future. Feminism and the politics of solidarity form part of my interests. In a recent interview, bell hooks spoke of the necessary steps to re-politicize feminism, and I would like to quote her: 'I think that we have to restore feminism as a political movement. The challenge to patriarchy is political, and not a lifestyle or identity. It's as if we have to return to very basic education for critical consciousness, around what visionary feminist politics really is about. And let's face it: visionary feminist politics is not about having a woman president. It's about having a person of any gender who understands deeply and fully the need for there to be respect for the embodied presence of males and females, without subordination' (Alptraum 2017, n.p.).

Is there more to the vision of a respectful and just life than a utopia? Can we establish ways of seeing this as beautiful, desirable?

Shirley A. Tate: One thing that the Black Power Movement did was spawn the Black Feminist Movement in the USA and a generation of Black feminist thinkers who produced seminal work within academic life. One of the areas of work which has been engaged in with vigour is that of Black beauty, because how one looks has long been the cause of suffering within enslavement and colonialism in the Global North and South West. Beauty has always been a political issue for Black feminists and Black men from WEB DuBois onwards, engaged in thinking through what Black anti-racist aesthetics could and should be about politically, in terms of beautification practices, and theoretically, in terms of critiquing white supremacist beauty norms.

Black anti-racist aesthetics—through just thinking 'Black is beautiful'— is about a basic education for critical consciousness and can be self- and life-affirming for Black women, men and children even today. What Black anti-racist aesthetics in the end demands is respect for Black difference and the end to whiteness as the major beauty norm which rules Black psyches. This might seem utopic because beauty is racialized, is embedded in our understandings of 'race' and is as such difficult to change. What we cannot have is a continuation of white feminists speaking of beauty as if it is a universal concept without any need for prefixes like 'Black', or for their repetition of pathological approaches to beauty as it relates to Black women and women of colour.

Katharina Fink: While being a strong and regulating force, it is the un/doings of these aesthetic ways of living that are important. Moroccan artist Yassine Balbzioui, whose artwork is featured on the cover of this volume, recently commented on this with his aesthetic practice. He chose to work with porcelain, a material historically celebrated for its refinedness, epitomizing middle- and upper-class values such as inheritance, temperance and 'taste' (see also Böllinger, this volume). By queering these notions—again, this is class, gender and race—through his artistic practice, he makes a powerful statement, which could be summed up as: beauty is experience. The richness of the object, the wonder and amazement of looking at it, feeling it, is based on the experiences this very object has made in its life, the moments that shaped its current appearance. It can be a powerful concept if connected to experience and performance, rather than a static meeting of norms. In the context of our discussion, I would also like to talk about art. What can art do in order to tackle beauty as a *dispositif*? What's the power of art to undo political normalizations of power, as inscribed in and on bodies—for example, Whiteness. Does it have any power at all? Which role can art play in questioning standardized beauty? Also, I think here of the work of Syowia Kyambi (see Kyambi and Soff, in this volume).

Shirley A. Tate: Beauty is experience. Experience brings to mind the second wave feminist practice of consciousness-raising to produce theories and politics based on the idea that 'the personal is political.' Subsequently, feminists critiqued experience as a primary basis for theory because personal experience was too often about similarity—of race, class, gender identification, education, able-bodiedness, national citizenship—rather than difference. Second-wave feminists then turned to seeing how subjects are discursively constructed, and by the end of the twentieth century, experience was not given the same weight as earlier in terms of feminist theory. On the other hand, Critical Race Theory (CRT) finds experience useful as a tool in more phenomenological accounts, which place the subject within networks of racialized intersectional power/knowledge that are subjected to genealogical analysis. CRT attempts to look at the link between intersectional race, racism and power by questioning the foundations of the neo-liberal social order. Its practitioners believe that racism is ordinary; the system of white supremacy serves material and psychic purposes for white people; race is socially constructed; different forms of racialization have different consequences; intersectionality and anti-essentialism are important in analyses; and people of colour or Black people have a unique perspective on experiences of oppression, which cannot be seen by whites.

Charles Mills' *The Racial Contract* (1997) supports this latter point when he says that white people have inherited a world which they themselves have made and in which they are surrounded by their own epistemologies of ignorance. CRT analyses place the power/knowledge of discursive practices as the locus of the emergence of meanings which build who we are and how we understand the world we live in. In my own approach to CRT, this is linked to a decolonial political critique drawing from Aimé Césaire (2000) of dis-alienation, of estranging oneself from those colonial discourses, which seek to fix us as being this or that as Black women and men. Rather, what dis-alienation enables is a 'becoming other' through narrations of the self that we analyse within a CRT approach.

Beauty is phenomenological. It is part of the lived experience of the racial epidermal schema which Frantz Fanon (1951) terms *'l'expérience vécue noir'* in the case of colonial Black women and men. We could also speak of the lived experience of whiteness as *l'expérience vécue blanc* and so on for other racialized groups. 'Beauty is experience' means that we have to start from beauty as a racialized notion *and* beauty as phenomenological. This means that my focus on beauty from a decolonial CRT perspective is based on 'the importance of lived experience, the intentionality of consciousness, the significance of nearness or what is ready-to-hand, and the role of repeated habitual actions in shaping bodies and worlds' (Ahmed 2006, 2). When we think from a decolonial CRT perspective, we also have to think of 'race' and beauty as performative (Tate 2005, 2009), so as to enable enactments of beauty within the sphere of intelligibility dictated by beauty norms. Art can play a role in the questioning of such standards through performativity, as it locates us as subjects. As subjects, art makes us face our ideas of beauty and ugliness and our affective responses to these as socially constructed and subjectively instantiated through our orientations as we move away from 'ugliness' because of visceral aversion and towards 'beauty' because of fascination and pleasure. Art can also play a role in questioning these orientations themselves in making us aware of the discourses and affects in which we are imbricated in terms of the binary beautiful/ugly.

Katharina Fink: So this is to the power of art and the paradoxes of the 'beautiful'. Thanks for this ongoing conversation, Shirley!

NOTES

1. Available at: http://www.bbc.co.uk/news/election-us-2016-37985967 (17 November 2017).
2. For an insightful discussion of the media reactions to the example of Semenya, who was forced to undergo a so-called sex verification test, see Gunkel (2016).
3. In 1851, Truth delivered her famous speech at the Women's Convention in Akron, Ohio, that was later given the name 'Ain't I a Woman.'

REFERENCES

Ahmed, Sara. 2006. "Toward a Queer Phenomenology." *GLQ: A Journal of Lesbian and Gay Studies* 12 (4): 543–74.

Alptraum, Lux. 2017. "Bell Hooks on the State of Feminism and How to Move Forward Under Trump: BUST Interview." *Bust Magazine*. Available at: http://bust.com/feminism/19119-the-road-ahead-bell-hooks.html (18 November 2017).

Césaire, Aimé. 2000. *Discourse on Colonialism*, edited by Robin D.G. Kelley. NYU Press.

Edwards, Bryan. 2010 [1794]. *The History Civil and Commercial of the West Indies*. Cambridge: Cambridge University Press.

Fanon, Frantz. 1951. "L'expérience vécue du noir." *Esprit Nouvelle Série* 179 (5): 657–79.

Gunkel, Henriette. 2016. "Queer Times Indeed? Südafrikas Reaktionen auf die mediale Inszenierung der 800-Meter-Läuferin Caster Semenya." *Feministische Studien* 30 (1): 44–52.

Kant, Immanuel. 2007 [1790]. *Critique of Judgement*. Translated by James Creed Meredith. Oxford: Oxford University Press.

Long, Edward. 1774. *The History of Jamaica*. London: T. Lowndes.

Mbembe, Achille. 2003. "Necropolitics." *Public Culture* 15 (1): 11–40.

Mills, Charles W. 1997. *The Racial Contract*. Ithaca and London: Cornell University Press.

Spillers, H.J. 2003. *Black, White, and in Color: Essays on American Literature and Culture*. Chicago: University of Chicago Press.

Tate, Shirley. 2005. *Black Skins, Black Masks: Hybridity, Dialogism, Performativity*. Farnham: Ashgate.

Tate, Shirley. 2009. *Black Beauty: Aesthetics, Stylization, Politics*. Farnham: Ashgate.

Tate, Shirley. 2015. *Skin Bleaching in Black Atlantic Zones: Shade Shifters*. Basingstoke: Palgrave Macmillan.

INDEX